How they fared in adoption: a follow-up study

STUDIES OF THE CHILD WELFARE
LEAGUE OF AMERICA

BENSON JAFFEE & DAVID FANSHEL

How they fared in adoption:
a follow-up study

COLUMBIA UNIVERSITY PRESS

New York and London / *1970*

Benson Jaffee is Associate Professor of Social Work in the School of Social Work, University of Washington, Seattle. David Fanshel is Professor of Social Work at Columbia University School of Social Work.

Foreword

THIS BOOK reports the findings of research into the life adjustment of one hundred adult adoptees. It inaugurates the collaboration of the Child Welfare League of America and Columbia University Press in the publication of a series of Child Welfare League of America studies. This cooperative venture adds strength and will serve to increase the availability and circulation of important professional literature in the child welfare field. Additional books in this series will be forthcoming in the near future.

Adoption has developed rapidly in the United States as one solution to the life problems of parentless children. In just one decade, nonrelative adoptions rose from fewer than 50,000 in 1957 to more than 83,000 in 1967. No other form of substitute care offers children—or adults seeking children—the quality of legal, psychological, and familial belonging that adoption creates. It is not surprising, therefore, that as a child welfare service it has absorbed a large share of community interest and of the energies of practitioners.

Certain questions are inherent in the very nature of adoption, and these have caused it to be subjected to close scrutiny by professional researchers and practitioners both inside and outside the field of social work. For example, can a family created in the image of a natural family really function in the same fashion as its biologically based counterpart? How much can ever be known about the inherited characteristics of the adopted child, and to what extent can nurture by his adoptive parents outweigh nature in his growing up? While the adoptive family possesses attributes in common with procreated families, in certain respects it is quite different from such families. Many in our culture view adoption as a rather exotic form of family life, and it is obvious that adoptive families comprise only a very small proportion of all families in our society. The question can therefore be raised as to whether adoptive parents are sufficiently able to cope with this minority status, both in themselves and in their growing child, that it will not interfere with their happiness.

Popular as well as professional literature about adoption is increasing. Yet, very little systematic research of families with adopted children who are now adults has been undertaken. This has been partly due to the fact that adoption as a social phenomenon has reached its present proportions only in relatively recent years and that there are consequently comparatively fewer families with adult adoptees available for study. Moreover, serious problems must be faced in locating such families and in establishing the kind of communication with them that is necessary for research purposes. Finally, any inquiry into the attitudes and relationships among people, particularly when reported in retrospect, involves many complexities and variables that pose hazards and challenges for current techniques of measurement.

At the same time, however, each well-conceived research effort of this type furthers our knowledge of the subject and contributes to the refining of our instruments. It was with this realization that the Child Welfare League undertook the research reported in the present study. Both the investigation and its publication by Columbia University Press as the initial work in the Studies series were made possible by the generosity of the Mildred E. Bobb Fund.

The study was conducted with the full awareness that the adoptive families cooperating in the investigation were products of agency practices in the early years that preceded the development of more professionalized approaches and skills. There is nevertheless a great deal to be learned from the results that are presented in this book, and that provide an essential frame of reference for future research on the life adjustment of adopted adults who were placed as children with the aid of more informed standards and procedures. Such comparative studies should throw powerful illumination, indeed, on the nature of adoption and on the theory and practice with which it is undertaken.

Joseph H. Reid, Executive Director
Child Welfare League of America, Inc.

New York City
June 1970

Preface

AN OPPORTUNITY to learn firsthand from adoptive parents about the intimate details of their experiences with their adopted children over the course of twenty or more years provided a stimulating experience to the writers of this book. For most investigators in the behavioral sciences, curiosity about human beings is both a motivation and a justification for their intrusion into the privacy of other people's lives; for us this curiosity was certainly an impelling factor in our decision to begin what was obviously going to be a difficult investigation. Attempting to find adoptive families and to obtain their cooperation in research after a hiatus of twenty to thirty years was admittedly a hazardous task. After considering a variety of alternatives for learning about adoption, however, we decided that there was much to be gained through research interviews with adoptive parents about what is involved in raising an adopted child. No one, we believed, could speak with as much knowledge about such experience as those who had lived through it themselves. We hope that the reader will agree that our effort was worthwhile inasmuch as it provides considerable food for thought for those interested in the institution of adoption services, particularly for future researchers interested in following up some of the leads we offer here.

This book is the product of our joint effort, which required an intimate sharing of all tasks through stages ranging from conceptualization and development of research procedures, through field interviewing, data analysis, and the interpretation of findings. Since we both have a background of social work education, experience, and commitment, tempered by considerable investment in the behavioral and social sciences, the reader can understand the derivation of our eclectic conceptualization of the research and its execution. Our concern was less with adhering to the favored research procedures of a specific academic discipline than it was with finding new ways of eliciting maximum information from the adoptive parents about the nature of the adoption experience.

It is difficult to acknowledge all who have been of help to us in this endeavor. The following are only a few to whom we are most indebted:

The Mildred E. Bobb Fund generously provided financial support for the undertaking. We deeply regret that the late Solomon I. Sklar, former trustee of the Fund, is not alive to receive the final product of our labors. He encouraged us to undertake this particular kind of adoption study with the conviction that adoptive parents had an important story to tell. Further encouragement was most helpfully given by his successor, William Victor Goldberg.

We are especially grateful to the staffs of the four participating adoption agencies who made their rosters of adoptive families and case records available to us. Their support and cooperation were indispensable in our execution of this research.

We received sound advice in the preliminary phase of research planning from Dr. Norman Polansky and Miss Elizabeth Herzog. Our colleagues at the Child Welfare League of America were helpful at all times in giving us the benefit of their experience with adoption. We are especially beholden to Joseph H. Reid, executive director of the League, for his constant support of our right to intellectual freedom in pursuing our research as we saw fit. We also benefited from cogent advice from members of the League's Research Advisory Committee, under the chairmanship of Dr. Julius B. Richmond.

Stalwart service was rendered by our caseworker-interviewers: A. Paul Parks, Miss Mary T. Davis, Mrs. Pearl Weiss, Miss Marjorie Stauffer, and Mrs. Rhoda Fishleder. The secretarial assistance we received from Miss Elissa Queyquep and Miss Shirley Bloom facilitated our work enormously. We are very appreciative of their help.

We feel most thankful to our research subjects, who permitted us entry into their homes so many years after their last contact with the adoption agencies, and who shared with us so much personal information about their experience with adoption. We hope that our research will prove of some benefit to the adoptive families who will come after them. We are sure that our one hundred families would consider this prospect ample reward for their cooperation.

Finally, we offer deep appreciation to our wives, Iris Jaffee and Florence Fanshel, for their patience and forbearance with our frequent absences in mind and body during the time of absorption in this study.

Benson Jaffee
David Fanshel

June 1970

Contents

xi

How they fared in adoption: a follow-up study

one / Introduction

INCREASINGLY over the past several decades, adoption has shown signs of being accepted as a social institution in the United States. There is greater public awareness of adoptive parenthood as a logical alternative for many of those couples who desire to have children of their own but cannot, because of infertility or other prohibitive factors such as the unusual jeopardy some women face in becoming pregnant. It seems likely that this public acceptance has been stimulated by the increasing number of programs on television and articles in popular magazines that have been devoted to this subject in recent years. As part of this trend, agencies have become quite responsive to the increasing public interest, and there are even signs that they are attempting to hark to vocal criticisms, from a variety of sources, about their modes of operation, e.g., their selection procedures, waiting periods, and fee systems.

It is estimated that in 1965 about 142,000 children were legally adopted in the United States.[1] Over the 15-year period ending in 1965, the number of children adopted annually has risen by more than 77 percent, from an estimated 80,000 in 1951. All told, more than 1.5

million children were adopted in the United States during this period.[2] The United States Children's Bureau estimates that as of 1966 there were in this country almost 2 million adopted children under 18 years of age.[3]

Of the 142,000 legally adopted children in 1965, approximately 76,700, or 54 percent, were adopted by nonrelatives.[4] More than two-thirds of these were placed with the aid of social agencies. Voluntary adoption agencies constituted 42 percent of the placements; public agencies, 27 percent. The remaining 31 percent of the adopted children were placed independently by their own parents or relatives, or through other individuals such as doctors, lawyers, or acquaintances of the parents.[5]

During the past decade, social workers serving adopted children and their parents have been carefully examining the quality of their practice.[6] However, much of the discussion in the professional child welfare literature about what constitutes good practice tends to have an indecisive tone. Although there has been rich clinical experience in this area recently, only rarely has it been underpinned by systematic research endeavors.

Pertinent to our study is the fact that little is known about the degree to which adoption results in a satisfactory family experience. This gap in information represents a serious shortcoming for those who undertake to work with adoptive families. Current knowledge about the nature of adoptive family life is limited to the observations of caseworkers during relatively short periods of contact with families; these contacts are usually restricted to the supervisory year following placement. Aware of this shortcoming, the Child Welfare League of America proposed to the Mildred E. Bobb Fund in October 1960 that a study be made of adoptive parents and their children who had been known to social agencies some twenty to thirty years earlier.

We hoped that a study of the adjustment of subjects who were adopted as young children and were now in their twenties would provide useful insights for practice. Despite the difficulty we foresaw in attempting to locate families after such a long hiatus, we felt there were decided advantages to be gained by looking at a sample of families in which the adoptees were now young adults rather than children in their teens or younger. We thought that at this late stage, the families would be sufficiently removed from the early childhood experience and the vicissitudes of child rearing to have developed some objectivity about the adoptive experience.

Another decided advantage in having research contact with families in which the adoptees were now adults was that we could construct a much more accurate picture of the overall life adjustment of these subjects than we could achieve by studying them as children. If, for example, an investigator were to study adopted children as adolescents, he would be seeing them when they were in transition to the responsibilities of adulthood. This is a stage commonly recognized as being turbulent, and a child's adjustment at this time may not be a reliable predictor of what he will be like as an adult. The young adult in his twenties presents a picture that already indicates fairly well what quality his lifetime adjustment pattern will assume in such important areas as sexuality, courtship and marriage, choice of vocation, and the quality of his personality. Looking at the individuals' adjustment in important situations, we would anticipate being in a relatively better position to discern well-established levels of functioning, while fully recognizing that an individual's mode of adjustment is never completed at any age level.

In a sense, the follow-up study was seen as a modest substitute to the long-term longitudinal study in which agencies might undertake to study adoptive families from the beginning of the placement experience until the children had achieved adulthood. The latter type of study is, of course, highly desirable since data secured as the child's life is unfolding would inspire greater confidence than when gathered on an *a posteriori* basis. However, the feeling of those who supported our research was that the results of a longitudinal study would not redound to the benefit of adoption agencies for many years to come. Therefore, the follow-up study was chosen because it promised earlier feedback to practice.

NATURE OF THE STUDY

In this book we report the findings of a study of a hundred families who adopted children during the years 1931–1940 through four social agencies in New York City.[7] The children were three years of age or under when they were adopted, and the adoptive families were living within a fifty-mile radius of the center of New York at the time. The four agencies participating in the study represented the three major religious groupings of New York City, and their cooperation therefore assured us of a cross-sectional sample of agency adoptions taking place within the decade of the 1930s.

At the inception of the study, we identified these agencies as being highly developed in their professional practice, and we anticipated they would be in an excellent position to contribute their expertise to the basic conceptualization of the research as well as to the development of research procedures, e.g., steps taken to locate families, the style and content of research interviewing, and so forth. We also expected that the staffs of these agencies would be of help in assessing the meaning of the findings and in suggesting implications for practice.

At the very beginning of this report, we offer the following caveat: It is important for the reader to bear in mind the fact that many of the families included in this study were exposed to a form of agency practice that was less well developed than it is today. A review of the records of these families and discussions with individuals who were acquainted with the operating procedures of the agencies during the period in which these adoptions took place revealed that there were a number of aspects of earlier agency practice that would be deemed inappropriate by the current staffs. As an example of this, we might cite the selection procedures formerly used by some of these agencies: A number of the case records reviewed by our research staff revealed a highly personalized approach to the selection of families. Sometimes, the element of personal friendship between a board member and a prospective adoptive applicant would enter into the determination of the suitability of the applicant. Needless to say, the intrusion of lay board members into the selection procedures involving specific individuals is now regarded as antithetical to professional practice.

Another example of outmoded practice would reside in the types of placements made. Thus, one family in the study was able to arrange for the adoption of a child while the adoptive mother was in the hospital recovering from the experience of having a stillbirth. The family received the adopted child the day the mother left the hospital in a fairly weakened physical and emotional condition. It is not likely that placement under such circumstances would be undertaken today.

These examples clearly reveal that the form of agency practice to which our study families were exposed was much less well developed than that which adoptive couples would encounter today in applying to the four agencies participating in our study. It therefore follows that the findings of our study cannot be interpreted as reflecting the likely outcomes of adoptions currently being completed by these agencies. To underscore this point, which is of great importance, we shall not use in this report the names by which the four agencies are presently known. Instead, we shall refer to them by the names they bore during the ten-year period when all the adoptions included in our study took place. They will thus be designated as follows:

Catholic Home Bureau	to be referred to as
Angel Guardian Home for	Catholic Home Bureau
Little Children	
Alice Chapin Nursery	to be referred to as
Spence Alumnae Society	Chapin Nursery/Spence Alumnae
Free Synagogue Child	to be referred to as
Adoption Committee	Free Synagogue Committee
Child Adoption Service	to be referred to as
of the State Charities	State Charities Aid
Aid Association	

The research we report here is based upon interviews that were quite detailed and far-ranging with adoptive parents of a hundred adoptees. The information we secured from these subjects represents their perceptions of the experiences they and their youngsters encountered from the time just preceding the introduction of the child into their home, through his growing-up period, to the situation prevailing at the time of the follow-up interview. It had been our original intent to use the adoptees themselves as the primary source of information and to secure their perceptions of the adoption experience as our principal data.

However, it soon became apparent that this was not a realistic expectation. For one thing, the agencies were loathe to approve a direct intrusion upon the adoptee in this research venture without first securing the parents' permission. It was reasoned that the seeking out of the adoptee without the intervening procedures would constitute a violation of the agreement made between the agencies and the parents. At the time of the consummation of these adoptions it had been understood that the agencies would withdraw from the family's life. There was an additional source of apprehension: there was no certainty that the adoptee had been informed by his parents that he was adopted. Neither was there any sureness that he was sufficiently stable emotionally to participate in a research interview that was seen as having potential for creating stress.

The wisdom of the decision not to seek out the adopted child without the parents' prior approval was subsequently validated in the field operations. We were told in interviews with four sets of parents that they had never informed their children of their adoptive status. We also encountered a number of situations in which we felt that the adoptee's current adjustment was obviously too precarious to expose him to the research procedure.

In addition to the issues stemming from the ethical concerns of the agency staff members and the researchers, our decision to interview the adoptive parents was dictated by the practical difficulties we could anticipate in attempting to locate the adoptees. While the adoptive parents were difficult enough to find after a hiatus of twenty to thirty years, the search for their children would have presented a much more formidable task. Like other young adults in this highly mobile society, we could expect that many of the young men in our sample would have moved to other parts of the country. We would also be confronted by an even more difficult task if we sought to locate the female adoptees, quite a few of whom presumably had married and whose names would thus have been changed. All in all, we saw the arguments against initiating direct contact with the adopted children as most compelling, and we therefore decided to focus our attention upon the parents in the first major phase of the research. It is this phase which is reported in the present volume.

The reader might well ponder over the accuracy of the reports provided by parents about their own experiences and that of their children with adoption. In undertaking this research excursion, we saw this as a legitimate issue but not one of such overriding importance as to vitiate the possibility of obtaining useful information from interviews with such subjects. We shared the belief of the agencies and the supporting foundation that adoptive parents have an unusually interesting and important story to relate about what they had lived through as parents. We were not aware of any previous attempt to inquire of a group of adoptive parents the nature of the experience encountered in raising to adulthood children not born to them. What were their satisfactions and joys in raising these children? What problems and painful experiences had they encountered? Did they see anything unique about the adoptive parent role that set it apart from the experience of other parents? While we recognized that the procedure of obtaining reports from parents alone might result in biased perceptions because individuals cathect their experiences in highly personalized ways, we felt that these subjective orientations were of themselves legitimate phenomena for research scrutiny.

While we were prepared to accept as informative the subjective responses of the parents, efforts were also made to make visible the degree of subjectivity characterizing their responses. For example, adoptive fathers and mothers were interviewed separately, making possible estimates of the degree of consensus prevailing between them in describing their own living experiences and those of their adopted children. Then, too, we made diligent attempts to secure access to the adoptees themselves so that they might participate in research procedures which would parallel much of the same ground that was covered in the interviews with the parents. Thirty-three adoptees were subsequently interviewed, and this separate research excursion will be presented in a future report.

NO CONTRAST WITH BIOLOGICAL FAMILIES

It is important to understand why we chose to give exclusive attention to adoptive families in preference to a study that would include a contrasting group of families with adult children who were biological offspring of the parents. This was a matter that was carefully considered and the decision to limit the bounds of the research stemmed from three basic factors:

(1) It was considered hazardous to contrast the adjustments of the two types of families, adoptive and biological, since such a comparison would presume an essential equivalence of these families. There are several aspects of adoption which give it a quality of uniqueness that would make comparisons unsound. For one thing, the adopted child is often one who has experienced separation from a parent figure who reared him prior to his placement in the adoptive home. It is frequently stated in the child development literature that such separations are potentially traumatic to children. The children often show immediate behavioral reactions to such changes even though it is not yet clear whether any long-range damaging effects can be attributed to separation experiences.[8]

The fact of separation is further confounded by the concomitant phenomenon of multiple mothering which entails the rearing of children by several maternal and paternal figures, each of whom may have had a different impact upon the child's developing personality. Whether this develops confusion for the child is a matter which is under investigation by child development researchers. Finally, little is known about the physical risks facing the child born out of wedlock whose mother may be prone to delay in seeking prenatal care and whose care of herself during gestation may not be of the same order as the woman bearing children within the marital relationship. Thus, it cannot be assumed that adopted children come into the world with the equivalent health status of nonadopted children.

(2) Furthermore, attempting on a post hoc basis, some two to three decades later, to locate a comparison group of biological families matched with the adoptive families on relevant nonadoptive characteristics would have posed formidable if not unsurmountable obstacles. For instance, to have controlled for the important variable of socioeconomic status (SES) would have required first resolving the very thorny problem of what point in the 20- to 30-year history of the adoptive families to choose for matching on this variable. While social class status would have exerted a continuous influence upon the entire life experience of these families, methodologically it would have been possible to select only one point in time for matching purposes. What

criteria could have been used to select that point? When would SES factors likely have had the greatest impact upon the subsequent adjustment of the adoptee? Would it have been at the time of placement? When the adoptee was five, ten, or eighteen years of age? We submit there would be no definitive or even consensually agreed-upon answers to these questions.

(3) Despite the hazards of comparison stated above, sheer curiosity might have nevertheless impelled us to seek to determine how biological parents looked back upon the experience of rearing their children. Contrast, even on a less than equitable basis, is the magnetic attraction for most research efforts. The economics of this research project, however, were such that it did not seem feasible for us to seek to match the adopted children with a control group and then replicate all of the research procedures to which the adoptive group had been exposed. As it was, the costliness of finding the adoptive families and subjecting them to elaborate interviewing procedures, followed by a formidable coding operation, proved to be so expensive that the goal of 175 to 200 families we initially established for this study had to be reduced to a sample of 100.

The reader is thus alerted to the fact that this research will not shed light upon the differences that might prevail between adoptive families and biological families. That is to say, we, the investigators and the reader, are in the common position of not being able to make any generalizations about the degree to which the outcomes of adoption reported in this study deviate from outcomes one could find in the population at large.

In view of the above, what then is the value of this study? For us and the agencies who cooperated in the research it was deemed useful to undertake the task of developing a portraiture of the adjustments of these families and to relate some of the significant outcomes to other variables known about the families. For example, one might ask whether the outcome of the adoptive placement was in any way related to the age of the parents at the time the child was placed in the home. In a like vein, one might wish to know whether there was any relationship between the number of years a couple had been married before they approached the adoption agency and the kinds of experiences they encountered as parents.

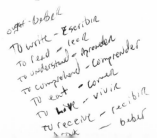

In other words, the design we chose, restricting the study to adoptive families, permits an internal analysis in which the sample can be broken down into various categories of adoption outcome. These subgroups may be further studied to discern the correlates of such outcome. In view of the paucity of research of this kind in the area of adoption, an exploratory level of design was deemed quite appropriate. Our hope was to secure information which would have a sensitizing function for agencies offering adoption services by providing a fairly full picture of those who have reared their children with relative success, as opposed to families where the child's life may have been unhappy and problematic. At the same time, we anticipated that the study would shed light upon variables that might be included in future studies where the designs would be more rigorous than the one employed here.

BROADENING THE KNOWLEDGE BASE
FOR ADOPTION SERVICE

What kinds of useful information might one obtain from adoptive families after they had lived through the experience of rearing their children? For the benefit of the reader, we make explicit the major questions to which this study is addressed:

1. What circumstances led to the adoptive parents' decision to adopt?
2. What was the nature of the infertility, if any, that caused them to resort to adoption? How many of the couples had their own biological children prior to and/or following adoption?
3. What was the nature of their and the child's initial adjustment to the adoptive experience?
4. What was the nature of the couples' experience in the parent role?
5. How do the parents currently perceive the ajustment of the adoptees in important life-space areas as they grew to adulthood? How did the adoptees' performance in these areas measure up to parental expectations?
6. What was the nature and quality of the parent-child relationships as the adoptees grew up?

7. To what extent do the parents report that the adoptees engaged in serious deviant or acting-out behavior as they grew up or in criminal behavior in adulthood? How many showed emotional problems, mental illness, or other aberrant forms of behavior?
8. At what age, how, and in what detail did the adoptive parents reveal to the adoptees and to others the facts of the adoptive status and the adoptees' biological background? How did the adoptees react to the content and the handling of this information?
9. To what extent did the adoptive parents attribute any of the adoptees' psychosocial problems to their adoptive status?
10. In general, how satisfied were the adoptive parents with their overall experience with adoption?

These questions concern some of the descriptive information available in this book. We trust that this kind of information will have value for agencies engaged in adoptive placements. We also assume that these findings will be of interest to the various professional groups concerned with adoption, e.g., lawyers, physicians, and clergymen, as well as to the larger audience of adoptive families and those who are contemplating the prospect of adoption. With respect to the immediate implications of the findings for practice, we would stress that the reader be mindful of the limitations of the study with respect to sampling, problems of recall, and the like, which will be set forth in Chapter III. It is our strong hope that these findings will not be grist for the mill of those who harbor basic hostility to the agencies who have the difficult professional task of selecting and providing supportive services for adoptive families. By the same token, we would like to believe that the findings will not be misconstrued by those who are so committed to the status quo in agency operations that they fail constantly to seek areas in which adoption practice can be made more effective. Either approach would be a disservice to the families who generously participated in this study and to those tens of thousands of families who will be adopting children in the future.

Aside from purely descriptive findings we have set forth in this book a substantial body of statistical analysis of these findings. It is important at this point to stress the fact that we have sought to identify variables that showed potential for being associated in meaningful fashion with the overall outcomes of adoption as reported by our subjects. There is no pretense of being able to make any causal inferences about the etiology of the various types of outcome. A much more rigorous study than was possible here would be required for such a purpose. We doubt whether the current state of knowledge about adoption yet permits the prior specification of variables required for this kind of research. It is rather our hope that leads developed in this research will spur others to even more painstaking studies in which greater sureness about significant variables in the lives of adoptive families will make it possible to determine more definitively why some children fare well in the adoptive experience while others encounter great difficulties. Needless to say, there is no assumption on our part that the range of difficulties experienced by adopted children is any greater than for those encountered by children reared by their biological parents.

two / Conceptualizing the study

WE APPROACHED the task of examining the experiences of individuals with the institution of adoption with certain notions about possible indications of dysfunction in the life of the family and possible sources of role strain. A basic challenge to us was the question of determining the behavioral indicators that might best be employed in scrutinizing a sample of adoptive parents. We believe these should take into account the stresses the parents might be subject to—perhaps of a different nature from those rearing their own biological offspring.

ENTITLEMENT TO THE CHILD [1]

After a review of the professional literature and after discussions with persons close to the phenomenon of adoption, the concept of *entitlement* emerged in our thinking as providing a useful perspective for understanding the dynamics of adoptive parent behavior. While the adopted child may be viewed as typically facing the task of resolving complex identity problems with respect to the two sets of parents who have played major roles in his life, we also considered it useful to think of a parallel identity challenge facing the adoptive parents. It was our conception that the typical adoptive parent is faced with the primary task of developing a feeling of entitlement to his child. We speculated that whatever hazards existed in adoption from the standpoint of parental behavior, these were likely to stem from the parents' inability to feel that the adopted children truly belonged to them. If this lack of security entered into the relationship, we anticipated that we would find these parents engaging in "as if" relationships, pretending that they were flesh and blood relatives with much of their emotional energies being spent in reenforcing this impression for themselves and for others. Clinicians usually refer to this type of behavior as "overly determined." We saw as an important undertaking for investigators in this field the task of determining whether a solid positive bond had indeed united adoptive family members as a result of successful living experiences together or whether the family showed itself to be vulnerable to disintegrative pressures.

Conceptually, we assumed that the successful resolution of the problem of entitlement would signify that the adoptive mother or father had mastered any basic doubts about his worthiness as a parent, particularly with respect to resolving the psychological insult associated with the problem of infertility. Professional writers in this field have long assumed that if the individual feels that he or she does not possess true masculinity or femininity because of an inability to procreate, this may well interfere with the development of a sense of parental entitlement to the child. Following this line of thinking, we speculated that a hazard in adoptive placements would reside in the possibility that the adoptive parent with unsuccessful identity resolution would harbor unconscious hostility towards the adoptee as the symbol of the failure to achieve fertility.

In attempting to develop operational measures of the adoptive parent's sense of rightful possession of his child, we identified three areas of parent behavior that appeared related to this basic concept, albeit in less than direct fashion: (1) the parent's risk-taking behavior; (2) the parent's manner of coping with normal processes of separation from the adoptee; and (3) the patterns employed by the parents in socializing the adoptee.

RISK-TAKING, SEPARATION, AND SOCIALIZATION

The physical care and protection of children are basic to the parental role and require the parent constantly to assess a variety of situations which may present potential risks to the health and well-being of his child. The average parent has come to accept a degree of such risk in raising his children, but from a theoretical standpoint this element might create a special problem for some adoptive parents. For example, we construed the overanxious use of medical facilities as possibly representing conflict in the adoptive parent about his entitlement to the adoptee. That is, the need to protect the adoptee's health in an excessively zealous fashion would reflect elements of defensive parental behavior. Similarly, an inability to allow the child to develop independently and to assume the kind of self-responsibility that is considered normal for his age group would be yet another manifestation of parental disablement.

For example, an adoptive mother who needed to accompany her youngster to school well beyond the time when his contemporaries were going unescorted, would likely reflect the type of internal parental conflict outlined above. Needless to say, the pressure of such internal conflict could also be indicative of behavior at the other end of the continuum. *Excessive* risk-taking by the adoptive parents—as exemplified by insufficient or negligent care of the adoptee's health or by unrealistically strong demands for premature independence on the part of the adoptee—might just as well betray unresolved parental feelings of unworthiness with which the adoptive parents consciously or unconsciously seek to cope by overcompensating for them.

This applies as well to risk-taking as extended to other areas of physical care and safety. Whether or not to allow boys to partake in physical-contact sports such as football is a typical parental decision which may involve the assumption of normal or excessive risks. The same holds true for the use of substitute care. The ability of the parents to make adequate and realistic use of baby-sitters, for example, is viewed as a test of their comfort in assuming parental responsibilities. Couples who cannot permit themselves any social life for an extended period after the adoptee's placement—as well as couples who carry on such active social lives that they jeopardize the formation of a relationship with the child—may well have conflicts about their right to have a child.

We thought it worth the effort to seek information from the adoptive parents about their past experience with respect to risk-taking, even though recollection of their own behavior might be impeded by the passage of so many years. Our aim was to order the subjects according to their tendencies to function within a range running from highly cautious and guarded behavior to relative freedom to excessiveness in the risk-taking area. We wished to examine how these tendencies might be linked to the outcome of the adoptive experience as measured by the various adjustment indices we intended to develop.

Aside from risk-taking, we saw other areas of child rearing as testing the parents' ability to undertake parental role obligations without neurotic conflict. One such area is the manner in which the parents dealt with problems of separation. Pollak has developed a model of what he considers to represent an emotionally healthy family.[2] This model includes among other parental tasks the ability to accept, and to further, normal separations of the child from the family unit, e.g., departures for school, sleep-away camps, college, and marriage. Pollak sees the growing-up experience of the child in the family as the training ground for the eventual total separation that must ultimately take place with the death of the parents.

In the unhealthy family the child is made to feel guilty when he seeks to separate himself out as part of his normal development. Various barriers are placed in his way by the parents. We viewed the handling of the phenomenon of separation as having particular significance in understanding adoptive families. We anticipated that parents whose sense of entitlement was tenuous would likely be the ones to suffer extreme anxiety with normal separations of the adoptee from the family unit. If each such separation were viewed as constituting a threat to the integrity of the family—on the grounds that what has been artificially put together is more vulnerable than nature's product —this might well become the seeding ground for serious emotional disturbances in the adopted child. We saw such parental orientation to separation as being fairly accessible to scrutiny in research interviews.

Yet another area that we anticipated would provide a clue about the security of the adoptive parents was that concerned with the socialization of the adoptee. The inability of a parent to apply suitable disciplinary measures when indicated would be an example of this type of impaired role behavior. We saw the underlying dynamics as likely taking the form of the parents' feeling that punishment could not be applied to the adoptee because the latter's affection for them was based upon something other than a biological relationship.

INFERTILITY AS A CENTRAL CONCEPT

Our examination of the practice literature revealed considerable interest and consensus of opinion among child welfare workers about infertility as a central issue in assessing the readiness of couples to assume the status of adoptive parents. The degree to which an individual has successfully assuaged the pain and assault upon his ego inflicted by his being infertile is seen by many writers as a key to understanding the dynamics of a couple's readiness to take on a child who is biologically unrelated to them.[3] If the adopted child personifies for the parents the fact that they have not been biologically adequate, it is reasoned that unconscious resentment may well influence the way they will relate to him.

The experience of social workers who have interviewed couples applying to adopt a child suggests a wide range of reactions to the request for information about the nature of the infertility, the medical diagnosis, the nature of the treatment received, and so forth. Not infrequently, situations are encountered in which the applicant is quite brittle when the topic of infertility is raised. Adoption workers also occasionally see wives who become so protective about their husband's sense of humiliation at being infertile, that they find it necessary to take the pose of being the source of the infertility, even when this is not the case. The reactions of adoptive applicants to discussions of infertility run the gamut from highly neurotic defensive behavior to apparent composure stemming from the individual's successful resolution of the problem.

There has not thus far been substantial research seeking to link the manner in which infertility is experienced by couples to their later performance as parents. However, there are many hunches, assumptions, and even myths about the infertility phenomenon. An example of one of the common sources of speculation is the alleged frequency of successful pregnancies following adoption in couples who have been presumed to be infertile. It is theorized that in some cases adoption promotes resolution of infertility by enabling individuals to improve their self-images through successful performance as parents; this is said to have the effect of facilitating relaxation which in turn promotes successful impregnation.[4] Another issue which has arisen about infertility deals with the suitability of couples whose physical examinations reveal no physical basis for infertility but who nevertheless have been unable to conceive their own child. The problem for the social worker is to assess the degree to which functional infertility may be related to major pathological patterns in the adaptation of the spouses to each other and in their intrapsychic functioning.

In a follow-up study which takes place some twenty to thirty years after a couple has been known to an adoption agency, it is obviously quite difficult to recapture with any degree of certainty the facts and the attitudes relevant to their infertility status at the time of the adoption application. Our approach in this research undertaking was to explore this area as systematically as possible through a content analysis of the existing agency case records and through depth interviews with the parents in which the recall of the subjects about the infertility condition was elicited. Because of the lack of consistent case recording within the four agencies, we did not expect that much could be mined from the content analysis. It was hoped, however, that the interviews would provide such information about whether the couple was in agreement about the locus of their infertility (i.e., in the husband, the wife, or in both), its nature (e.g., low sperm count, tilted womb, etc.) the nature of the medical help sought, and the attitude of the couple about the condition.

REVELATION

In considering the adjustment of adoptive families during the years in which their children grew to adulthood, we saw as central to the purposes of this study the determination of how "the telling" or the revelation of adoption was handled. This subject holds more than academic interest since there has been a fair amount of controversy in professional circles about how best to tell children of the facts of their adoption. Some investigators have developed the perspective, based upon the psychoanalytic treatment of adopted and nonadopted children, that revelation of adoptive status ought to be postponed until the child is fairly old—perhaps in his late teens—when he can cope with the emotional turmoil that such knowledge is likely to stimulate.[5] While agencies have long stressed to couples the need to tell adoptive children the truth about their status, professional practice has not yet had the benefit of research which can shed light upon the consequences of revelation at various ages or of divulging to the adoptee the information concerning the marital and social status of his biological parents. There seems to be a fair amount of professional consensus that the adoptive mother's and father's handling of revelation is apt to provide useful clues about their overall adjustment as parents. As set forth in the professional literature, it would appear that the adoptive parent who chooses to "bury" the biological parents, or who resorts to other fabrications about them, is reflecting his own unsatisfactory resolution of infertility.

In developing a guide for the interviews to be conducted with the adoptive parents, we specified various kinds of information that we desired about the manner in which revelation was handled. We were interested to know first whether the adoptee had ever been told he was adopted, and if so, at what age and under what circumstances the initial revelation had taken place, and what information the adoptee had been given at the time. Also we desired to ascertain how frequently the topic had been discussed within the family over the years, the adoptee's reaction to these discussions, and the parents' recall of whether they had experienced any discomfort in their handling of the subject. In addition, we wished to determine the extent to which the adoptive parents had tended to make the fact of adoption visible to their associates, friends, and neighbors. We anticipated that extreme secretiveness about the adoptive status might be related to the outcome measures we would develop.

CONCEPTUALIZING THE OUTCOME OF ADOPTION

In attempting to develop a rationale for assessing the outcome of the adoption experience, we recognized that we needed to differentiate among a number of salient factors. By whose standards would we assess the outcome: the parents'? the adoptees'? the broader community's? The resolution of this problem proved to be far from simple.

In the preliminary interviews conducted with adoptive parents solicited as pretest research subjects through the *New York Times*, we discovered occasionally that the parents and their adopted child differed in the way they evaluated both past and present family life experiences.[6] For example, an adoptee might have succeeded in completing his college education and might currently express pleasure about his achievement. Yet, the parents might well express a discordant note because of the adoptee's failure to complete the professional education required for pursuing the same kind of career pattern followed by his adoptive father.

To cite another type of conflict, the adoptee may have married someone from a different social or religious background and appear quite pleased about his marital situation while his parents might show considerable distress about this deviation from their wishes. In other types of situations, the adoptee and his parents might be in complete accord in approving the total economic dependency of the former upon his parents extending through the third decade of the child's life. From a societal viewpoint, the failure of the child to take financial responsibility for himself might well be seen as an indication of considerable disablement. From the viewpoint of the family, however, this type of arrangement might cause little or no discomfort.

We gradually came to the conclusion that the appraisal of the outcome of a human being's life experiences involved rather profound philosophical issues. We believed that in any research dealing with the assessment of individuals it would be important to build into the evaluative procedures some measures reflecting the subjective orientations of the key actors as well as measures of a more objective kind. These orientations were deemed to have as much cogency as the allegedly more objective societal expectations involving some notion of normative behavior for a cross section of the population in the same age range.

We also recognized that there was considerable hazard in attempting to characterize, with one stroke of the brush, the totality of a human being's life as being entirely successful or unsuccessful. It was more congenial to our outlook to address ourselves to different areas of the adoptee's life space and to describe his adjustment within each of these areas. This would give recognition to the fact that a person could perform with considerable self-satisfaction and adequately meet societal standards in certain areas while yet revealing dysfunctional adjustment in other life-space areas. Looking at the life of Vincent van Gogh, for example, one might view his performance in the creative-artistic sphere as having afforded him much individual satisfaction and having resulted in tremendous societal gain, although he simultaneously experienced a strong element of personal torment and psychological disablement.

It was not our intent to ignore the societal implications of the adjustment of the adopted children covered by our research. Thus, the interviews with the parents were designed to elicit a wide array of information related to potentially deviant or inadequate social behavior as commonly defined in our society. For example, there was interest in learning whether any of the adoptees had histories of antisocial behavior as children or adults. We also obtained data about the degree of emotional pathology experienced by the adoptees, including any history of hospitalization in mental institutions. The research interview also covered such phenomena as alcoholism, abrogation of role responsibilities such as poor work records, neglectful parental behavior, and severe marital disharmony, including separation or divorce. There was also discussion with the parents about the heterosexual relationships of the adoptees including problems in courtship and marriage.

Another area considered by us to be of central importance in evaluating the nature of the adoptive experience was the quality both past and current of family relationships. We saw this as a highly complex phenomenon since patterns of family living in part reflect the specific cultural milieu in which our families might be embedded. Thus, for one type of family, open expression of hostility and frequent altercations might have the quality of severe pathology reflecting serious disharmony, whereas in other family units this same type of manifest behavior might be more culturally acceptable and would not have such profound implications.

An attempt was made to build into the research procedures various lines of interrogation about the nature of each family's life experiences. Questions in our interviews and items in our questionnaire covered such dimensions as the degree of closeness the family maintained over the years, the amount of warmth that prevailed in their relationships, the frequency with which conflict broke out, and the depth of such conflict. We also inquired about the degree to which the family shared activities as the adoptee grew up, the frequency of contact among nuclear family members after the adoptee had achieved adulthood, and similar indicators of relationship. While we recognized that the concepts of closeness and warmth are not easy to distinguish, we hoped, through this multifaceted scrutiny of family life, to be able to discern those families where alienation and extreme disenchantment with each other had occurred and those families where a strong sense of solidarity had taken hold.

One aspect of the research exploration of the adjustment of the adoptees that was quite striking to us was the fact that their lives were unfolding even as the research was proceeding. Thus, one adoptee suffered a fatal accident within weeks of our interview with his adoptive parents. Another adopted child, after years of severe social and personal maladjustment, had very recently seemed to be settling down in a fairly high-level job and, for the first time, appeared to be "straightening himself out."

We were aware that the issue of *prevalence* of disordered living as construed by epidemiologists is usually defined in terms of the number of persons in the population who are afflicted with a given disorder at a given point in time. In this study, our orientation was somewhat different. The appraisal of the adoptee's adjustment took into account disorders that might have occurred in the past but that had since been overcome. This is a more stringent approach to the assessment of morbidity in individuals. We considered it important to include past history of dysfunctioning because a major intent of our study was to sensitize agencies about the variables associated with negative outcome at *any* stage in the adoptee's life. Practically speaking, if one set of parents has been able to provide a child with a relatively stress-free living experience during his growing-up years *and* in his current adulthood, such a family can be construed as having accomplished more than the family in which the adoptee's development and maturation have been hectic and stressful in nature, even though he may have eventually achieved a normal adjustment as an adult at the time of the study.

The gist of our discussion above is that the atttempt to characterize the outcome of adoptions is fraught with many contingencies which must be taken into account when attempting to assign families to some kind of adjustment continuum. For the layman, and this is unfortunately often true of the professional as well, hedging the evaluation of adjustment with "if's, and's, and but's" may engender some irritation and perhaps be seen as an evasion of the central evaluative task. Typically, the researcher is confronted with the exasperated query of the person interested in the outcome of adoption: "All I want to know is whether these children grew up to be bank robbers or bank presidents!" Our response to such a view of the evaluation task is: "Life just ain't that simple."

three / The study method

THE PRECEDING two chapters have introduced the reader to the background of this study, to its objectives and general design, and to the manner in which we conceptualized its principal dimensions. To complete the first section of this report concerning the nature of the study the current chapter will present the methods used in the investigation. Beginning with a discussion of the subjects of the research it will then deal with the sampling methods employed, the procedures used to locate the sample families, and the representativeness of the final sample. Next, each of the three sources of data for the study will be considered and the various data-collection instruments described in some detail. Finally, the qualifications and training of the research interviewers will be treated briefly.

Sufficient attention will be devoted to each of these topics to provide the reader with an understanding of the major methodological decisions made at various junctures of the study. Should he be interested in a more detailed examination of these decisions and of other methodological aspects of the study, the reader is referred to Appendix A, *Additional Notes on the Study Method.*

The sample

As indicated in Chapter I, the research reported in these pages is a study of the perceptions of a sample of *adoptive parents* concerning the development and adjustment of their adopted children. The adoptees are the subjects of the inquiry: the focus of concern is upon their life adjustment. However, their story is told not by themselves but by their adoptive parents, intimate coparticipants in their life experiences. Most likely it is not exactly the same story that the adoptees themselves would have recounted,[1] but we believe that it is nonetheless a valid and important account which can yield revealing insights into the dynamics of adoptive family life.

THE POPULATION SAMPLED

Ideally the total universe from which the sample was drawn should have consisted of all families with whom children were placed for adoption by the four participating agencies during the period specified for the study, viz., 1930–1940. However, various practical considerations dictated that the population actually used be somewhat more circumscribed than this, and it was therefore delimited in three respects.

1. *Age of the adoptee at placement* We confined the study to families whose adopted children had been three years of age or younger at the time of placement. This step was taken for two reasons: first, we desired to study the adjustment of a sample of children who had been placed at a relatively early age and who consequently had experienced a substantial period of time in the status of adopted child. In terms of the placement age range prevailing in the four participating agencies two to three decades ago, the age of three seemed a reasonable cutting point which would permit the achievement of this objective. Considering the relatively modest size of the sample being studied, we deemed it desirable to achieve as much homogeneity as possible with respect to (a) the antecedent life experiences they were apt to have encountered prior to placement, and (b) their consequent

potential for adjusting satisfactorily in their adoptive homes. Again, the age of three presented a desirable dividing point. The special adjustment problems experienced in adoptive placement by older children as a group would have tended to obscure the factors entering into the adjustment of the children placed at younger ages who were the prime subjects of the study.

2. *Race* There were so few nonwhite families with whom the four agencies had placed children during the 1930–1940 decade that had any of them fallen into the sample it would have been impossible in the statistical analysis to separate out and control for race as a factor in the life adjustment of the adoptees. Consequently, the universe we sampled was confined to white families.

3. *Geographic area* As mentioned earlier, the Fund financing the study required that it be confined to adoptions arranged by agencies located in New York City. However, since a number of placements had been far beyond the New York metropolitan area, both time and financial limitations under which we operated required that the geographic base of the universe of families to be sampled also be delimited in some way.

This universe was consequently restricted to those families who at the time of adoption placement had been living within a 50-mile radius of the center of Manhattan. This area included all five boroughs of New York City, all of Nassau County and part of Suffolk County on Long Island, lower Connecticut, and a portion of New Jersey. Within it had lived the overwhelming bulk of the white families with whom the four participating agencies had placed children three years of age and under for adoption during the 10-year period studied.

When the universe had thus been narrowed, it consisted of 1,136 families divided into four agency roster groups. The number of families comprised in each component roster was as follows:

	NUMBER OF FAMILIES
Catholic Home Bureau	154
Chapin Nursery/Spence Alumnae	283
Free Synagogue Committee	373
State Charities Aid	326
Total	1,136

SAMPLING PROCEDURE

Because the initial contact had to be with the adoptive parents, the sampling unit became the adoptive *family* as represented by the adoptive father's name listed in the agency roster. However, we wished our final sample to consist of an equal number of families with whom boys and with whom girls had been placed in order to explore whether there were significant differences in the problems encountered by adopted children of each sex. The families appearing on each agency roster were therefore identified as to the sex of the child they had received to permit stratified sampling on this basis.

A random sample of 50 families was drawn from each agency roster, providing a total target sample of 200 or 17.6 percent of the sample universe. We believed that a sample of this size was sufficiently large to permit the type of statistical analysis contemplated and adequate to represent the population from which it was drawn. In addition, a reserve sample of 20 families, again evenly divided on the basis of the sex of the adoptee, was selected from each roster to be used in the event that the agency's primary sample became exhausted by attrition before yielding the requisite number of adoptive families for study. This occurred in 18 instances, and families were drawn from the reserve sample in such a manner as to preserve the equal sex distribution of the sample adoptees.

LOCATION PROCEDURES

One of the central and at the same time most arduous tasks faced by any investigator undertaking a follow-up study after a lapse of a number of years is that of locating the subjects he wishes to study. The well-known mobility of the American population presents a severe challenge to the ingenuity and resourcefulness of the researcher in his attempt to follow the peregrinations of the families or individuals in whom he is interested and to trace them to their current abodes. That this aspect of a retrospective study calls for considerable inventiveness is amply attested to in the descriptions of the location procedures used in at least three recent major follow-up studies in the child welfare field.

In finding our subjects, we were confronted with a major task which was in some respects more taxing than that encountered by some of the investigators recently reporting.[2] Because this problem is a basic one in follow-up studies and because it is only by researchers sharing their respective solutions to it that a common and effective body of coping techniques can evolve, we have included in Appendix A a detailed account of the various approaches which we explored. Most were found unfruitful for purposes of this inquiry, and the reasons why are also presented.

At this point, it will suffice to state that the only resource which proved at all productive was the current telephone directories of the thirty to forty principal communities within the study area. These directories were combed carefully on two separate occasions, and it was this intensive searching which ultimately yielded all the sample families whom we were able to locate.

NATURE OF THE FINAL SAMPLE

How effective were our location procedures? Table 3–1 summarizes the results, showing the numbers of families from both the primary and reserve samples who were finally found by means of the telephone directory search.

Of the primary sample of 200 families, we were successful in locating 121, or three-fifths. Somewhat more "finds" were realized from the Catholic Home Bureau sample roster than from the rosters of any

Table 3–1 / Number and percentage of primary and reserve sample families located and not located—total for all agencies

	PRIMARY SAMPLE		RESERVE SAMPLE	
	NO.	PERCENT OF TOTAL	NO.	PERCENT OF TOTAL
Total families	200	100	80	100
Locations attempted	200	100	18	23
Actually located	121	61	9	11.5
Not located	79	39	9	11.5
Locations not attempted	—	—	62	77

of the other three participating agencies.[3] Once the primary sample had been exhausted, the reserve sample was tapped for 18 families, half of which were successfully located. Of these 18 families, 16 were drawn from the reserve of 20 families for Chapin Nursery/Spence Alumnae.[4] All told, therefore, 130 families were finally found, which constituted 60 percent of the 218 families whose current whereabouts we had made efforts to trace.

However, inability to locate families was not the only source of attrition to which our original sample was exposed. Another source was the refusal of families to participate in the study once they had been painstakingly tracked down. About one-fifth of the 130 found, 25 families, did not consent to cooperate in the project.[5] Many of these would not explain why. They maintained merely that they did not wish to be involved in any way. Some were skeptical of the value to be derived from such a study while others offered such explanations of their refusals as family illness, vacation plans, or just sheer unavailability at any time in the foreseeable future.

Ultimately 100 families were included in our study,[6] 25 from each of the four agency rosters. This was a rather drastic reduction in the 200 initially envisaged. Such a cutback in the size of the study was dictated by the compelling factors of cost and time in two major areas: the location of sample families, and the conduct of the adoptive parent interviews. Reference has already been made to the difficult and time-consuming nature of the first task. Finding sample families to interview proved far more expensive than we could have anticipated at the outset of the study. In addition, the eventual length of the interview with each adoptive parent, plus the time required to process it, turned out to be substantially greater than we had originally expected and thus also worked severely to deplete an already tight budget. Consequently, we decided to circumscribe the study and limit it to 100 adoptive families, the first 25 interviewed from the sample roster of each of the four participating agencies.

THE QUESTION OF REPRESENTATIVENESS

To what extent can our 100 families be considered representative of the population from which they were drawn? To put the question differently, to what degree would it be justified for the reader to conclude that the findings contained in this report characterize not only the limited group of families interviewed but also the 1,136 families who comprise the balance of the universe from which the 100 originally came?

Although quite germane, these questions cannot be readily answered in simple, unequivocal terms. On the face of it, the inability to locate two-fifths of the primary sample would seem to bring into question representativeness of the three-fifths who were found unless the two groups were highly comparable with regard to the major variables considered salient in the life adjustment of children. Such a comparative appraisal was not possible in the present study simply because data regarding the relevant variables were not available for the unlocated families. Most of these variables would have manifested themselves in the lives of the adoptees only subsequent to placement, and, as mentioned earlier, the large majority of families had had no contact with the placing agencies following the legal adoption proceedings. Moreover, the skimpy and uneven quality of the case records prevented comparison of the located and unlocated families on even some of the major antecedent variables for which data might normally be expected to be contained in case records and which were later found to be significantly related to outcome.

Further, these same recording limitations prevented us from examining the differences with regard to the independent variables which existed between the located families who consented to participate and those who refused to do so. Added to this was the fact that in the very brief telephone conversations with the latter families, it was well nigh impossible to learn much concerning the important intervening life experiences which might have had a strong impact upon the ultimate adjustment of the adoptees. Adoptive parents who were suspicious of the study were also loathe to divulge information regarding how their children had fared over the years or, for that matter, how they were faring presently. Occasionally, in an effort to rationalize his not participating in the study, a parent would comment that the adoption had "worked out fine." Besides being rare, however, such comments were relatively meaningless.

Several factors would thus seem to prompt at least the raising of the question of whether the interviewed families can be considered adequately to represent the agency roster universes from which they came. At the same time it seems to us that this question cannot be answered unequivocally in the negative because sufficient unimpeachable evidence is lacking to permit such an answer. The only variable on which the 100 participating and the 79 unlocated families are definitely known to be dissimilar is the propinquity of their current residences to the center of Manhattan. And there seems no firm basis for concluding that this factor alone would differentiate the two groups in ways of direct relevance to the purpose of this study.

We make the assumption that the families who could not be found in the phone directories had moved out of the study area by the time the present research got under way. However, this in itself should not cause surprise, nor can it be considered in any way deviant or unusual behavior. The great mobility of the American population is well documented, and the fact is that a minimum of two decades had passed since the adoptions had been legally consummated. There is every reason to expect that sometime during this period these families would have moved from their former addresses for one of a number of perfectly commonplace reasons. That such moves took them more than fifty miles away can be considered largely fortuitous, particularly when we discovered that some of the located families had also at one point settled beyond the boundaries of the study area only to relocate once more within it prior to the inception of the study.

There would appear, then, no solid grounds for concluding that the factor of residence within or beyond the study area would be likely, in and of itself, to differentiate the located and unlocated families in ways or on variables of significance to this study. At the same time, it must be conceded that all the implications and ramifications of the residence factor are not really known or understood. Moreover, the two sources of sample attrition described above did deprive the final group of 100 families of its intended random quality, and there is no way of assessing the nature or the extent of the biases which such attrition may have introduced into the study. Consequently, we believe that caution and restraint are indicated in reaching conclusions about the generalizability of this investigation's findings. These should, we suggest, be interpreted exclusively rather than inclusively. They should, in other words, be taken to represent data and conclusions drawn from, and for the most part applicable only to, the life experiences of the adoptive families who actually participated in the study.

What are the implications of such a stance for the usefulness of this report? If its findings cannot be generalized to adoptive families other than those actually studied, are these findings of any real value? We emerge from this study believing that they are. We view the issue of generalizability as not looming nearly as large in an exploratory excursion as it does in studies of more sophisticated design. As mentioned earlier, the present inquiry was conceived of as a frankly exploratory piece of research. It was undertaken while awaiting results of the few recently launched longitudinal investigations in the adoption field whose findings will not be available for several years to come. In the meantime, this study was seen as opening up an area which had formerly received almost no systematic research attention, viz., the dynamics of adoptive family life and the long-term adjustment of adopted children. We hoped to be able to shed some beginning light upon these important subjects and to provide clues to aspects of them which might profitably be studied at some time in the future.

Sources of data

In order to achieve the study's objectives, information was obtained from three major sources by means of four principal research techniques. In essence, we used a multitrait, multimethod approach somewhat similar to that suggested by Campbell and Fiske.[7] The primary source of data was naturally the adoptive parents themselves. In lengthy and detailed interviews they provided us their perceptions of their experiences with adoptive family life and of their adopted children's past and present levels of adjustment. They also completed an extensive questionnaire designed to explore some of the same areas which were covered in the interview and also to tap some of the attitudes of the parents concerning certain generic aspects of the adoption phenomenon and certain approaches to child rearing.

A second source of data was the sample families' case records. Although by and large these contained relatively sparse information, they were mined for whatever data they could furnish regarding the adoptive parents' personal and social characteristics, their motivations for adopting, and also the adoptees' preadoptive life experiences. Finally, data were also gathered from the caseworker-interviewers in the form of professional judgments and evaluations of four aspects of the adoptive parents' experience with and handling of adoption.

The present report will address itself to the data obtained in the parent interviews, from the interviewer ratings, and from the review of the case records.[8] The nature of the several instruments and procedures used to obtain this information will now be considered further in a general way. In Appendix A the reader will find a more detailed discussion of some of the more technical aspects of the design, testing, and limitations of the instruments and of the decisions which were made to cope with problems arising during their use.

THE CASE RECORD REVIEW

Prior to the interview with each family—and, in most instances, even before that family had actually been located—the agency record of the adoption application, study, and placement process was read and a fairly detailed schedule completed.[9] The purpose of this review was twofold: to glean from the record any information which might facilitate the location of the family, and to gather whatever data were available regarding the characteristics and background of both the adoptive parents and the adoptee to serve as the independent variables in our inquiry.

The scantiness of the case record contents, already mentioned, severely restricted their usefulness for these dual purposes. Nevertheless, the record review did prove of some limited value. A number of families were found to continue to live at the addresses last listed in the case records or in supplementary files. In several other instances, these addresses furnished leads through which we were able to track the families to their current residences. Finally, in a few cases, references in the records to summer homes or to longstanding vacation haunts provided fruitful clues to the location of families whom we might otherwise never have found.

With respect to the background and characteristics of the adoptive parents, the case records did contain almost universally basic data concerning the age of the couples at application, former marriages, and socioeconomic data. Generally, there was also information concerning the applicants' preferences as to the age and sex of the children they were requesting. However, very little was found in the majority of records about the nature or cause of the infertility that had led to adoption application or regarding the couples' feelings and attitudes about this barren condition. This notable lacuna in what would currently be considered essential information is not surprising, of course, when one realizes that prior to the 1940s the staffs of the four agencies were almost uniformly untrained.

Similarly, the case records were relatively unproductive of data concerning the background and characteristics of the adoptees. Information *was* uniformly available regarding the sex and age of the children at placement, but the records were very uneven with regard to the children's preplacement histories. Both the amount and quality of recording concerning this crucial factor varied markedly from record to record both within and among agencies, ranging from no information at all or simply brief pencilled notes to full case histories, including some diagnostic summaries.

Consequently, although it was possible to develop a somewhat crude count of the *number* of preadoption placements experienced by all hundred adoptees, we were not able to include among our independent variables measures of the nature or quality of these placements or of the circumstances under which they were made. This places a limitation upon the significance of the conclusions we can draw regarding the relationship between the number of prior placements to which adoptees were exposed and the nature of their subsequent adjustment in the adoptive homes. Finally, there was no basis for using IQ as an antecedent variable since in a sizable proportion of the cases this information was also lacking. We knew for certain only that each child had received a physical examination prior to placement and that he had been found sufficiently physically sound to be adopted. We had no way of knowing the status of his intellectual or emotional health at the time.

THE INTERVIEW

Without question, the interview with the adoptive parents constituted the heart of our study. It was these in-person discussions which produced the wealth of data upon which the findings of this report are based. It is thus appropriate to describe in general terms the content of the interview, its format, and the data-recording instrument used in connection with it. Once again, however, we have allocated to Appendix A the detailed discussion of the important but somewhat technical methodological considerations which entered into our decisions to design and structure the interview in the following manner.

Content Since the interview was our major source of data, we made an effort to cover in some depth the various salient dimensions of the overall adoptive experience that pertained to the adoptee's adjustment. Guided by an extensive 36-page interview outline,[10] the interviewer explored the adoptive parents' perceptions of the nature of this adjustment in virtually all of the adoptee's major life-space areas. The full scope of this coverage will become apparent as this report unfolds. The following listing of the principal areas should, however, suffice to give the reader a sense of the breadth of subject matter encompassed by the interview:

1. the history and current status of the adoptive family;
2. the events leading up to the adoptive couple's application for a child;
3. the adoptive parents' first meeting with the adoptee, and their early living experiences with him;
4. a description of the adoptee at various stages of his development with respect to his adjustment in a variety of life-space areas;
5. the general family situation as the adoptee grew up;
6. the childrearing patterns used by the adoptive parents in the adoptee's upbringing;
7. the timing and approach of the adoptive parents in revealing to the adoptee his adoptive status, the nature and amount of information divulged, and the adoptee's reaction to this information;

8. the nature of the current relationship between the adoptee and his adoptive family;
9. the adoptive parents' assessment of the adoptee's personal and social adjustment;
10. the adoptive parents' overall assessment of their experience with adoption.

The interview was markedly developmental in its orientation. That is, in discussing major adjustment areas with the adoptive parents, we sought to obtain a panoramic view over time; a picture of the developmental progress evidenced by the adoptee throughout the two to three decades of his life. Thus, we queried the adoptive parent about how his son or daughter had fared in every basic area of his life space (e.g., school performance, personality adjustment, social relationships, etc.) during three specific age periods: below age 10, age 10 to 17, and age 18 and over. The composite or overall adjustment record in each area was then utilized to develop a final summary measure of the adoptee's adjustment in that sphere of his functioning.[11]

Site We sought whenever possible to schedule interview appointments at the Child Welfare League offices, which assured optimal interviewing conditions and guaranteed privacy from interruption. However, our overriding concern was to *obtain* the interview, wherever it had to be held, and every effort was therefore made to maximize the convenience of the adoptive parents in the scheduling of time and place. The result was that the large majority of families elected to be interviewed in their own homes most frequently during evening hours in order to guard against intrusion by the adoptees, other family members, friends, or neighbors.

Designation of adoptee to be focus of interview As we began contacting sample families to arrange for interviews, we discovered that several of these families contained two or more adoptees who were equally eligible for inclusion in the study, the criteria for eligibility being: (1) adoptive placement not later than age three, (2) by one of the four participating agencies, and (3) a current age of between 21 and 30 years. This situation posed a problem for us. The depth and scope of the data we wished to obtain concerning the adjustment of a given adoptee had already resulted in a very lengthy interview, which made it unfeasible to include a second adoptee within its purview. At the same time, budgetary limitations clearly ruled out a second interview with a given set of adoptive parents. These circumstances therefore required that we designate in an unbiased fashion a single adoptee to be the principal focus of attention in each family. We did this in advance of each interview by selecting from a table of random numbers the ordinal position of the adoptee who was to be the subject of the study in the event that more than one adoptee qualified for inclusion.

When such a situation was encountered, the interviewer identified the subject of the interview for the adoptive parents at the outset of the interview and explained to them the rationale behind the decision to concentrate on that sibling. The interviewer adhered firmly to the randomly designated choice as the primary focus of attention in the face of frequently expressed parental preferences for concentrating upon the other child, but he also encouraged them to bring into their stories any comparative information regarding the other adoptee which the parents thought might be interesting or relevant. Often such encouragement was gratuitous because the adoptive parents found themselves literally incapable of discussing their two children separately. In such instances the interviewer was frequently hard put but did his best to help the parents to individualize the adopted siblings.

An important consequence of the decision to focus upon only one adoptee should be noted. In several two-adoptee families the parents reported drastically differing life histories and dramatically contrasting current adjustments for the sibling who was and the sibling who was not the subject of the interview. More than once the comment was heard that had the focus been upon the undesignated adoptee, the story forthcoming would have been diametrically the opposite of the one that actually did unfold. In some instances, it was the unselected sibling who had manifested severe problems in many or in all life-space areas, and some of the parents of these children remarked that had it not been for the subject-adoptee, their experience with adoption would have been a totally disastrous one. Conversely, the random designation procedure also resulted in focusing attention upon several problem-ridden adoptees whose adopted siblings emerged as relatively well-adjusted and stable individuals. In both cases, the interviewers attempted to obtain as clear a picture as possible of the sibling's adjustment without shifting the interview orientation away from the subject. Such information was incorporated in the interviewers' diagnostic summaries of these adoptive families. However, the reader should be aware that the findings contained in the body of this report are, except where indicated, based exclusively upon the data concerning the hundred adoptees randomly designated as the subjects of the study.

Format and conduct In general, the interview format was an informal, unstructured one. The adoptive parent was engaged by the interviewer in a free-flowing discussion of the various aspects of his child's adoptive experience, with the interviewer following the parent's lead in the fashion of a casework interview and exploring topics in greater or lesser depth as this seemed indicated. The interviewer was guided by the detailed outline, but its topics did not have to be covered in any predetermined order. The form in which these were broached was totally unstructured, save for the question which uniformly initiated each interview: "Before we start discussing specifics, is there anything in a general way you would like to tell me about your adoptive experience?" Aside from this more or less standardized inquiry, the interviewer could phrase questions in the manner he deemed most appropriate and most likely to evoke the fullest and most meaningful response from the particular adoptive parent. He was free to use his professional judgment regarding when and how to introduce specific topics and how long to pursue them, provided only that all of the major areas of the outline were touched upon at some point in the interview.

We selected this unstructured approach to interviewing after careful consideration of its relative advantages and disadvantages compared with the more traditional, formal, structured format. We concluded that the free-flowing, casework-type interview would afford the interviewer the greater leeway we believed was required to explore the very personal and possibly emotion-laden material called for by the study. It would permit the interviewer to "feel his way" in opening up to examination potentially sensitive areas which presumably many adoptive parents had long since ceased to reflect upon and had not discussed with strangers for two to three decades. Not only would this format enable the interviewer to minimize the parents' possible discomfort; it would provide him the latitude to pursue in depth potentially productive leads which could not easily be followed in a structured interview where the interviewer is confined to items in a precoded schedule.

At the same time, we hoped to compensate for the methodological limitations and deficiencies of this approach through the use of an interview codebook, which will be described shortly. An extensive field pretest of our instruments led us to believe that our decisions concerning the form of the interview and its underlying rationale were basically sound; that the interview content did in fact tap meaningful dimensions of the adoptive experience; and that the unstructured format was workable.

In more than three-fifths (62) of the 100 sample families, we were able to interview both adoptive parents. In the remaining families, several different factors led to our being able to interview only one of the two adoptive spouses.[12] All told, 89 adoptive mothers and 73 adoptive fathers were interviewed.

In instances where both parents in a family participated in the study the "respondent" was considered to be the adoptive *family* consisting of two partners. Together they were seen as constituting a single source of information concerning the family's experience with adoption, and their composite responses were so treated in the final data analysis. This meant that the interviewer was free to discuss only a portion of the outline topics with each partner provided that between them he explored all the essential areas.

When the separate interviews had been completed, both parents were again seen jointly to discuss two topics which had purposely been left untouched in the individual interviews because it was considered more advantageous to cover them when the partners were together. One of these was the couple's overall assessment of the satisfaction which they had derived from the total adoptive experience. The other was our desire to interview their adopted son or daughter. We believed that the optimal point for introducing this latter topic was at the end of the contact, after the interviewer had had the opportunity to establish the best possible rapport with the parents, and after they in turn had become identified with the study's objectives.[13]

Naturally, the above interview format was inapplicable where only one adoptive parent participated in the study. Since that parent was the sole source of information regarding the family's adoptive experience, the interview continued without interruption until the interviewer was satisfied that all possible topics had been covered. This took on the average approximately two hours. Then, in most instances, the questionnaire was left with the interviewee to be completed and mailed back at the earliest convenience.[14]

Taping the interview All but six of the hundred sets of parent interviews were tape recorded. In two instances where taping was not achieved, a language barrier prevented the interviewers from communication with the couples well enough to allay their anxiety and fear and to convince them of the confidentiality with which the tapes would be used. In the other four instances, the interviewees had tended to be resistive and suspicious from the outset of our initial contact with them, even prior to learning about our desire to tape the interviews. For the remaining ninety-four families, our request to record the interviews occasioned very little anxiety. The casework interviewers were surprised and impressed by the ease with which the adoptive parents adjusted to and became apparently oblivious of both the recorder and the microphone lying in front of them. Our study thus offers additional evidence to buttress the frequent reports in the literature that taping constitutes no real barrier to free communication and rapport even in interviews where the subject matter is very personal and considered "sensitive."

The interview tapes were of great value in at least three aspects of the study. First, and perhaps foremost, they made possible the delayed completion of the voluminous interview codebooks which will be described shortly. Optimally, a codebook should have been filled out directly following a given interview, but this was oftentimes precluded by the press of other work or by sheer fatigue. For example, it was frequently not possible for an interviewer to spend approximately three hours interviewing, particularly during the evening, and then return home or to the office and immediately devote the additional three to four hours required to complete the codebook. After a lapse of several days or even weeks, when he was able to begin this task, the wealth of detail demanded in the codebook items would most likely have begun to fade from memory. Undoubtedly, the quality of the study's basic data would have been impaired had not the interviewers had the opportunity to replay the interview tapes to refresh their memories either prior to or during the completion of the codebooks.

A second valuable purpose served by the tapes was their use in assessing the reliability of codebook entries, a procedure described in detail in Appendix A. Briefly capsulized, in the absence of typescripts there would have been no other way without the tapes to check on the reliability of the interviewers' translation of discursive interview material into objective codebook data. Finally, the tapes proved invaluable in the training of interviewers. No amount of verbal orientation could give the prospective interviewer as clear an understanding of the nature of the interview he would be conducting and as good a feel for the desired quality of interviewing and the problems he might confront as listening to one or two tapes of "live" interviews.

THE CODEBOOK

It was noted earlier that although we decided upon an unstructured, free-flowing interview, we were also cognizant of the limitations of this type of format. Chief among these is the fact that the discursive interview can present a problem in data analysis. Once the data are gathered, they must subsequently be coded or in some way translated into a structured and categorized form amenable to statistical manipulation.

Our solution to this problem was to couple the unstructured interview with a codebook by means of which the oral reports of the adoptive parents were converted into objective, categorized items which could be coded and treated quantitatively through use of an electronic computer. One such codebook was completed by the interviewer for each set of adoptive parents interviewed as soon as possible after the termination of the interview. We hoped in this way to capitalize upon the advantages of both the unstructured and the structured interview formats while compensating for the deficiencies of each. Our interviewers had the leeway we believed they required to gear the interviews to the particular needs and modes of relating displayed by individual parents. They were also able to explore topics in varying degrees of detail in order to mine particularly rich veins of information which might unexpectedly be revealed during the course of the interview. At the same time, upon the completion of each codebook, the basic data were in such form that we could readily proceed with the coding for statistical analysis.

Special scoring and coding procedures were required to cope with certain features of the interview format and of the kind of information we sought to obtain from the adoptive parents. A detailed consideration of these procedures is reserved for Appendix A, but, in summary, they permitted (a) the coding of inferential as well as definitive information, and (b) the scoring in a single codebook of both disparate and concordant information furnished by the two members of any adoptive parent couple.

Because the codebook data were to comprise the source of the study's major findings, including our measures of the adoptees' overall adjustment, it was essential that we be quite certain that these data were reliable. Consequently, two types of reliability checks were undertaken. As indicated above, one concerned the reliability of the basic codebook entries themselves. These were derived from what was essentially a content analytic process in which the interviewer *coded* —rather than made judgments from—the information furnished by the adoptive parents in their oral reports and then converted this coded material into prestructured codebook items. We needed to determine whether other researchers, exposed to the same parental reports, would code them in the same way. Only to the extent that they *would* tend to do so with a fair degree of certainty could we be satisfied that our primary data were reliable and that we could place confidence in their meaningfulness.

We therefore assessed the reliability of a 20 percent random sample of the one hundred completed codebooks, confining our check to those data which bore upon all of the major dependent or outcome variables. The rationale for this decision, as well as a detailed presentation of the statistical methods employed, will be found in Appendix A. Suffice it to say at this point that the codebook data were found to be reliable at a substantially high level of statistical signficance.

The question of reliability also arose, in connection with the coding of the codebook items for machine card punching, preparatory to computer analysis. The accuracy of this coding was tested by each of two coders recoding a random sample of twenty codebooks originally coded by the other. Thus, 40 percent of all the codebooks were involved in the check which revealed an unusually low rate of miscodings.

THE INTERVIEWERS' RATING INSTRUMENT

The third source of data for the findings presented in this report consisted of interviewer ratings of a number of characteristics pertaining to each parent's functioning, feelings, and attitudes in the role of adoptive mother or father. These ratings called for professional judgments to be made by the caseworkers who comprised our interview staff.

With the rating instrument,[15] the adoptive parents were rated on fifteen different scales assaying four major dimensions of the parental experience with adoption: (1) the parents' overall satisfaction, stress, and investment in the adoption experience, (2) their feelings about their inability to procreate their own children, (3) their attitudes and feelings about their child's adoptive status, and (4) their relationship with the adoptee. On each scale, the interviewer located the parent on a nine-point continuum with the aid of three anchoring illustrations. The resulting quantitative ratings were supplemented by the interviewer's diagnostic summary of the most salient aspects of each family's experience with adoption. This summary touched upon at least three topics not covered by the rating scales, viz., the parental handling of the revelation of adoptive status, the adoptee's current overall adjustment, and the adjustment of his siblings, both biological and adopted.

In analyzing the rating data, the separate father and mother scores on each scale were averaged to obtain a single rating representing the parental pair on that item. Of course, where only one parent had been interviewed, his rating was utilized in the data analysis. In instances where an interviewer believed that the interview had provided him no basis whatsoever for rating a given parent on a specific item, his rating of the other parent on that item was used.

The reliability of ratings was tested in the same manner and with respect to the same random sample of twenty cases selected to assess the reliability of the codebook data. Nine of the fifteen ratings were used for this purpose. The rationale for the choice of these scales and a discussion of the nature and results of the reliability test will be found in Appendix A. At this point, it can be stated that the ratings were found to be only moderately reliable, ranging from correlations of .43 to .82. The highest reliability was achieved for the rating dealing with the extent of the parents' satisfaction with their current relationship with the child. The lowest reliability occurred for the rating dealing with the amount of defensiveness shown by the parents in discussing their relationship with the child.

The study staff

The profesional study staff consisted of six part-time interviewers plus the two writers of this work. All interviewers were professionally trained caseworkers, most with considerable casework experience. One had had substantial previous experience in research interviewing.

This group of interviewers was subjected to the same attrition process which frequently characterizes studies where interviews must be scheduled to meet the convenience of prospective interviewees, and where it is consequently possible to provide interviewers with only intermittent work. Moreover, reference has already been made to the fact that a large portion of interviews in our study had to be conducted during the late evening hours at the homes of our sample families, which were oftentimes located a good distance from New York City. These factors, together with the interviewer's need to carry a rather heavy tape recorder, tended to discourage some of the female interviewers and contributed to the attrition rate. Thus, although at its peak the interviewer staff numbered eight, including the writers, almost three-fourths of the interviews (seventy-two) were conducted by three male interviewers. Forty-nine of these families were interviewed by the two writers.

All interviewers underwent a thorough training program before undertaking their first interviews, and all were subjected to ongoing

supervision once out in the field. The intensity of this supervision varied with different interviewers, depending primarily upon our assessment of the general quality of their early interviews. However, the
high degree of reliability found in the codebook data would seem to
attest, at least in part, to the common base from which all of the interviewers operated as a result of their training and supervision.

*four | Describing the
adoptive families*

IN THIS CHAPTER we present for the reader the general findings of the
study as a prelude to the more detailed analyses to be reported subsequently. Since expository writing about a large array of descriptive
variables can be tedious and difficult for the reader to absorb, we
have sought to add interest to our presentation by discussing the characteristics of the families according to their classification into three
groups representing the overall outcome of the adoption experience.[1]

Group I is composed of 33 families in which the adoptees evidenced the most favorable life adjustment over the years. Designated
as "low-problem" adoptees, they constitute the top third of the 100
adoptees ranked on the basis of their overall adjustment scores. Group
II represents the families of the 34 adoptees who achieved an adjustment which we have classified as "middle-range" in nature, while
Group III consists of the families of the 33 adoptees who manifested
the most problematic outcomes and whom we have classified as
"high-problem" adoptees.

These three outcome categories should be understood by the reader to represent relative rather than "pure" groupings. We do not intend to infer that the adoptees in Group I encountered no problems; nor do we wish to create the impression that adoptees falling into Group III necessarily manifested many problems in all the life-space areas we examined. Rather, the tripartite classification is meant to provide only an overall estimate of the general quality of the adoptees' life adjustments and their families' experiences with adoption as perceived and reported by the adoptive parents. Subsequent chapters of this volume will be devoted to detailed statistical analyses of the correlates of overall adoptee functioning as well as their adjustment in each of the several life-space areas entering into the overall measure.

Composition of the adoptive families

We inquired into several aspects of the composition of the adoptive families at the time their children were placed with them. Were there, for example, other children in these families prior to the adoptee's entrance? Forty-one of the families participating in the study answered "no" to this question: their only child was the adoptee who was the subject of the research interview. Of these families, 46 percent had adoptees in the high-problem group, a much higher percentage than was true for the families where there were two or more children in the family unit.[2] Only two families in the high-problem group had previously adopted other children prior to adopting the child who became the subject of our study, while there were ten such families in the middle-range group and six in the low-problem group. It is thus noteworthy that the parents of high-problem adoptees stand out as having been relatively limited in their prior experience as parents. They show a fairly marked difference in this respect from the families who seemed to fare better in the adoption experience.

Since there has been interest among students of fertility in knowing whether adoptive mothers become pregnant after they adopt a child, this material was covered in the interview with the adoptive parents. We found that twelve of the one hundred couples had succeeded in having a baby through biological means *after* they had adopted a child. With respect to the three categories of outcome, we found that three families in each category had each had one biological child born to them. In addition, two families in the low-problem group and one in the middle-range group had had two children born to them. Eight of the low-problem, ten of the middle-range, and seven of the high-problem families went on to adopt another child subsequent to the adoption of the subject of our inquiry. Two families, cited above, had had the experience both of adopting a second child and then of having a biological child born to them; one of these was in the high-problem group, and one in the middle-range group.

Table 4–1 concerns the number of siblings of the adoptee who were present in the adoptive family. The table's three columns represent the total number of siblings in the family and includes both those in the home before the adopted child was placed and those who subsequently entered the family system. For two out of every five of the adoptive families, the adoptee who was the subject of the research interview was an only child. In 50 percent of the families, the family unit had contained an additional child, while about one-tenth of the families had had two or more other children. Only one family in this last category had contained three or more siblings.

The families with only one single adoptee subject—i.e., no siblings—are sharply distinguished from the other families with respect to adoptee outcome or adjustment. In 46 percent of the no-sibling families, the adoptee fell within the high-problem grouping. This was true of only 26 percent of the adoptees who had had one sibling and of 11 percent of those who had had two or more siblings. The problems experienced by the single-child families in the care of the adoptee might be viewed as lending support to the theory propounded by

Table 4–1 / Number of siblings in adoptee's family

	NO SIBLINGS	ONE SIBLING	TWO OR MORE SIBLINGS
Group I (low problem)	30%	36%	34%
Group II (middle range)	24	38	55
Group III (high problem)	46	26	11
Total cases	(41)	(50)	(9)

Pollak to the effect that a healthy family requires certain structural supports, e.g., a child of each sex.[3]

We had anticipated that disenchantment with adoption might be a factor tending to discourage parents in the high-problem group from applying for additional adopted children. However, this was something about which the adoptive parents were seemingly not conscious when they spoke of the matter at the time of our interviews with them. Moreover, our assumption was not borne out by a comparison of the reapplication experiences of parents in each of the outcome groupings. A total of five sets of adoptive parents reported that they had actually made efforts to adopt another child following the placement of the subject of our study but had not succeeded. This was true for one family each in the low-problem and high-problem categories and for three families in the middle-range grouping. In addition, almost identical numbers of families in the three outcome categories reported having given consideration to the matter of adopting another child but not having followed through with this.

When the adoptive parents who had reared only one adoptee were asked why they had not sought a second adoption, twenty-six sets of such parents reported that the agency had either rejected them or discouraged them from reapplying, or that they had been confronted with financial, health, or other circumstantial situations that had served to deter them. Ten of the high-problem and nine of the low-problem families gave the latter reason, as opposed to only three families from the middle-range group. We found it of interest that none of the families reported as a reason for failing to seek the adoption of a second child the fact that they had been discouraged because of their experience with the adoptee, even in cases where the parents had rather stark stories to tell.

Social characteristics of the adoptive families

SOCIOECONOMIC STATUS

The measure of socioeconomic status (SES) employed by us in this study was a three-factor index in which each factor was given equal weight. These included the 1950 income of each adoptive family, the prestige rank of the adoptive father's occupation, and the extent of the adoptive father's education. Every family received a score for each of the three factors, and these were summated to provide an overall SES index score.

We chose 1950 income because it represented the families' financial situations at the time the one hundred adoptees were between ten and twenty years of age. This figure would more adequately characterize the financial climate prevailing throughout most of the children's important developmental years than would the families' incomes either at the outset of adoption or at the point that the study was launched. The prestige ranking of the adoptive father's occupation was based upon the "Revised Scale for Rating Occupation," developed by Warner, Meeker, and Eells.[4]

We present the income distribution of the study families in Table 4–2 below. Most of the one hundred families fell within the middle-income brackets. One in ten reported an income under $5,000, and somewhat more claimed an income of $30,000 or more. The income of more than half the families ranged between $5,000 and $15,000 during the year in question, the median income for the total sample being $11,053. When income is examined across outcome groups, it is readily apparent that on the average the families with adoptees in the low-problem category were financially the most advantaged, those with adoptees in the high-problem category, the least advantaged. Thus, so

Table 4–2 / *1950 income of study families*

1950 INCOME	GROUP I	GROUP II	GROUP III	TOTAL
Under $5,000	12%	12%	6%	10%
$ 5,000–$ 9,999	31	35	43	36
$10,000– 14,999	6	29	21	19
$15,000– 19,999	12	—	9	7
$20,000– 29,999	21	12	9	14
$30,000– 39,999	15	3	—	6
$40,000 and over	3	9	12	8
Total cases	(33)	(34)	(33)	(100)
Median income	$15,625	$10,500	$10,357	$11,053

far as this component of SES is concerned, the higher average adoptive family incomes appear to be associated with a better overall life outcome for the adoptees even though some families with substantial incomes have adoptees located in the high-problem grouping.

The distribution of the prestige ratings of adoptive fathers' occupations on the Warner, Meeker, and Eells scale is presented in Table 4-3. The occupations of almost two-thirds of the adoptive fathers in the sample fall within the two highest rankings on the scale, and almost three-fourths fall within the three highest prestige rankings. Illustrative of the occupations listed within each of these rankings are the following: [5]

> Highest prestige rating (rank 7)—lawyers, doctors, dentists, engineers, high school superintendents, proprietors and managers of businesses valued at $75,000 and over, regional and division managers of large financial and industrial enterprises, certified public accountants, etc.

> Second highest rating (rank 6)—high school teachers, trained nurses, newspaper editors, proprietors and managers of businesses valued at $20,000-$75,000, assistant managers and office and department managers of large businesses, salesmen of real estate, of insurance, etc.

> Third highest rating (rank 5)—social workers, grade school teachers, librarians (not graduate), proprietors and managers of businesses valued at $5,000-$20,000, all minor business officials, bank clerks, cashiers, supervisors of railroad, telephone, contractors, etc.

Table 4-3 / Prestige ranking on Warner, Meeker, Eells scale of adoptive father's occupation [6]

PRESTIGE RANKING (LOW TO HIGH)	GROUP I	GROUP II	GROUP III	TOTAL
1	3%	—%	—%	1%
2	6	3	3	4
3	12	6	12	10
4	9	21	6	12
5	3	9	15	9
6	21	29	27	26
7	46	32	37	38
Total cases	(33)	(34)	(33)	(100)
Mean rank	5.5	5.5	5.6	5.5

It can also be seen from the "mean rank" line in Table 4–3 that with regard to this component of SES the three outcome groups are virtually identical.

With respect to the educational achievement of the adoptive fathers, the third component of our SES index, the Group III families stand out sharply from the families in the other two adjustment groups. As can be seen from Table 4–4, more than one-half the fathers of high-problem adoptees had completed their college education, with one-fourth having had professional or graduate education beyond the undergraduate level. By contrast, less than a third of the fathers of adoptees in each of the other two groups had completed four years of college education, and fewer had gone on to take additional professional or graduate training. At the other end of the educational spectrum, only 12 percent of the adoptive fathers of high-problem adoptees had failed to secure any high school education, whereas this was true of 15 percent of the adoptive fathers in the middle-range outcome group and of 24 percent of the fathers of low-problem adoptees.

Our overall measure of socioeconomic status was developed by summating each family's three component scores. The range ran from a low of 3 to a high of 21. No family scored at the very bottom in all three areas, but one family of a low-problem adoptee received the low SES score of 4. Also, one family received a score of 21, having been

Table 4–4 / Extent of education of adoptive father [7]

HIGHEST EDUCATIONAL LEVEL ATTAINED	GROUP I	GROUP II	GROUP III	TOTAL
Less than 5 years of grammar school	6%	6%	—%	4%
5–8 years of grammar school	18	9	12	13
Some high school	6	18	9	11
Completed high school	31	18	12	20
Some college	9	20	12	14
Completed college	18	12	31	20
Professional or graduate education	12	17	24	18
Total cases	(33)	(34)	(33)	(100)

rated the highest in each of the three subareas. Table 4–5 presents the full distribution of SES scores for the 100 families in our sample and reveals a fairly even spread over most of the range and a median score of 13.4 for the sample as a whole. Our three outcome groups differ to some degree in the proportions of families falling at different levels on the SES continuum. However, no marked or dramatic differences are found to distinguish one group from the other two. This is particularly evident in the very narrow spread among the mean SES scores for the three outcome groups. In other words, the index we have utilized suggests only a limited relationship between the socioeconomic status of the adoptive families based largely upon their characteristics at the time of adoption and the subsequent course of the adoption experience. We will examine this relationship in greater depth in a subsequent chapter reporting upon the correlational analysis of the several independent and outcome variables. The reader can anticipate that the relatively weak linkage between SES and outcome we have here tentatively advanced will be seen to be more firmly grounded.

RELIGIOUS AFFILIATION

As we noted in Chapter I, the choice of agencies to participate in the current study was determined in part by our desire to obtain a cross-

Table 4–5 / Socioeconomic Status (SES) Scores of study families (based upon 1950 income, prestige ranking of adoptive father's occupation, and extent of adoptive father's education)

SES SCORES (LOW TO HIGH)	GROUP I	GROUP II	GROUP III	TOTAL
Scores 4–6	15%	3%	3%	7%
Scores 7–9	9	18	18	15
Scores 10–12	15	26	12	18
Scores 13–15	15	23	31	23
Scores 16–18	34	21	18	24
Scores 19–21	12	9	18	13
Total cases	(33)	(34)	(33)	(100)
Mean score	13.3	13.1	13.9	13.4

sectional sample embracing adoptive parents of the three major religious faiths. Pursuing this objective, the Catholic Home Bureau was invited to participate because of its service exclusively to Catholic clients. Similarly, the Free Synagogue Committee was approached as an agency which, during the 1930s and 1940s, had a completely Jewish clientele. Finally, we anticipated that both Chapin Nursery/Spence Alumnae and State Charities Aid would contribute a predominantly, if not totally, Protestant group of adoptive parents to the sample.

With equal size subsamples of twenty-five from each agency, we anticipated that the religious composition of the one hundred families would be one-half Protestant and one-fourth each Jewish and Catholic. Were this to prove true, it would facilitate our subsequent data analysis since any variables examined on the basis of placing agency or correlated with agency of placement would also simultaneously constitute an analysis by religious affiliation. This was indeed our rationale for the use of "agency" in the correlational analyses in later chapters of this report.

Perusal of Table 4–6, below, will reveal that this approach was largely but not fully justified. The total column of that table shows that only 42 percent rather than the expected 50 percent of the families belonged to Protestant denominations, while an unanticipated 5 percent of families were of Catholic religious persuasion over and above the 25 percent expected. Finally, 3 percent of our couples represented mixed religious marriages. Examination of religious affiliation by placing agency revealed that the original expectations had been

Table 4–6 / Religious distribution of study families
by outcome

	GROUP I	GROUP II	GROUP III	TOTAL
Protestant	43%	36%	49%	42%
Catholic	36	32	21	30
Jewish	15	29	30	25
Mixed marriage [8]	6	3	—	3
Total cases	(33)	(34)	(33)	(100)

correct in three out of four instances: all twenty-five families adopting from Catholic Home Bureau had in fact been Catholic, all twenty-five adopting from The Free Synagogue Committee had been Jewish, and all twenty-five obtaining children from Chapin Nursery/Spence Alumnae had belonged to some Protestant denomination. It was only with regard to the religious affiliation of the State Charities Aid families that we encountered some variation from our expectation. Seventeen of these families had classified themselves as Protestant, but five had designated themselves as Catholic, and three had reported mixed marriages. Neither the agency records nor the interviews with these latter three families provided information regarding the specific religion in which the adoptee had been raised.

The consequence of the religious distribution of the sample is that throughout this report our findings relating agency of placement to other variables can, by and large, also be regarded as constituting the relationship of religious affiliation to these same variables. However, while the agency-religion correspondence can be regarded as perfect when the findings pertain to families adopting through three of the agencies, it must be viewed as only approximate where State Charities Aid families are concerned.

In interpreting the above table, some interesting facts emerge when we examine the religious identifications of families within each of the three outcome groups. Thus, Protestant families who comprised approximately two-fifths of the total sample are somewhat overly represented in the high-problem outcome group, where they make up almost half of the total. The pattern of distribution is even more exaggerated for the Jewish families who are especially heavily concentrated in the middle-range and high-problem outcome groups. By contrast, our Catholic families are more than well represented in the low-problem group and underrepresented in the high-problem group.

SURVIVAL STATUS OF ADOPTIVE FAMILIES

To the extent that adoptive placement is viewed as an effort to provide a child with a substitute for the biological family of which he was deprived, it is to be hoped that the adoptee will be able to enjoy and benefit from a "complete" family, i.e., two adoptive parents living together and, if possible, one or more siblings. Toward this end, all adoptive agencies require as part of their application procedure physical examinations of the prospective adoptive parents to determine whether there are any health conditions that might be predictive of less than normal longevity for either of the two partners. Such examinations were required by the four participating agencies during the decade 1930–1940. Although the case records contained scant information concerning the results of these examinations, it can be assumed that the one hundred couples involved in the present study satisfied the four agencies on this score to the point where all were successful candidates for adoptive parenthood.

We sought to determine how many of the one hundred adoptees had in fact grown up in intact families. For those who had suffered the loss of one or both adoptive parents, we wished to determine when such losses had been sustained.

In Table 4–7 we see that 65 percent of the families were still intact with both adoptive parents alive and living together at the time of the field study. This is almost the identical proportion of intact families reported by Skeels and Skodak in their thirty-year follow-up of ninety-three adoptive couples with whom a hundred children had been placed in early infancy in the early 1930s.[9] During the interval between the placement of the children and the inception of the current study, 20 percent of the adoptive fathers and 8 percent of the adoptive mothers had died. The percentage death rate for the fathers

Table 4–7 / Family status of study families at inception of study

	GROUP I	GROUP II	GROUP III	TOTAL
Family intact: adoptive parents alive and living together	58%	73%	64%	65%
Adoptive father deceased	24	18	18	20
Adoptive mother deceased	12	—	12	8
Adoptive parents separated or divorced	6	9	6	7
Total cases	(33)	(34)	(33)	(100)

was very similar to that found by Skeels and Skodak, viz., 24.4 percent, but the death rate for the mothers was substantially lower than that reported by those two investigators, viz., 21.5 percent.

The adoptees in the middle-range outcome group sustained the smallest loss by death of their adoptive parents. Almost three-quarters of the families in this group remained intact at the time of the inception of the study, whereas this was true of somewhat less than two-thirds of the families in the high-problem category and less than three-fifths of the families of low-problem adoptees. Proportionately more adoptees in this last group had lost their adoptive fathers by death, and equal proportions of adoptees in Group I and Group III had suffered the death of their adoptive mothers. No adoptive mothers had died among the Group II families. Fairly equal proportions of adoptive parents in the three outcome groups had been divorced or separated.

It is noteworthy to us that although a higher proportion of low-problem adoptees (42 percent) had been deprived of one of their adoptive parents through death, separation, or divorce, they had nevertheless made the most favorable subsequent life adjustment.[10] In other words, solely on the basis of these data, one could be led to conclude that the death of an adoptive parent or the dissolution of the adoptive parents' marriage does not necessarily augur poorly for the eventual adjustment of the adoptee. Admittedly, such a formulation would be partial and incomplete. It fails to take into consideration such essential components as the quality of the relationships enjoyed by the adopted child with both parents prior to, and with the surviving parent following, the death or absence of one parent. It also neglects the age at which the child suffered the loss, a factor which we now consider.

Table 4–8 presents the data concerning the age of the adoptees at the time of the death, separation, or divorce of their adoptive parents. The reader will notice that in only three of the thirty-five instances when the adoptive family was thus afflicted was the adoptee five years of age or under. Those first five years are acknowledged by most social workers and child development specialists to be the most crucial ones for the child in the development of object relationships and thus the ones in which he is most vulnerable to the damaging conse-

Table 4-8 / Age at which adoptees experienced death, separation, or divorce of their adoptive parents

AGE OF ADOPTEE	GROUP I	GROUP II	GROUP III	TOTAL
5 or under	—%	6%	3%	3%
6–10	6	—	3	3
11–15	9	6	12	9
16–20	12	6	9	9
21–25	15	3	3	7
26 and over	—	6	6	4
No death, separation, or divorce in family	58	73	64	65
Total cases	(33)	(34)	(33)	(100)

quences of the loss of a parent. All told, only six of the thirty-five adoptees were deprived of their adoptive parent up to the age of ten.

In this connection, we call the reader's attention to the fact that according to Table 4-8, 42 percent of the low-problem adoptees—a total of fourteen—had suffered the loss of an adoptive parent. However, we see that for 27 percent (or nine) of the adoptees, this loss was sustained when they were sixteen years of age or older, and for none of them did it occur when they were age five or younger. As we suggest above, this age distribution may well be one of the two critical factors which account for the appearance of these adoptees in the low-problem category notwithstanding the relatively large numbers of them whose adoptive families did not remain intact.

Considering the survival of the one hundred adoptees we can report that all were alive at the time the study was launched. In 1962, after interviewing one adoptive father but before an interview could be arranged with the adoptee himself, the latter was killed in an automobile accident. Thus, as of the completion of the study, ninety-nine of the adoptees under investigation were still alive. The one fatality comprised 2 percent of the forty-nine male adoptee subjects, which is below the 5 percent estimate of expectancy of deaths for white males born in 1930 and alive one year later.[11]

Events leading to adoption

During the interview, our subjects were asked to recall the period preceding their agency applications and to relate the circumstances leading to their decision to adopt. While the recall of material which took place twenty to thirty years prior to the interview might seem to the reader beyond the reach of the average person, the interviewers employed in this study were impressed with the vividness of the information about their experiences which many of the adoptive parents provided. While the accuracy of their recall quite likely suffered from the passage of a considerable period of time,[12] it nevertheless appears useful to set forth explicitly what the responses of the subjects were.

PRECEDING EVENTS

The parents were asked whether the decision to adopt a child followed any unusual event in their lives. For example, did the request take place right after the death of their biological child? Or did it perhaps come after a stillbirth or a miscarriage? In analyzing the responses of our one hundred participating families, we found eighty-one of them reporting that no unusual event had occured prior to their seeking to adopt. Of the remaining eighteen couples, five spoke of the death of a biological child before adoption, and another nine made reference to a stillbirth or miscarriage. Four additional sets of parents indicated that there had existed before their application a period of upsetness relating to other kinds of problems.

In Table 4–9, we present the responses of the adoptive parents according to the three categories of outcome. While the differences are not striking, it is noteworthy to find that only one family in the low-problem group told of the occurrence of a stillbirth or a miscarriage prior to adoption, whereas three in the middle-range group and five in the high-problem category reported such experiences. While the differences are not statistically significant, we feel they are suggestive and warrant further investigation as a variable that might be related to the performances of adoptive families.

Table 4-9 / Events preceding decision of parents to adopt

	GROUP I	GROUP II	GROUP III	TOTAL
Normal period (No unusual event)	88%	79%	76%	81%
Death of own biological child	6	6	3	5
Stillbirth or miscarriage	3	9	15	9
Period of upsetness	3	3	6	4
Other	—	3	—	1
Total cases	(33)	(34)	(33)	(100)

Motivation The adoptive parents were asked to recall their state of mind at the time they approached the agency to apply for adoption. We desired to identify the nature of their motivations to adopt and specifically whether they were aware of any reservations they might have experienced about the general idea of adoption. Almost two-thirds of the adoptive parent couples showed consensus in stating they had been highly motivated to adopt, and only three couples conceded that both spouses had been less than completely enthusiastic about the prospect. Of interest is the fact that in seventeen cases out of a hundred the couple agreed that the woman had been highly motivated to adopt but the man less so. In eight cases the adoptive parents disagreed with respect to the depth of motivation of one or both parents. In Table 4-10 we show the parents' reports of their motivations according to the three outcome categories.

A few differences are noteworthy. We were particularly struck by the fact that more than one-fourth of the couples with low-problem adoptees reported that the woman had been highly motivated and the man less so. This was a substantially larger group than acknowledged such divergent motivation among the parents of the middle-range (15 percent) and high-problem adoptees (3 percent). We would have anticipated a reverse finding, viz., that there would have been more instances among families with adoptees in the high-problem group where the man would have been reported to be less than highly motivated. Since the finding surprised us, we have conjectured that perhaps the large number of reportedly low-motivated fathers in the low-problem category might reflect a lack of defensiveness in this group and security in the knowledge that their adopted children had fared quite well.

The reader might also note in Table 4–10 the extent to which spouses in the high-problem grouping tended to disagree in reporting their depth of motivation. Six of the thirty-three couples (18 percent) in this category presented conflicting reports, as did two couples (6 percent) in the middle-range category, but this was true of none of the couples in the low-problem group. The lack of agreement among parents of the high-problem adoptees suggests some connection between the relatively unhappy experiences these parents had to report to the researchers and the possibly lower degree of shared communication between the partners in these families.

Infertility An interview topic about which we anticipated considerable sensitivity concerned the source of the couple's infertility, if this had been the reason the couple had applied to adopt.

Table 4–10 / Parents' report of the depth of their motivation to adopt

	GROUP I	GROUP II	GROUP III	TOTAL
1. *Parents agree that:*				
a. *Both were highly motivated*	61%	71%	61%	64%
b. *Both were less than highly motivated*	3	—	6	3
c. *Woman was highly motivated; man less so*	27	15	3	17
d. *Man was highly motivated; woman less so*	—	6	—	2
2. *Parents disagreed on depth of motivation of one or both parents*	—	6	18	8
3. *Parents agree on high motivation of one parent; other not covered*	6	3	3	4
4. *Not covered/Unable to determine*	3	—	3	2
Total cases	(33)	(34)	(33)	(100)

Table 4-11 / Adoptive parents' reports about source of infertility

	ADOPTIVE MOTHERS' REPORTS				ADOPTIVE FATHERS' REPORTS			
	GROUP I	GROUP II	GROUP III	TOTAL	GROUP I	GROUP II	GROUP III	TOTAL
Couple not infertile; other reason for not having children	15%	20%	12%	16%	12%	18%	3%	11%
Prior miscarriages or stillbirths	3	15	12	10	3	3	18	8
Man reported as source of infertility	9	—	6	5	6	3	6	5
Woman reported as source of infertility	21	32	37	30	18	26	34	26
Cause reported as undetermined	28	15	15	19	18	3	15	12
Parents refused to divulge information	3	3	3	3	3	3	—	2
Both parents reported as source of infertility	—	3	—	1	—	9	—	3
Not covered in interview	3	—	—	1	6	6	3	5
Partner not interviewed or interviewer unable to determine information	18	9	15	14	34	29	18	27
Other	—	3	—	1	—	—	3	1
Total cases	(33)	(34)	(33)	(100)	(33)	(34)	(33)	(100)

Our interviewers were trained to seek information from the respondents about this matter without antagonizing them to the point of jeopardizing their willingness to continue in the interview. As it turned out, there were few direct refusals to divulge information, but at the same time there were a fairly substantial number of persons whose responses could not be coded because of the vagueness of information secured from them.

According to the reports of 30 percent of the adoptive mothers, the principal source of infertility had been the woman herself. This is evident from Table 4–11 which shows that in only five of the one hundred cases did the wife state that her husband had been the cause of the inability to have children and that in only a single instance was failure to procreate seen as having been the joint responsibility of both partners. One-tenth of the mothers attributed the absence of biological children to prior miscarriages or stillbirths, while in one-fifth of the adoptive mother interviews we were informed that the cause of infertility had never been medically determined. Finally, 16 percent of the women told their interviewers that as couples they and their husbands had not been infertile and that other reasons, e.g., health problems, had accounted for lack of biological offspring. Interestingly, as may be seen from Table 4–11, the reports of the adoptive fathers yielded a quite comparable picture of the bases of infertility.

When we compared the three outcome groups according to the kinds of infertility reported by the respondents, we were struck by the almost complete absence of reports of prior miscarriages or stillbirths among parents of low-problem adoptees. Among families where the adoptees had evidenced a highly problematic adjustment, there was a somewhat higher proportion of cases in which the woman was reported as a source of infertility than was true for families whose children had shown low-problem outcomes. While these findings are suggestive, they are far from clear-cut.

Our respondents were asked to provide details about their efforts to secure medical help to overcome their infertility. In only about one-third of the cases in each category of outcome did both husbands and wives agree that they had made strong efforts to secure such help. Another 16 percent reported moderate efforts in this direction. Thus, for the sample as a whole, one might say that about half the couples had made any real attempts to obtain medical help to overcome their incapacity to procreate. The other families had either already established their ability to have children or simply had not extended the necessary effort to overcome their infertility.

Sex preference There has been recent research interest in the sex preferences of adoptive applicants. In one study for example, it was found that the rate of rejection by the agency of couples wishing to adopt a female baby was significantly higher than the rejection rate among applicants preferring a boy. Those asking for male children showed a statistically greater number of completed adoptions than those requesting female children.[13] Kirk, in reporting on ten years of adoption research, suggests the sex preference of adoptive couples is a very revealing variable.[14]

Out of our sample of a hundred families, seventeen reported that they had felt a strong desire for a boy at the time they had applied for a child, and four reported having had a mild desire for a boy. Twenty-two couples said that they had very much wanted a girl, while nine recalled having felt a mild desire for a girl. Twenty-eight couples told us that they had had no preference when they came to the adoption agency, feeling they could have taken a child of either sex. In fourteen instances, we found that either the two partners disagreed in their recollections of the sex of the child they had preferred at application or that one parent remembered having specified a child of a given sex while the other parent reported having had no preference on this score.

In examining the sex preference of parents according to the three categories of outcome, we found that in general the parents whose adopted children had fared best in their life adjustment had showed a greater tendency to be specific about the sex of the child they had wanted than had been true of the parents of adoptees with the most problematic adjustments. Thus, whereas more than one-third (36 percent) of the parents of adoptees in both the low-problem and middle-range outcome categories had voiced either a strong or mild desire for a girl when applying for a child, less than one-fifth (18 percent) of parents of high-problem adoptees had expressed desires of similar specificity and intensity. At the same time, a strikingly higher proportion of couples in the latter category than in the low-problem category indicated a disparity in their retrospective reports of sex preference at the time of adoption. Again, while these findings are not dramatic, they do suggest to us how different were the patterns of communication prevailing among the parents of adoptees in the two polar outcome groups.

Age preference We also queried the respondents about their recollections concerning their preferences for the age of the child they had desired at the time they approached the agencies. Had they been thinking of an infant exclusively or perhaps an older child? In Table 4–12 we have set forth the age preferences expressed by the parents according to the three outcome categories. For the entire sample, more than one-third stated that they had wanted an infant, a child under six months of age. Another 20 percent indicated that they had desired a baby, a child up to one year of age. Five percent of all the couples indicated they could have taken a child up to two years of age, and 2 percent would have been willing to accept a child up to three years.[15] For 13 percent of the couples, the two partners gave divergent reports about what age they would have found acceptable. We were interested to note

Table 4–12 / Reported age preferences of parents at the time they applied to the agency

	GROUP I	GROUP II	GROUP III	TOTAL
Infant: under 6 months	27%	26%	55%	36%
Baby: up to 1 year	21	21	18	20
Up to 2 years	9	3	3	5
Up to 3 years	3	3	—	2
Disparity in age preference expressed between man and woman	15	12	12	13
No preference expressed by either parent	18	32	9	20
Other	3	3	—	2
Not covered in interview	3	—	3	2
Total cases	(33)	(34)	(33)	(100)

that one-fifth of the couples indicated that they had specified no preference about age and could have been flexible in this matter. They often attributed the decision to place a very young child in their home to the desires of the agency.

In looking at the distribution of age preferences according to the grouping of families by the three outcome categories, we find a striking difference between the reported desires of parents of high-problem adoptees and parents whose children showed more positive outcomes. Fully 55 percent of the couples in the former outcome category stated that they had preferred an infant, a child under six months. By contrast, such a preference was reported by less than half that proportion of couples whose adopted children fell in the low-problem and middle-range adjustment groups. We might conjecture that those couples who strongly desired to simulate biological parenthood, perhaps to the point of concealing their infertility from the community, would have gravitated toward infants. This is a striking difference, and its implications will be examined in the more systematic analysis reported in subsequent chapters.

Also of interest is the fact that while 18 percent of the parents of low-problem adoptees and 32 percent of the parents of middle-range outcome adoptees told us that they had had no age preferences, a comparable stance had been taken by only 9 percent of the couples whose children had shown the most problematic adjustment. There had apparently been greater flexibility about the age of the prospective adoptee in the two groups where the children actually fared best over the years.

Biological parents We asked the adoptive parents about the kinds of information they had been given concerning the adoptee's biological background. What had they been told, for example, about the marital status of the natural parents? Approximately half our total sample couples (53 percent) said they had been informed that their children had been born out of wedlock. This was true, however, of more parents of high-problem adoptees (61 percent) than of adoptees now classified as showing low-problem or middle-range adjustments (52 and 47 percent, respectively). At the same time, a substantially larger number of adoptive parents of low-problem adoptees (7) than of middle-range (3) or high-problem (1) adoptees had been led to believe that their children had been born to married couples.

In reviewing the responses of the adoptive parents, we were struck with how little most of them knew about their children's biological parents. Only 35 percent of the interviewees had even a modicum of information about the natural mother's education, and only 25 percent knew about the natural father's education. At least half of the adoptive parents had absolutely no knowledge whatsoever on this topic. In this respect, the parents of high-problem children were somewhat better informed than the other parents, but any conclusions about the implications of this fact would be most hazardous. Only about half of the adoptive couples had been given any information about the nature of the relationship which had existed between the biological parents (e.g., whether they had known each other well, had planned to marry, and so forth) but this knowledge, too, tended to be somewhat skimpy. With the exception of the parents of high-problem adoptees, only a minority of the adoptive parents had been provided with any information about the social characteristics of the biological families. The same held true with respect to the natural father's occupation and the health of the natural mother and father.

Similarly, less than one-quarter of the parents had obtained even a limited amount of information about the biological mother's and father's intelligence. All in all, we were impressed with the paucity of information reportedly available to these families. Further, there is some suggestion in the data that the adoptive parents of the high-problem adoptees possessed more information than did their counterparts with low-problem children. One might speculate as to whether such information constituted a burden for the former group rather than strengthening their positions as adoptive parents.

In connection with the matter of information about the biological parents, an effort was made to keep track during the interviews with the adoptive parents of any invidious references made by them to the "weak stock," "poor inheritance," or "inadequate endowment" of the adoptee. In only three instances did a parent of a child in the best adjusted group make such a comment and in only two instances for parents of middle-range outcome adoptees. However, in six interviews

with parents of high-problem children both parents made such re-
marks, and in another five interviews one of the two parents commented in this fashion. Thus, derogatory comments about the adoptee's background were made in one-third of the interviews with
parents whose children had displayed the most problematic adjustment. This differentiation among the three groups is not surprising. If
an adoptee had turned out to the parents' satisfaction, as most of the
low-problem children had, there would have been no stimulus for the
parents to have had serious question about the child's biological inheritance.

OTHER PREADOPTIVE CHARACTERISTICS

A section of our interview with the adoptive parents covered the
adoptee's history prior to his placement in the adoptive home. Twenty
percent of the parents stated that they had received no information regarding their children's preadoptive health. Two-fifths reported having received information that the child had had no health problem or
health deficiency, and 10 percent acknowledged having received information about a specific health problem. These figures apply about
evenly for the three outcome groups. An even larger group of parents
(31 percent) reported not having received information about the
child's intelligence prior to placement. However, about the same proportion had received information to the effect that the child was normal in this area. No family in our sample reported having received information prior to placement that their adoptee was intellectually
deficient in any way.

With respect to the child's preplacement personality, almost two-
fifths of the sample couples said they had received no information
about this, and only one family in each of the three outcome categories reported having been provided information which indicated that
the child had had a personality problem. Similar findings were reported with respect to the child's developmental patterns prior to
placement, except that three sets of parents of high-problem adoptees
had been told of deficiences from which their children had suffered
prior to their placement in their adoptive homes.

Early adjustment in the
adoptive home

The parents were asked to recall their early experiences with the adoptee after they had brought him home. For example, we asked how he had adjusted during the first three months in their home. Surprisingly, almost all the parents claimed to be able to recall this period in fairly detailed fashion. It was obviously an exciting one for them, and the research questions evoked many emotion-charged memories about this experience. As might be expected, the parents of the low-problem adoptees were almost uniform in reporting that their children had adjusted very well right from the beginning. Only one family in that category reported a child who had evidenced moderate problems during the initial period.

The families with adoptees in the middle-range outcome category and in the high-problem group reported 62 and 70 percent of their children, respectively, as having adjusted very well. Six children (or 18 percent) in each category of outcome had showed moderate problems, and two children (6 percent) now in the middle-range group had demonstrated severe problems. Four families in the middle-range group and two families with currently high-problem adoptees revealed situations in which the parents disagreed about whether or not the adoptee had showed problems during the initial period. We might note, therefore, that the middle-range and high-problem outcome groups do not seem particularly distinguishable from each other with respect to reports about the early experience of the child but that both are somewhat differentiated from the low-problem group.

We asked the parents to tell us how long it had taken them to feel that the adoptee was really theirs. Eight out of ten parents reported that they felt this almost instantly, often in less than a week. Others reported having begun to feel this way within a few months. By and large, it appeared from the parental reports that they had taken hold with their children almost right away, and there was no appreciable difference in this connection among the responses of the parents of adoptees in the three outcome categories.

five / *Describing*
the adoptees

WE NOW PROCEED from the essentially self-descriptive material provided by the adoptive parents to their characterizations of and experience with the adoptees over the years. We also include in this chapter information gleaned from the individual case folders which were made available to us by the participating agencies. In keeping with the format already established, we present the descriptive data about the adoptees according to the three outcome categories we have labeled "low problem," "middle range," and "high problem."

Child characteristics

Sex As discussed in Chapter III we designated one child in each adoptive family to be the focus of attention in the research interview. We had designed our sampling procedure in such a way as to insure adequate representation of children of both sexes. As a consequence, our sample of 100 adoptees consisted of almost equal proportions of males and females; 49 and 51, respectively. In Table 5–1 we show the distribution of the two sexes according to the three outcome categories. It is noteworthy that females were found to show more satisfactory outcomes: 40 percent were in the low-problem group as opposed to 27 percent of the males. Male children were more heavily represented in the high-problem category. This finding of differential outcome according to sex of the adoptee parallels the results of the investigation of independent adoptions by Witmer, et al.[1] That study, conducted in the State of Florida, showed remarkably similar findings: of the girls, 41 percent were rated as showing good adjustment compared to 29 percent of the boys. Why adopted male children should show more problems in adjustment as they grow up is a matter worthy of investigation.

It is possible that the sex of a child has different meaning for some parents in the context of adoption than it would under conditions of biological parenthood. In his report about his research in adoption, Kirk comments that adoptive fathers from traditional backgrounds may be reluctant to adopt male children because of the importance placed upon continuity of the family line.[2] That is, there would be a reluctance to accept adopted male children since they really could not be viewed as rightful heirs. This suggests that boys placed in this type of family would be exposed to ambivalent attitudes and possibly covert rejection.

Age at placement There has been considerable concern in the child welfare literature about the possible effect of the *timing* of the placement of a child with an adoptive family. Yarrow's research suggests that the older an adoptive child is at the time of transfer from a foster home to an adoptive home, the more apt he is to show behavioral symptoms in the postplacement environment.[3]

Table 5–1 / Sex of the adoptees (percentaged across)

SEX	GROUP I	GROUP II	GROUP III	TOTAL CASES
Female	40%	33%	27%	(51)
Male	27%	35%	38%	(49)

It was of interest to us to note that contrary to our expectations adoptees in the high-problem group had a lower mean placement age than their counterparts in either the low-problem or the middle-range outcome categories. High-problem adoptees had a mean age of 12.0 months when placed in their adoptive homes, contrasting with 15.6 months for the middle-range adoptees and 16.2 months for the low-problem subjects. In subsequent analysis, we will ascertain whether the fact of early placement was correlated with other background characteristics of the children and their parents.

Agency placing adoptee   In Table 5-2, we provide the distribution within each of the three types of outcome for the four agencies participating in the study. The reader will observe that the Catholic Home Bureau families showed the largest proportion of cases in the low-problem group (31 percent). The Chapin Nursery/Spence Alumnae agency and the State Charities Aid contributed almost as large a grouping (27 percent each). Finally, the smallest proportion in this positive outcome group (15 percent), were adoptees placed by the Free Synagogue Committee.

With respect to the high-problem category, State Charities Aid and Catholic Home Bureau accounted for the smallest proportion of the cases, 15 and 18 percent, respectively, whereas Chapin Nursery/Spence Alumnae contributed the largest proportion (37 percent). The Free Synagogue Committee provided a sizable grouping within this lowest ranking category (30 percent). We observe that children adopted through Chapin Nursery/Spence Alumnae tended to show a U-shaped distribution with very few cases in the middle group (12

Table 5-2 / Outcome by agency placement

PLACING AGENCY	GROUP I	GROUP II	GROUP III
Catholic Home Bureau	31%	27%	18%
Chapin Nursery/ Spence Alumnae	27	12	37
Free Synagogue Committee	15	29	30
State Charities Aid	27	32	15
Total cases	(33)	(34)	(33)

percent). The Catholic Home Bureau and State Charities Aid adoptees were skewed in the direction of the low-problem category whereas the Free Synagogue Committee adoptees were skewed in the direction of the high-problem category. We shall subsequently examine the social characteristics of the families according to agency identification to determine whether the differences in adoptee adjustment for each agency can be explained by the characteristics of the families.

Preadoptive placements Information concerning the preadoptive placement history of the adoptees was abstracted from agency case records. Reference was made in Chapter III to the uneven state of these records, a situation which frequently necessitated sifting through numerous indirect allusions to such placements scattered throughout the record contents before an adequate chronological sequence could be reconstructed.

For our purposes, a preadoptive placement consisted of any sojourn by the adoptee for a period of at least two weeks in duration in any agency boarding home, hospital or maternity home, foster home, or any other congregate living arrangement which occurred prior to the time the child was placed by the agency in the home of the adoptive couple in our study sample. If, for example, a child had been placed in an agency boarding home, subsequently removed and hospitalized for two weeks or more, and then returned to the same boarding home, this was counted as three placements. Our rationale for this method of counting number of placements was that for an infant or very young child each removal and replacement brought with it a rupture of the tenuous relationships he had begun to develop during the placement. From the perspective of current child development theory each such discontinuity in relationships is potentially traumatic to the child and could adversely affect the degree of his security as well as his subsequent ability to form warm and lasting interpersonal relationships. Hence, we desired to obtain as all-inclusive a measure as possible of the separation experiences suffered by the adoptee.

The mean number of preadoptive placements for the total group of 100 adoptees was 3.2 (with standard deviation of 1.4). The range and mean number of placements experienced by the adoptees in each of the three outcome categories is as follows:

Low problem: 2.88 placements (with standard deviation of 0.31)

Middle range: 3.32 placements (with standard deviation of 1.2)

High problem: 3.18 placements (with standard deviation of 1.7)

While the low-problem adoptees had been exposed to fewer place-ments, the differences among the three outcome groups in this regard were quite modest.

Description of child at various stages of his development

MANNERISMS AND TEMPERAMENT

We asked the parents to reflect upon their adoptee's mannerisms and temperament over the years. Had they felt that he was similar to them in this regard or somewhat different? We viewed the parental re-sponses to this question as potentially reflecting the degree to which close identification had developed between them and the adoptees. The responses of our subjects, as presented in Table 5–3, reveal an in-teresting difference as seen within the three categories of outcome. For the total sample, only 10 percent of the parents made any claim that the adoptee had closely resembled both parents. However, this was true for almost 20 percent of the parents with adoptees in the low-problem outcome group but for only 6 percent of parents of mid-dle-range adjustment children.

Almost half the total sample of parents saw the adoptee as being somewhat similar to both parents or to either the father or mother alone. A comparable proportion of parents whose children fell in the low-problem and middle-range categories reacted this way, but such a response was given by only about one-third (36 percent) of the parents of high-problem adoptees. A particularly striking finding was that only 6 percent of the parents of low-problem adoptees described their children as being not at all similar to either parent while this was true of more than one-fourth the parents of middle-range out-come adoptees and more than one-third the couples with adoptees classified in the high-problem category.

*Table 5–3 / Extent to which adoptive parents saw
adoptee's mannerisms and temperament as similar
to their own over the years*

	GROUP I	GROUP II	GROUP III	TOTAL
1. *Very similar to both parents*	18%	6%	3%	9%
2. *Somewhat similar to both parents*	18	23	6	16
3. *Very similar to mother or father*	18	9	9	12
4. *Somewhat similar to mother or father*	12	12	21	15
5. *Not at all similar to either parent*	6	26	37	23
6. *Parents gave disparate responses*	4	9	6	6
7. *Other*	9	—	3	4
8. *Not covered/Unable to determine*	15	15	15	15
Total cases	(33)	(34)	(33)	(100)

It was no doubt easier for the parents of low-problem children to see them as similar to themselves; hence the rarity of disclaimers about such similarity. That it was difficult for the parents of high-problem adoptees to see their children as being like themselves was perhaps also to be expected. Whether the perception of the adoptee as being different from the parents preceded and contributed to the negative outcome is a question that cannot be adequately answered in a retrospective study. The reader, however, will shortly discern how this finding is a prelude for even more pronounced differences between the three outcome groups with respect to the parents' perceptions of the characteristics of their children in a variety of life-space areas.

GENERAL HEALTH

As we were interested in securing information about the nature of the adoptee's overall health condition over the years, parents were asked to characterize their child's physical health in a general kind of

Table 5-4 / Adoptive parents' reports of adoptee's predominant health over the years

	GROUP I	GROUP II	GROUP III	TOTAL
Excellent health	52%	41%	33%	42%
Good health; occasional illness	45	41	55	47
Fair health; frequent illness	3	3	6	4
Poor health	—	3	—	1
Disparate responses by parents	—	6	3	3
Other	—	6	3	3
Total cases	(33)	(34)	(33)	(100)

way. We find in Table 5-4 that for almost nine out of ten families, the adoptee's health was described as being either excellent, with virtually no illness of any kind or good, with only an occasional minor illness. Only one adoptee was described by his parents as having suffered poor health.

However, despite the overall positive assessment of the children's health status, we note in the table that there is a tendency to depict health conditions in a way which parallels the grouping of the cases into the three types of outcome. Thus, only 33 percent of the parents of high-problem adoptees reported that their children had enjoyed excellent health compared to 52 percent of the parents of low-problem adoptees. While the differences are not dramatic, they nevertheless reflect aspects of the total life situations of the children which suggest that almost all life-space areas are implicated in the overall adjustment of the children and their parents.

The parents were also asked whether the adoptee had sustained major illnesses or physical handicaps as they grew up. It can be seen from Table 5-5 that 57 percent of our sample answered this question in the negative, 37 percent reported one or more major illnesses, and 4 percent provided disparate responses. It is again of some import that 79 percent of the low-problem children had had no illnesses or handicaps of a major kind, whereas this had been true of only 56 percent of the middle outcome and 36 percent of the high-problem adoptees. More than half those in the last category had had one or more serious illnesses, a rather telling finding.

While about two-fifths of the families reported that their children had suffered at least one serious illness, question remained as to whether the illness had affected the children's functioning. Eighteen families reported that the specified illness had had no such effect or that it had been a source of only slight impairment in adoptee functioning. Twelve families reported moderately impaired functioning, and four reported severe impairment. In the last group, all the adoptees fell within the high-problem outcome category, i.e., Group III. There were no reported cases of severe impairment in the other two groups although seven adoptees with middle-range adjustments were considered to have been moderately impaired, compared to three in the low-problem group and two in the high-problem category. Thus, while physical illness had not been a widespread problem, it had been sufficiently a factor in the lives of these adoptees to have constituted a handicap.

We also asked the parents whether the reported illnesses had created emotional problems for the adoptees. It emerged that there were seven cases in the high-problem outcome category where the physical illness was considered to have brought with it a moderate or serious emotional problem, while there were only three such cases in the middle-range group and only one case in the low-problem group. Thus, 21

Table 5–5 / Reports of major illnesses or physical handicaps experienced by the adoptee

	GROUP I	GROUP II	GROUP III	TOTAL
No major illness or physical handicaps	79%	56%	36%	57%
One or more major illnesses or physical handicaps	21	38	52	37
Disparate responses by parents	—	3	9	4
Not covered	—	3	3	2
Total cases	(33)	(34)	(33)	(100)

percent of the high-problem adoptees had suffered from emotional problems that were linked by their adoptive parents to physical impairments.

In pursuit of our interest in the overall functioning of the adopted children, we asked the parents to inform us about the extent to which the adoptee had suffered from any of a number of ailments which could theoretically have had an emotional etiology. For example, had the adoptee been troubled by chronic colds, headaches, stomachaches or intestinal disorders, allergies, skin disorders, respiratory difficulties, or obesity or underweight?

When we tabulated the responses we found the typical report of parents to be that the adoptee had not suffered from any of the conditions we had specified. For the total sample, only thirty-six of our one hundred subjects had suffered from one or another of these types of disorders. The three outcome groups did not differ from each other in number of such symptoms. When we asked the parents of adoptees who had been afflicted by symptoms whether they attributed these ailments to the children's emotional upsetness, half of them made firm negative statements, three were uncertain, and seven parents answered in the affirmative.

SCHOOL PERFORMANCE

In our effort to assess the nature of the adoptive experience, we considered the adjustment shown by the adoptee in the area of education to be a particularly sensitive indicator of the adequacy of his social functioning. We asked the parents to characterize the level of the adoptee's school performance for each of the three age categories that had been established. The distribution of the parents' responses is set forth in Table 5–6.

To examine first the earliest age period: we see that the parental assessment of the adoptee's overall school performance is distributed in each outcome category in a way as to reflect the multidimensional adjustment model underlying the formation of the outcome groups. Thus, while more than one-fourth of the low-problem children were considered to have performed in excellent fashion, this was true of about one-tenth the adoptees in the middle-range outcome group and of only 3 percent of those in the high-problem category. Combining the "excellent" and "good" performance descriptions, we find that 61 percent of the low-problem, 32 percent of the middle-range, and only 18 percent of the high-problem adoptees had performed at an excellent-to-good level. Furthermore, whereas only 3 percent of the Group I children were described as having below average or very poor academic functioning, this was true of 18 percent of the adoptees in the middle-range group and 43 percent of the Group III children. We thus find a clear-cut differentiation among the three outcome groups with respect to level of school performance in their earliest school years.

The reader will note that the parental responses were similarly distributed for the age period 10 to 17 years, i. e., the junior high and high school levels. However, we found a less striking difference between the low-problem and the middle-range categories for the age period eighteen and over, although there was a quite pronounced

Table 5–6 / Parents' reports of level of adoptees' school performance during three age periods

	BELOW AGE 10 OUTCOME GROUP [a]			AGE 10–17 OUTCOME GROUP [a]			AGE 18 AND OVER OUTCOME GROUP [a]		
SCHOOL PERFORMANCE	I	II	III	I	II	III	I	II	III
Excellent	27%	12%	3%	21%	12%	—%	15%	9%	—%
Good	34	20	15	37	18	12	18	23	6
Average	24	35	24	30	35	12	21	18	9
Below average	3	15	19	3	20	27	6	6	9
Very poor	—	3	24	—	3	31	3	—	15
Other	—	—	3	—	—	6	—	—	—
Disparate parent response	12	15	12	9	12	12	—	6	3
Not applicable (no college attendance)	—	—	—	—	—	—	37	38	55
Not covered	—	—	—	—	—	—	—	—	3
Total cases	(33)	(34)	(33)	(33)	(34)	(33)	(33)	(34)	(33)

[a] Group I = Low problem; Group II = Middle range; Group III = High problem.

difference between these two groups and the high-problem group. Of the latter group, 55 percent had not attended college, so there was no level of performance to speak of for them during this age period. This contrasted with 37 percent of the low-problem adoptees who did not go to college and 38 percent of the adoptees in the middle-range group. Among the adoptees who had attended college, a greater proportion in the high-problem category had reportedly performed at a below-average level than was true of the adoptees in the other two outcome groups.

We asked the parents about a variety of problems the adoptee may have experienced in school over the years. The problem areas about which we inquired included physical disabilities affecting school performance, slowness of comprehension of school material, failure to tap the adoptee's intellectual capacity, creativity, or learning ability, the extent of low motivation to learn, relationship problems with teachers or other adults and with peers in the academic environment and, finally, other kinds of school-focused problems such as restlessness, truanting, school phobias, and the like.[4] Not unexpectedly, our data disclosed that, with one exception,[5] in each of these areas the adoptees now classified in the high-problem category had revealed substantially more problematic behavior than had the adoptees in either of the other two outcome groups. Not only had a greater proportion of them reportedly evidenced such difficulties; substantially more of them had experienced more severe problems in each area than

Table 5–7 / Parents' reports about school problems
of adoptees: low motivation to learn

	GROUP I	GROUP II	GROUP III	TOTAL
Major problem	—%	9%	40%	16%
Moderate problem	3	18	18	13
Minor problem	3	6	6	5
No problem	94	58	12	55
Disparate parent response	—	—	6	2
Not covered	—	9	18	9
Total cases	(33)	(34)	(33)	(100)

had been true for their counterparts in the other outcome categories. In each problem area, furthermore, the adjustment of the low-problem adoptees had been characterized by fewer and less extreme problems than had been manifested by the middle-range outcome adoptees.

The distribution of the three classes of adoptees with respect to the problem of low motivation to learn—as set forth in Table 5-7—may be considered roughly illustrative of the general nature of their distribution in the other problem areas. We note, for example, that more than nine out of ten low-problem adoptees were described as *not* having experienced low motivation. By contrast, six out of ten adoptees in the middle-range outcome category and only about one in ten of their fellow adoptees in the high-problem group were reported to have been free of this problem. At the other end of the spectrum, three-fifths of the adoptees with the least positive outcomes were said to have had major or moderate problems regarding motivation to learn, while this was the case for about one-fourth of the middle-range adoptees and for only 3 percent of the low-problem adoptees. None of the latter group was reported to have encountered major problems in this area.

When we inquired of the parents concerning special efforts they might have made to promote their children's school achievement, a total of twenty-one sets of parents reported definitely that they had *not* promoted the adoptee's school achievement in any special way. Twelve of these were parents of low-problem adoptees, seven were parents of adoptees in the middle-range category, and only two were parents of high-problem adoptees. In families where the adoptees had been given assistance, the usual form of help had been close supervision of homework, and here differences among the outcome groups were not marked. Two of the families of high-problem adoptees had hired tutors or special teachers for their youngsters, and this had also been true of one family whose adoptee had displayed a middle-range adjustment.

Of particular interest is the fact that five of the high-problem adoptees had been sent to private or other special schools involving a living-away arrangement, whereas only one adoptee in each of the other two outcome groups had had similar experiences. We consider this a noteworthy finding, especially since in several instances, the parents of high-problem adoptees attending these out-of-town schools implied that they had been institutions tending to specialize in schooling for children with academic difficulties. We had, moreover, other indications in the interviews that the parents of high-problem adoptees had tended to promote the school achievement of their children in a variety of ways. It appears that these efforts often did not achieve the desired results.

Aside from the level of the adoptee's school performance as described by the parents, we considered it important to understand the parents' attitudes about their youngsters' overall academic performance. We recognized that satisfaction with the same level of performance might not be uniform for all the parents. For example, even though some adoptees had functioned only moderately well in high school, we found their parents to be very satisfied with this because their expectations had not been pitched at a high level. By contrast, other parents in our sample expressed dissatisfaction with the adoptees' academic performance even though the latter had completed college. Recognition was thus given to the subjective component in evaluating an adoptee's school performance.

In examining the parents' responses, we again found that parental satisfaction was inversely related to the adoptee's position within the three categories of outcome. The data contained in Table 5–8 make this quite clear. They show, for example, that during the period of the elementary school years 88 percent of the parents of low-problem adoptees were very satisfied with their children's academic performance. Such satisfaction was voiced by 32 percent of the parents of middle-range adoptees but by only 18 percent of the parents of adoptees in the high-problem category. Of the parents of the best adjusted adoptees, 12 percent were moderately satisfied, while this was true for 29 percent of the parents of middle-range outcome adoptees, and 12 percent of the parents of adoptees classified in the high-problem category. Perhaps even more striking, no parents of low-problem adoptees expressed dissatisfaction with their children's academic functioning during the age period below ten, whereas 21 percent of the parents of middle-range adoptees and 49 percent of the parents of high-problem adoptees voiced either moderate or great dissatisfaction with their children's performance in this life-space area.

Table 5–8 / Adoptive parents' reports of satisfaction with adoptee's academic performance

	BELOW AGE 10 OUTCOME GROUP			AGE 10–17 OUTCOME GROUP			AGE 18 AND OVER OUTCOME GROUP		
	I	II	III	I	II	III	I	II	III
Very satisfied	88%	32%	18%	79%	35%	6%	48%	23%	3%
Moderately satisfied	12	29	12	9	26	15	6	18	15
Moderately dissatisfied	—	15	21	6	21	24	6	6	6
Very dissatisfied	—	6	28	—	3	37	—	—	12
Disparate parent response	—	15	18	6	12	9	3	9	6
Other	—	—	3	—	—	—	—	—	—
Not covered	—	—	—	—	—	9	—	—	3
Unable to determine	—	3	—	—	3	—	—	6	—
Not applicable (no college attendance)	—	—	—	—	—	—	37	38	55
Total cases	(33)	(34)	(33)	(33)	(34)	(33)	(33)	(34)	(33)

Examination of Table 5-8 shows a fairly considerable group of adoptees in each of the three adjustment categories who did not go to college. However, for those who did attend, a fair amount of dissatisfaction was expressed concerning the performance of adoptees with the most problematic overall adjustment.

SOCIAL RELATIONSHIPS

We were interested in determining the extent to which the one hundred adoptees had been able to enjoy satisfying social experiences as they grew up. With this in mind, we asked each of the parents to tell us to what extent they thought their children had tended to be socially gregarious over the years. An interesting finding emerged. The low-problem adoptees came out as the most gregarious, but they were closely approximated by the high-problem children, with the middle-range outcome adoptees showing the least gregariousness. Thus, for the period below age ten, about four-fifths (79 percent) of the low-problem and three-fifths (63 percent) of the high-problem adoptees were considered to have been either very or moderately gregarious, whereas approximately one-half (53 percent) of the middle-outcome adoptees were so described by their parents. We noted quite similar trends for the other two age periods investigated.

When we asked the parents to tell us about their reactions to their children's choice of own-sex friends, almost all the parents of low-problem adoptees (97 percent) reported having been very much satisfied. On the other hand, such reports were given us by the parents of only 68 percent of the middle-range and 15 percent of the high-problem adoptees. This is a striking difference. In addition, 24 percent of the parents of high-problem adoptees indicated actual *dissatisfaction* with their children's past choice of friends. A similar finding was revealed when parents were asked about their satisfaction with the adoptee's other affiliative activities. Only about one-fourth (27 percent) of the parents of the high-problem adoptees expressed satisfaction in this area as compared with almost three-fourths (71 percent) of the parents of middle-outcome adoptees and nine-tenths (91 percent) of the parents of adoptees falling into the low-problem outcome category.

We further asked the adoptive parents to review in their own minds the degree to which the adoptee's overall social situation as he grew up had been *for him* a source of happiness or a source of stress. For example, had the adoptee's social situation required him to struggle with problems of social isolation, self-doubt, or embarrassment? In this area we found very little difference among the three outcome categories. Slightly more than half of the adoptees in each category were described as having experienced very great happiness with respect to ther social situations and little or no stress. Another fourth were said to have been moderately happy with some modicum of stress.

The adoptees who had experienced substantial or almost constant stress varied from 10 percent in the high-problem group to 16 percent in the middle-range group. Thus, our data suggest that, from a social point of view, the high-problem adoptees had been no less happy than those with more favorable outcomes in the low-problem and middle-range categories. This is suggestive of some of the reports about juvenile delinquents which have indicated that such problematic children are almost as completely socialized with respect to the pleasures they derive from group experiences as are children who are more law-abiding and well adjusted in other areas of living.[6] In other words, the child who is suffering from school problems, conflict with his parents, and the like does not necessarily have the same problems with respect to having an active and gratifying social life with other children. The friends of the high-problem adoptees in our sample may well have been youngsters who were experiencing problems similar to those of the adoptees themselves. Despite this, they may have represented the only source of gratification in the troubled adoptees' lives.

In further exploring the adoptee's social life as he grew up, we inquired into his general leisure-time activities over the years and asked whether the parents had ever felt concerned about problems in this sphere. We found that generally, for the various types of difficulties considered, the adoptees in the low-problem and middle-range outcome categories had rarely caused serious concern for their parents. There had been more substantial concern for the adoptees who showed high-problem outcomes. Thus, only one adoptee each in the two former groups had caused their parents to be concerned about too much investment in play activity to the point of neglecting school work. Five such situations were reported by the parents of high-problem adoptees. Only one adoptee in the middle-range group, a girl, had engaged in leisure-time activities not appropriate to her sex and had been described by her parents as a tomboy when younger, but there were two such cases among the high-problem adoptees. Also in this latter group there were two cases where the parents told of having been perturbed because the adoptees had engaged in potentially destructive or delinquent activities. One adoptee in the middle-range outcome group had been the cause of concern to his parents because his leisure pursuits had been of a solitary nature, and this was true of two adoptees classified in the high-problem group.

During the period below ten years of age, two-fifths of the high-problem adoptees had evidenced leisure-time activity problems that had disturbed their parents. During the 10- to 17-year age period, the proportion of high-problem children whose leisure activities had distressed their parents increased to 51 percent of the adoptees in that outcome category, while this was true of the behavior of only 12 percent of the adoptees in the middle-range and 6 percent of the adoptees in the low-problem categories. Our data would thus tend to support the view that for troubled children, the adolescent period is a time of increased incidence of leisure-time activity problems. When the data were organized for problems emerging after the age of eighteen, we found a general decline in the reported incidence of problems, although 27 percent of the parents of the high-problem adoptees still spoke of leisure-time activity problems in that age period as compared with 6 percent of the parents of adoptees in each of the other two adjustment groups.

With respect to leisure activities, we were also interested in determining the degree to which our sample adoptees had showed outstanding talents. Those in the low-problem category were reported to have fared somewhat better in this regard than those in the other two outcome categories. Almost two-thirds of the adoptees in the former group were described as having displayed one or more outstanding talents, whereas almost half of those in the middle-range and high-problem categories had, according to their parents, manifested such talents. The talents described were in such areas as art, music, athletics, and drama. Five of the adoptees in the low-problem group were described by their parents in rather glowing terms as being very outstanding athletes.

Finally, in the social relations sector of the adoptees' life-space, we explored their functioning in the area of heterosexual relationships. We inquired into the general nature of these relationships, asking the parents whether and to what extent they had been perturbed over the years regarding a number of matters: the adoptee's refusal, extreme reluctance or slowness to develop such relationships, his ineptitude or lack of self-confidence in this area, his overactive interests or precociousness, his tendency to be promiscuous, and the like. When we tabulated the responses, we found that none of the parents of low-problem adoptees had voiced any serious concern with respect to either the adoptee's current or past heterosexual behavior, and only two had expressed moderate concern. Similarly, only one parent of a middle-outcome adoptee had talked of having been troubled by the adoptee's preoccupation with heterosexual relationships, and only nine parents in this group had told of their moderate concern about such problems.

On the other hand, thirteen sets of parents (39 percent) of adoptees in the high-problem group had reported having been greatly distressed over their adopted children's heterosexual relationships. These included two sets of parents who had been concerned about the adoptee's failure to develop normal relationships, two couples who described their children as having been precocious, and two parents who characterized their children as having been promiscuous. In two families, adoptees had manifested more than one such problem, and two couples reported other nonspecified types of problems in the heterosexual adjustment of their adopted children.

Along these same lines, inquiry was made about the degree of conflict that may have prevailed between the parents and the adoptee over heterosexual matters. During the 10- to 17-year age period, there was reportedly no conflict at all in families of low-problem adoptees, while some conflict was reported in six families in the middle-range, and seven families in the high-problem outcome categories. This distribution was not materially different during the eighteen and over age period. However, while 97 percent of the parents of low-problem adoptees and 82 percent of the parents of middle-outcome adoptees stated affirmatively that there had been no conflict whatsoever over heterosexual matters during this later period, only 54 percent of the parents of high-problem adoptees made such statements.[7]

PERSONALITY

What kind of child had the adoptee been as he was growing up? What was the nature of his adjustment? What personality problems had he manifested? The description of the adoptee presented by his parent with respect to these dimensions of his functioning was considered a highly significant area of inquiry. For purposes of general overview, the parents were asked to describe their child's predominant mood state as he grew up. Had he tended to be a cheerful youngster, generally characteriezd by a happy demeanor, or had he tended to be morose, dissatisfied, or a generally unhappy youngster?

Table 5–9A presents the responses of the parents to this global query for the three outcome groups. The data show that the adoptees in the low-problem category were almost uniformly described in

Table 5–9A / Parents' report of adoptee's general mood during three age periods

ADOPTEE'S HAPPINESS	BELOW AGE 10 OUTCOME GROUP			AGE 10–17 OUTCOME GROUP			AGE 18 AND OVER OUTCOME GROUP		
	I	II	III	I	II	III	I	II	III
Generally happy	97%	82%	52%	94%	79%	46%	91%	82%	43%
Generally moderately happy	3	15	15	3	18	18	3	12	21
Generally unhappy	—	—	15	—	—	24	3	—	24
Disparate parent response	—	—	9	—	—	3	—	3	3
Other (e.g., parent deceased)	—	—	6	3	—	6	3	—	3
Not covered/Unable to determine	—	3	3	—	3	3	—	3	6
Total cases	(33)	(34)	(33)	(33)	(34)	(33)	(33)	(34)	(33)

Table 5–9B / Parents' report of adoptee's tenseness during three age periods

ADOPTEE'S TENSENESS	BELOW AGE 10 OUTCOME GROUP			AGE 10–17 OUTCOME GROUP			AGE 18 AND OVER OUTCOME GROUP		
	I	II	III	I	II	III	I	II	III
Generally very tense	6%	17%	12%	3%	11%	15%	3%	11%	18%
Generally moderately tense	9	6	15	9	6	18	15	6	15
Generally not tense	76	65	49	79	71	43	73	68	46
Disparate parent response	3	3	6	3	3	9	3	6	6
Other (e.g., parent deceased)	3	—	3	3	—	3	3	—	6
Not covered/Unable to determine	3	9	15	3	9	12	3	9	9
Total cases	(33)	(34)	(33)	(33)	(34)	(33)	(33)	(34)	(33)

blithesome terms. In only one instance (3 percent in Table 5–9A) was it stated that an adoptee in this group had been generally unhappy, and this pertained to the period when he was eighteen years of age or older. It is also apparent that none of the adoptees in the middle-range grouping were reported to have experienced periods of general unhappiness as children. In sharp contrast, however, one out of four of the adoptees in the high-problem group was described as having been generally unhappy during the two older age periods and 15 percent in the earliest age period. Only two-fifths to one-half of the youngsters in this outcome category were described as having been generally happy over the three age periods.

Another reflection of the general emotional state of the adoptee was the degree to which he was described as having been tense as he grew up. This is portrayed by the data in Table 5–9B which reveals that the high-problem adoptees had also tended to be more tense, though not dramatically so, than their counterparts in the two other outcome groupings. All in all, our data appear to add up to the finding that the adoptees with the most problematic overall adjustment were fairly well differentiated from those in the other two outcome groups with regard to their general emotional demeanor over the years in which they grew to adulthood.

PERSONALITY PROBLEMS

The parents were queried about specific personality difficulties with which the adoptees had been afflicted as they grew up. These included the following problem entities: speech problems, sleep disturbances, phobias, considerable restlessness, considerable aggressiveness, excessive fears or anxiety, and enuresis. In addition, the parents were asked to describe any other difficulties the adoptees had encountered in the personality area. The presence of any problems in this sector of the adoptee's life-space was conceived of as being a potential indicator of a more generalized state of maladjustment.

For each of the problem categories about which our interviewers inquired, there was only an occasional response indicating that the adoptee had been perceived by his parents to have revealed such a difficulty. Thus, only four adoptees were said to have suffered from speech disorders as they grew up, and in only one case was this said to have been severe. Similarly, only eight children had suffered from sleep disturbances, with only two situations in which this condition was considered to have represented a severe problem. Other reports of personality disturbance included two cases of phobias, seven of considerable restlessness, eight of considerable aggressiveness, four of excessive fear or anxiety, and four cases of enuresis.

All in all, thirty-eight adoptees were reported to have suffered from at least one of the personality problems specified in our interviews or others described by the parents. Of interest is the distribution by outcome category of the adoptees who had experienced no problems of any kind in the area of personality that the parents had considered worthy of mention. This was the case for 85 percent of the adoptees in the low-problem group and for 53 percent of those in the middle-range outcome category. It is striking that only 9 percent of the high-problem adoptees were described as having been problem-free in this area.

In Table 5–10 information is provided about the extent to which the parents had sought professional help for any personality problems the adoptees might have manifested. Since the high-problem grouping contained the largest number of adoptees with reported personality

Table 5–10 / Help sought by parents for adoptee's personality problems

	GROUP I	GROUP II	GROUP III	TOTAL
ADOPTEE REPORTED TO HAVE PERSONALITY PROBLEMS:				
Psychiatric help sought	3%	9%	27%	13%
More than one type of help sought (e.g., psychiatry, casework, clinical psychology, etc.)	3	3	18	8
Other	3	9	6	6
No help sought	6	26	31	21
Not covered	—	—	9	3
ADOPTEE REPORTED TO HAVE NO PROBLEMS (NO HELP SOUGHT)	85	53	9	49
Total cases	(33)	(34)	(33)	(100)

difficulties, it is not surprising that 51 percent of the adoptees in this category were described as having received help with their problems from a variety of sources. Some 27 percent were said to have received psychiatric assistance. By way of contrast, only 21 percent of the adoptees in the middle-range adjustment group had received some kind of help, with 9 percent having received psychiatric assistance. Among the adoptees in the low-problem category, only 9 percent had reportedly ever received professional help of any kind, 3 percent having received psychiatric attention. About a third of the high-problem group represented cases in which the parents indicated they had not sought professional help for their children even though they reported the adoptees having evidenced personality problems.

One additional way of obtaining the parents' perspective on the adoptee's personality was to get them to talk about the degree to which they had been pleased with his personality over the years. We recognized that while some children might have shown fairly severe problems one could also expect variation among the parents in their tolerance for even profound personality difficulties. Table 5–11 presents this material for the three outcome groups. As one might anticipate, there is a strong association between the degree of pleasure with the adoptee's personality expressed by the parents and the adoptee's location within the three outcome groupings. Thus, nine out of ten parents of low-problem adoptees were described as having been

Table 5–11 / Parents' general response to adoptee's personality over the years

	GROUP I	GROUP II	GROUP III	TOTAL
Highly pleased	88%	56%	18%	54%
Moderately pleased	3	20	9	11
Moderately displeased	3	—	13	5
Moderately annoyed	—	—	9	3
Highly displeased	—	—	15	5
Disparate response	3	18	15	12
Other	—	3	18	7
Not covered	3	3	3	3
Total cases	(33)	(34)	(33)	(100)

Table 5-12 / Emotional climate prevailing between
adoptee and parents during three age periods

	BELOW AGE 10 OUTCOME GROUP			AGE 10–17 OUTCOME GROUP			AGE 18 AND OVER OUTCOME GROUP		
	I	II	III	I	II	III	I	II	III
ADOPTEE AND FATHER									
Very happy relationship	85%	79%	40%	82%	73%	37%	73%	74%	40%
Moderately happy relationship	6	15	30	6	15	24	6	14	21
Somewhat unhappy relationship	—	—	15	—	—	12	—	—	12
Very unhappy relationship	—	—	12	—	—	24	—	—	15
Disparate parent response	—	—	3	—	6	3	—	6	6
Other (e.g., parent deceased)	3	3	—	6	6	—	15	6	6
Not covered/Unable to determine	6	3	—	6	—	—	6	—	6
Total cases	(33)	(34)	(33)	(33)	(34)	(33)	(33)	(34)	(33)
ADOPTEE AND MOTHER									
Very happy relationship	94	79	46	85	76	40	82	82	34
Moderately happy relationship	—	15	24	3	15	15	3	12	30
Somewhat unhappy relationship	—	—	9	—	—	9	3	—	6
Very unhappy relationship	—	—	15	—	—	21	—	—	21
Disparate parent response	—	3	3	6	6	12	6	3	3
Other (e.g., parent deceased)	—	—	3	—	—	3	—	—	—
Not covered/Unable to determine	6	3	—	6	3	—	6	3	6
Total cases	(33)	(34)	(33)	(33)	(34)	(33)	(33)	(34)	(33)

highly pleased with their children's personalities over the years. By comparison, this type of report was given by a little more than half the parents of middle-range adoptees and by less than one-fifth the parents of high-problem adoptees. All told, 54 percent of the parents in the total sample stated they had been highly pleased with their children's personalities.

A striking difference occurs in the parental reports of *displeasure* in this area. Of the parents of high-problem adoptees, 37 percent said that they had been displeased in varying degrees with the adoptee's personality, but such a reaction was given by no parents of middle-outcome adoptees and by only one set of parents of a low-problem adoptee. Many of the youngsters in the high-problem category were viewed by their parents as having provided them with a living experience fraught with a good deal of tension and unhappiness.

FAMILY RELATIONSHIPS

We sought to learn as much as possible about the manner in which the adoptee had related to his parents. The parents' qualitative evaluation of this relationship was seen as providing one important indicator of the overall outcome of the adoptive experience. In Table 5–12 we present information obtained from the parents about the emotional climate which prevailed between themselves and their children during the three age periods specified by our interviewers. This information is presented to show separately the adoptee's relationship to his father and to his mother.

It should again be noted that examination of these reported relationships shows a high correlation between the degree of happiness said to have prevailed in the relationship with each parent and the nature of the adoptee's overall outcome. The difference is quite noteworthy when the children in the high-problem grouping are compared with those in the more favorable outcome categories. Thus, in speaking about the period before the adoptee was ten years old, 85 percent of the parents of low-problem adoptees reported a very happy relationship between the child and his father, and this was true of 79 per cent of the parents of middle-range outcome adoptees.

Table 5-13 / Conflict between adoptee and parents during three age periods

	BELOW AGE 10 OUTCOME GROUP			AGE 10-17 OUTCOME GROUP			AGE 18 AND OVER OUTCOME GROUP		
	I	II	III	I	II	III	I	II	III
ADOPTEE AND FATHER									
Very frequently	—%	—%	12%	—%	—%	12%	—%	—%	12%
Somewhat frequently	—	—	9	—	6	6	—	6	9
Occasionally	—	3	24	—	9	24	—	6	18
Almost never	100	85	46	97	79	37	88	79	43
Disparate response	—	3	9	—	—	15	—	3	6
Other (e.g., parent deceased)	—	6	—	3	6	6	9	6	12
Not covered/Unable to determine	—	3	—	—	—	—	3	—	—
Total cases	(33)	(34)	(33)	(33)	(34)	(33)	(33)	(34)	(33)
ADOPTEE AND MOTHER									
Very frequently	—	—%	12	—	—	15	—	—	15
Somewhat frequently	—	3	12	—	9	6	—	6	3
Occasionally	6	18	15	9	12	18	9	12	21
Almost never	94	76	52	85	67	40	85	73	49
Disparate response	—	—	6	—	9	15	—	3	3
Other (e.g., parent deceased)	—	—	—	6	—	6	6	—	9
Not covered/Unable to determine	—	3	3	—	3	—	—	6	—
Total cases	(33)	(34)	(33)	(33)	(34)	(33)	(33)	(34)	(33)

However, only 40 percent of the parents of high-problem adoptees described the adoptee-father relationship in this manner. Of the parents of children in the latter grouping, 27 percent indicated that a somewhat or very unhappy relationship had prevailed between the father and the child during the younger age period, 36 percent of these parents gave similar reports for the adoptee-father relationship during the 10- to 17-year age period, and 27 percent for the period 18 years and over. None of the parents of adoptees in the two more favorable outcome groups reported an even slightly unhappy relationship during any of the three periods.

Findings similar to those cited above were obtained with respect to the adoptee-mother relationship. Again, only modest differences emerged between the reports of parents of adoptees in Group I and Group II, but more profound differences were revealed between the reports of these families and those whose children were classified in Group III. As has been true for other variables deemed to have evaluative implications, these data confirm the impression of fairly substantial adjustment difficulties for the high-problem adoptees. However, we have also noted that a fairly sizable proportion of this same group apparently enjoyed very happy relationships with their parents. Thus, one should not assume that *all* the adoptees in the high-problem category were embroiled in relationship difficulties with their parents. Also, for the sample as a whole it is obvious that a substantial majority of the parents reported favorably about this area of family life.

Another way of looking at the parent-child relationship is to think in terms of the conflict that might have prevailed between the two generations, and our interviewers inquired into this topic. Table 5–13 presents information concerning the frequency of adoptee-parent conflict during the three age periods covered by the study and deals separately with the adoptee's relationship with each of his parents. Examining the adoptee-father relationship first we note the expected finding that conflict was seen as almost never having been a problem at any age period in the families of low-problem adoptees. Very similar findings characterize the father-adoptee relationship in families of middle-range outcome adoptees.

However, a somewhat different picture emerged in the families of the high-problem children. In that category, about one child in five had suffered conflict with his father either very frequently or some-what frequently during each of the three age periods, and this propor-tion is almost doubled when one adds those reporting occasional fa-ther-child conflict. There is thus again revealed a distinctive difference between the high-problem adoptees and their counterparts in the two other outcome categories. However, a previously expressed caution should be repeated here: not all the high-problem adoptees had expe-rienced conflict with their fathers. A fairly sizable group of parents of such adoptees reported no conflict to speak of during each of the spec-ified age periods.

In examining the reported conflict between the adoptee and his mother, the data do not appear to be substantially different from the data reported for the child-father relationship. Again, it should be noted that almost none of the low-problem adoptees were reported to have experienced conflict with their mothers, and similar accounts were given by the parents of almost three-fourths of the middle-range outcome adoptees. However, about two out of five of the high-prob-lem adoptees were said to have experienced varying degrees of con-flict with their mothers during the three specified age periods.

CONFIDING IN PARENTS

One measure of the relationship between a child and his parents as he grows up is the degree to which he confides in them about a va-riety of matters that concern him. We asked the parents to describe the degree to which this kind of sharing had been characteristic of their relationship with the adoptees. Table 5–14 presents the responses of the parents. It is of interest to note that in each outcome category decidedly more frequent adoptee-mother confiding was reported to have occurred during all age periods than was true for adoptee-father confiding. Thus, for example, 72 percent of the low-problem children were said to have confided very frequently in their mothers below the age of ten but only 39 percent in their fathers. The same tendency was also apparent during the other two age periods.

Another rather striking finding was that a much greater propor-tion of the low-problem adoptees were said to have confided very fre-

Table 5-14 / Adoptee's tendency to confide in parents during three age periods

	BELOW AGE 10 OUTCOME GROUP			AGE 10–17 OUTCOME GROUP			AGE 18 AND OVER OUTCOME GROUP		
	I	II	III	I	II	III	I	II	III
ADOPTEE CONFIDING IN FATHER									
Very frequently	40%	12%	12%	37%	12%	9%	27%	12%	12%
Somewhat frequently	30	44	21	33	47	21	37	41	21
Rarely	6	26	37	6	29	40	6	26	28
Never	—	3	21	—	3	21	—	3	15
Disparate parent response	6	6	—	6	3	—	6	3	3
Other (e. g., parent deceased)	3	3	3	3	6	3	9	9	9
Not covered/Unable to determine	15	6	6	15	—	6	15	6	12
Total cases	(33)	(34)	(33)	(33)	(34)	(33)	(33)	(34)	(33)
ADOPTEE CONFIDING IN MOTHER									
Very frequently	73	24	18	67	21	15	64	18	15
Somewhat frequently	12	49	15	12	49	9	18	46	9
Rarely	3	21	37	—	24	43	3	21	40
Never	—	3	18	3	3	21	3	6	21
Disparate parent response	—	—	—	—	—	—	3	—	—
Other (e. g., parent deceased)	—	—	3	6	—	6	—	—	9
Not covered/Unable to determine	12	3	9	12	3	6	9	9	6
Total cases	(33)	(34)	(33)	(33)	(34)	(33)	(33)	(34)	(33)

quently in both of their parents than was true of the middle-range and the high-problem adoptees. This was one of the few characteristics in which the low-problem adoptees tended to stand out from their fellow adoptees in *both* other outcome categories. As an example, during the earliest age period covered only 24 percent of the middle-range adoptees and 18 percent of their high-problem counterparts were said to have confided very frequently in their mothers, whereas this was reported to have been true of 73 percent of the low-problem children. Comparable proportions prevailed for the two subsequent age periods.

The high-problem adoptees were quite differentiated from their middle-range fellows in that a substantially greater proportion of the former were said to have rarely or never confided in either of their parents. For example, 54 percent of the Group III adoptees, as contrasted with 24 percent of the Group II adoptees, reportedly rarely or never confided in their mothers during their early childhood. This much higher proportion of high-problem nonconfiders in their mothers was also characteristic of the two older age periods for which we obtained data. All in all, one is impressed with the fact that the matter of confiding in the parents seems to be directly correlated with the overall outcome of the adoption.

Summary

The descriptive data concerning the adjustment of the adoptees over the years points up the obvious differences existing for the three groups we had organized by overall outcomes. Differences were noted in the sexes and ages of the adoptees placed with families in these categories, differences with respect to the agencies arranging the placements and differences in family composition. The early expectations of parents with regard to the sex and age of the child desired showed some differentiation by outcome categories. We also found that more mothers of high-problem adoptees reported miscarriages as the reason for their not having had a child of their own than was true of the women with adoptees classified in the other two outcome categories.

Distinctive differences were noted between the adoptees in the three outcome groups with respect to levels of educational performance, manifestations of personality disturbance, and the quality of family relationships. These differences reflected the basis upon which the three outcome groups had been organized for research purposes.

six / Background
for adoption

IN CHAPTER IV, we described the one hundred adoptive families we studied with regard to a variety of background variables: personal, social, and economic. These attributes are referred to as antecedent or independent variables because they existed prior to the families' experience with adoption. As recent mental health surveys [1] have shown, they are also theoretically capable of influencing the entire nature of the adoptive experience as well as the outcome of that experience for the adoptees. For this reason, we used these variables descriptively in Chapter IV to characterize these families after they had been trichotomized on the basis of the adoptees' overall past and current adjustment. In the present chapter we will be concerned with a correlational analysis of these variables, which is undertaken to determine in what ways they are meaningfully interrelated. Our purpose will be to provide additional insights into the characteristics and background of both the couples and the children who together entered into the unique relationship called adoption.

The findings we will present in the following pages will be based principally though not exclusively upon the correlations which proved statistically significant or near significant.[2] However, the matrix of intercorrelations among all the background variables is available from the Child Welfare League of America.

Characteristics of the adoptees

AGE AT PLACEMENT

Practice theory in child welfare has for a long while stressed the potential risks of adjustment difficulties attendant upon the adoptive placement of older children. Our data enable us to shed limited light upon this proposition because, by design, all of our subjects were three years of age or younger at the time of placement. Thus, the meaning of the phrases "older at placement" and "younger at placement" is relatively circumscribed. Nevertheless, a span of three years does provide a range within which to explore the various correlates of *later* or *earlier* adoptive placement. The outcome correlates of age at placement will be examined in Chapter XIV; here we address ourselves to the associations between the adoptee's age at placement and other important independent variables included in the study.

In Table 6–1 we see that adoption through two of the agencies participating in the study is strongly related to the adoptees' age at placement. Children placed by Catholic Home Bureau tended to be older when placed whereas children adopted through the Free Synogogue Committee were, by contrast, likely to be younger at placement. Chapin Nursery/Spence Alumnae and State Charities Aid adoptees tended to fall between these two extremes.

We found a significant positive relationship between a child's age at adoption and the number of preadoptive placements he was apt to have experienced: the older he was when his adoptive parents received him, the more likely he was to have had a greater succession of temporary preadoptive placements in a variety of settings. These settings were most commonly agency boarding homes, hospitals, or other kinds of congregate living arrangements. The association is not unexpected since the older the child at the time of placement in the

Table 6–1 / Correlations [a] between age of adoptees
at placement [b] in adoptive home and other selected
independent variables

VARIABLES	CORRELATIONS
Placing agency: [c]	
Catholic Home Bureau	−58 **
Chapin Nursery/Spence Alumnae	19
Free Synagogue Committee	43 **
State Charities Aid	−05
Characteristics of the adoptee:	
Sex (female; MALE) [d]	10
Number of preadoptive placements (one; EIGHT OR MORE)	22 *
Characteristics of the adoptive parents:	
Children in the family prior to adoptee (none; ONE OR MORE)	−14
Children in the family after adoptee (none; ONE OR MORE)	09
Motivation to adopt (high for one or both parents; LESS THAN HIGH FOR ONE OR BOTH PARENTS)	−14
Presence or absence of infertility (not infertile; ALL OTHER RESPONSES)	−02
Strength of effort to overcome infertility (all other responses; STRONG EFFORT)	−18
Sex preference: girl (girl desired; ALL OTHER RESPONSES)	15
Sex preference: boy (boy desired; ALL OTHER RESPONSES)	−02
Preference for age of child (infant or baby; ALL OTHER RESPONSES)	35 **
Age of adoptive father at application (20–24 years; 50 YEARS OR OVER)	−01
Age of adoptive mother at application (20–24 years; 50 YEARS OR OVER)	−03
Socioeconomic status (SES) (low; HIGH)	−42 ** c
Partial correlations, controlling for:	
Catholic Home Bureau −20 *	
Chapin Nursery/Spence Alumnae −40 **	
Free Synagogue Committee −34 **	
State Charities Aid −42 **	

adoptive home, the more opportunity there was for him to suffer turn-over in his prior living arrangements.

A strong negative correlation is apparent between the adoptee's age at placement and the socioeconomic status (SES) of the adoptive family. The lower the status, the more apt was the family to have received an older child for adoption. The strong relationship existing between the two variables is partially explained by the fact that placement had been effected by Catholic Home Bureau. We have already noted that children placed by this agency tended to be older. In a subsequent section of this chapter, we shall see that Catholic Home Bureau adoptive families also tended to be located at lower SES levels. We therefore hypothesized that it was adoption through Catholic Home Bureau that might explain at least part of the seemingly perplexing relationship between age of the child at placement and the family's SES.

It can be seen in Table 6-1 that this hypothesis was substantiated when we computed a partial correlation between these two variables, controlling for adoption through Catholic Home Bureau. The original correlation dropped noticeably (from $r = -.42$ to $r_{12.3} = -.20$), which indicated that adoption through Catholic Home Bureau had in fact been responsible for a sizable portion of the negative relationship we observed between SES and age of the adoptee at placement. When we controlled for the fact of adoption through the Free Synagogue Committee and Chapin Nursery/Spence Alumnae, the original correlation also decreased, though not nearly as much, revealing that adoptive placement by these agencies had also contributed in small measure to the original finding. However, all four partial correlations remained statistically significant, i.e., the higher the adoptive parents'

NOTES TO TABLE 6-1

* Significant: $p < .05$. ** Significant: $p < .01$.

a Decimal points omitted for this and all following tables.

b Direction of age variable: *under 4 months;* 36 MONTHS OR OVER.

c This nominal variable was dichotomized as follows for purposes of correlation analysis: $0 =$ family adopted through agency; $1 =$ family did not adopt through agency.

d For this and all following tables in the present chapter, the variable is presented parenthetically immediately following the variable name. The low pole is given first in italicized form; then the high pole in capital letters.

socioeconomic status, the more likely they were to have received an infant or young baby.

In Chapter IV we saw that the one hundred adoptees as a group had experienced an average of slightly more than three temporary placements before being adopted. The number of such preadoptive placements is a variable which, according to child welfare paractice theory, has implications for the subsequent emotional well-being and social adjustment of the adoptees. We will, however, defer to a later chapter consideration of whether our findings do or do not lend support to this proposition. At this juncture, we will confine ourselves to an examination of the relatively few significant correlations we uncovered between the number of preadoptive placements experienced by our adoptee subjects and various other independent variables.

We have already seen that the older a child was when placed in his adoptive home, the greater the number of preadoptive placements he was apt to have had. We also discovered that children who had been adopted through the Free Synagogue Committee were significantly more likely to have experienced fewer such prior placements, whereas the opposite was the case among children adopted through State Charities Aid. For reasons which we cannot readily discern, there is almost no relationship between the number of prior placements and the sample adoptees who came to their adoptive parents through either of the other two agencies participating in the study.

We also see in Table 6–2 that couples who had previously had no other children, either biological or adopted, were more likely to have received adoptees with a history of more rather than fewer preadoptive placements. There seemed to be no immediately obvious explanation of this finding. We speculated at first that it might be due to the fact that applicant couples with "marginal eligibility" because of age or other personal characteristics had demonstrated the greater flexibility suggested by Kadushin [3] and had been willing to accept children whose history of several different prior placements had made them somewhat less desirable adoptee candidates. However, we had to as-

Table 6-2 / Correlations between number of
adoptee's preadoptive placements [a] and other
selected independent variables

VARIABLES	CORRELATIONS
Placing agency: [b]	
Catholic Home Bureau	−02
Chapin Nursery/Spence Alumnae	04
Free Synagogue Committee	19
State Charities Aid	−21 *
Characteristics of the Adoptee:	
Sex (female; MALE)	−06
Age at placement in adoptive home (under 4 months; 36 MONTHS OR OVER)	22 *
Characteristics of the adoptive parents:	
Children in family prior to adoptee (none; ONE OR MORE)	−21 *
Children in family after adoptee (none; ONE OR MORE)	−03
Motivation to adopt (high for 1 or both parents; LESS THAN HIGH FOR 1 OR BOTH PARENTS)	−08
Presence or absence of infertility (not infertile; ALL OTHER RESPONSES)	−06
Strength of effort to overcome infertility (all other responses; STRONG EFFORT)	01
Sex preference: girl (girl desired; ALL OTHER RESPONSES)	00
Sex preference: boy (boy desired; ALL OTHER RESPONSES)	−07
Preference for age of child (infant or baby; ALL OTHER RESPONSES)	13
Age of adoptive father at application (20–24 years; 50 YEARS OR OVER)	11
Age of adoptive mother at application (20–24 years; 50 YEARS OR OVER)	08
Socioeconomic status (SES) (low; HIGH)	−17

* Significant: $p < .05$.

[a] Direction: one preadoptive placement; EIGHT OR MORE PLACEMENTS

[b] Direction: family adopted through agency; FAMILY DID NOT ADOPT THROUGH AGENCY

sume that the association occurred by chance upon finding no significant relationship between any of the personal characteristics of the adoptive parents and the number of preadoptive placements experienced by the adoptees. The latter variable is related only to the parents' SES, an association which we will discuss in greater detail below.

Characteristics of the adoptive parents

PRESENCE OR ABSENCE OF INFERTILITY

In current adoption practice theory, the infertility of adoptive applicants and the manner in which they have coped emotionally with this condition are regarded as primary diagnostic and screening considerations in the application process. As we indicated in Chapter III, infertility was not accorded this centrality during the 1930s and the 1940s, a reflection of the minimal professionalization of the staffs of the four participating agencies. The case records of our one hundred sample families contained sparse reference to any exploration of the reasons why couples had not procreated, and many records contained no allusion at all to this topic. Consequently, the following findings concerning the relationship between various aspects of infertility and other independent variables are based solely upon information provided by the adoptive parents in their research interviews.

As can be seen from Table 6–3, there were no significant correlations between the adoptive couple's fertility status and either the placing agency or any of the adoptee characteristics. However, among couples where either or both partners reported that the couple had been infertile prior to adoption, the woman was very apt to be identified by herself and/or by her husband as having been responsible for the infertility. Many such couples were likely to have made substantial efforts to overcome their barren state through seeking medical aid, but a number of them reported that the specific cause or reason for this condition had never been determined. We were interested and somewhat puzzled, however, to find that other of our data showed a statistically significant relationship between such reports of undetermined cause and the couples' socioeconomic status. Higher SES cou-

Table 6–3 / Correlations between fertility and infertility of adoptive couple at the time of adoption [a] and other selected independent variables

VARIABLES	CORRELATIONS
Placing agency:	
Catholic Home Bureau	—06
Chapin Nursery/Spence Alumnae	04
Free Synagogue Committee	04
State Charities Aid	—01
Characteristics of the adoptee:	
Sex (*female;* MALE)	01
Age at placement in adoptive home (*under 4 months;* 36 MONTHS OR OVER)	—02
Number of preadoptive placements (*one preadoptive placement;* EIGHT OR MORE PLACEMENTS)	—06
Characteristics of the adoptive parents:	
Children in family prior to adoptee (*none;* ONE OR MORE)	—07
Children in family after adoptee (*none;* ONE OR MORE)	—01
Motivation to adopt (*high for one or both parents;* LESS THAN HIGH FOR ONE OR BOTH PARENTS)	—10
Strength of effort to overcome infertility (*all other responses;* STRONG EFFORT)	55 **
Sex preference: girl (*girl desired;* ALL OTHER RESPONSES)	—02
Sex preference: boy (*boy desired;* ALL OTHER RESPONSES)	08
Preference for age of child (*infant or baby;* ALL OTHER RESPONSES)	—18
Age of adoptive father at application (*20–24 years;* 50 YEARS OR OVER)	04
Age of adoptive mother at application (*20–24 years;* 50 YEARS OR OVER)	02
Socioeconomic status (SES) (*low;* HIGH)	07

** Significant: $p < .01$.

[a] Direction: *couple not infertile or did not suffer prior miscarriages;* ALL OTHER RESPONSES.

ples were more likely than lower SES couples to inform us that the basis for their infertility had never been ascertained ($r = -.27$).

On its face, this finding seemed to us to be somewhat at odds with reasonable expectations. The more affluent families should ostensibly have been more able than their less well-to-do counterparts to have afforded the costly medical examinations and procedures necessary for arriving at an accurate diagnosis of the reason for their infertility. Moreover, being by and large more educated persons and perhaps more sophisticated in their knowledge of what steps might be taken to learn why they could not have their own children, they might reasonably have been expected to be more motivated than lower SES couples to pursue vigorously whatever avenues were open to them in this regard.

However, the above reasoning rests upon several important assumptions: that SES was the sole major factor distinguishing the two groups in their efforts to determine the cause of their barrenness; that high and low SES couples *desired* equally strongly to discover and overcome the obstacles to their being able to procreate; and that the etiology of the infertility among couples of differing socioeconomic status was the same or could equally readily be determined. Obviously, these are hazardous assumptions to make in the absence of any data which would permit testing their reasonableness. We are thus unable to explain the above finding but suggest that it may be a fruitful area for further investigation.

MOTIVATION TO ADOPT

In the interview we asked our adoptive parents how highly motivated they had been to undertake adoption at the time they had applied to the agency for a child. For purposes of correlation analysis, the resulting responses were grouped into two categories: reports that both members of the couple had been highly motivated to adopt, and reports that one or both partners had shown less than high motivation to take this step.

We found that the presence or absence of such motivation was correlated significantly with adoption through two of the four placing agencies in our study. If a couple had obtained their child through

Catholic Home Bureau, they were likely to report that both spouses had been highly motivated. By contrast, parents in families which had acquired their children from State Charities Aid were equally apt to admit that one or both partners had been less than highly motivated to enter into adoption.

Our data provide no basis for explaining these disparate reporting tendencies nor the comparable though less pronounced disparity between reports of couples adopting through Chapin Nursery/Spence Alumnae and the Free Synagogue Committee.[4] We would have had to gather substantially more background and personality data than we did in order to assess the extent to which the divergent tendencies reflected the strong need of the couples adopting through two agencies to deny less than high motivation and the greater ability on the part of couples adopting through two other agencies to be candid and frank with respect to this topic. In addition, the reader should bear in mind our earlier cautionary note regarding the documented unreliability of retrospective data concerning parental child-rearing behavior. We can safely assume that in the realm of highly charged emotions and attitudes relating to the desire to adopt, the accuracy of recall some two or three decades later would be even more subject to the affect of memory loss, repression, and distortion.

OTHER CHILDREN IN THE FAMILY

More than three-fourths (78 percent) of our sample families had been totally childless prior to having applied for the adoptee who was the subject of our inquiry. They had not had any biological offspring nor had they previously ventured into adoption. Our data reveal that this status correlates modestly though significantly with three other independent variables. Among such previously childless families, our adoptee subject tended more often to be male; conversely, among families already consisting of one or more children, our adoptee was more apt to be female. This difference, however, was in fact partly a reflection of socioeconomic differences among the two types of families, as was revealed by the partial correlation controlling for the effect of SES ($r = -.20$—sig.; $r_{12.3} = -.17$—not sig.).

Children adopted by childless couples were also likely to have been placed toward the early part of the 1930–1940 decade, since they tended to be older at the point we launched our study. Finally, previously childless adoptive parents were prone either to have adopted a second time or to have had their own biological child or children. One can interpret a subsequent adoption as either evidence that the couple's initial experience had been a rewarding one and/or as a reflection of the prevailing belief that it is not desirable for a child to be an "only child." That some of these families subsequently had their own biological children is not as easily interpreted. Reports of a satisfactory adoptive experience being followed by a couple's being able to procreate for the first time are frequently heard. However, our data shed no light on such reports nor on the causal relationship implicit in them.

SEX PREFERENCE

We saw in Chapter IV that for our sample as a whole a slightly greater preference for girls than for boys was manifested by couples upon first applying to the four agencies. In examining our data for purposes of the present analysis, however, we noted a marked tendency in the opposite direction on the part of couples who adopted through Catholic Home Bureau. In contrast with applicants at the other three agencies, Catholic Home Bureau couples had been prone *not* to specify a preference for girls when describing the characteristics they desired in a child.[5] Our data provide no sound basis for explaining this finding.

The correlation analysis reveals that applicant couples who explicitly requested a child of a given sex were likely to have expressed that desire rather strongly. However, applicants who asked for girls tended to have presented their sex preference with more intensity than did couples requesting boys, and the former, not unexpectedly, were more apt to have been given children of the desired sex.

All in all, though, the expressed desires of applicants for children of either sex tended to have been fulfilled by the four agencies. However, the correlation between a request for a girl and the fulfillment of that request ($r = .70$) was substantially stronger than the comparable relationship between the expressed desire for a boy and compliance with that request by the agencies (r = —.50).[6] This may well be attributable partly to the above finding that couples desiring girls had expressed their preferences with more vigor than had applicants who asked for boys.

In addition, as indicated in the preceding section of this chapter, couples who requested females when applying for the adoptee who became the focus of our study were likely already to have been parents of one or more adopted or biological children at the time that the adoptee was placed with them. Not surprisingly, these couples were apt to have added no further children to their families. Being predominantly middle class families, they probably shared with nonadoptive parents in their socioeconomic stratum the prevailing norm of relatively small families. Moreover, another factor militating against further increases in family size may well have been the agencies' reluctance to place additional children in homes which had already received one and sometimes two adoptees.

AGE PREFERENCE

The propensity for adoptive applicants to request infants or very young babies is well known to every adoption agency. As we saw in Chapter IV, our sample families were no exception to this tendency: almost three-fifths of them specified the desire for an infant or a baby no older than one year. However, in this connection Catholic Home Bureau families as a group again appeared to depart from the more general trend. We see from Table 6-4 that couples applying to that agency showed a modest but still noteworthy tendency *not* to stipulate the desire for an infant or a baby.[7] This is all the more noteworthy in view of the fact that for the entire sample as a whole, we discovered a significant positive correlation (r = .35) between expressed preference for an infant or a baby and the agencies' willingness to place younger children in such homes.

Once again there is no immediately self-evident explanation of the lesser tendency of Catholic Home Bureau families to request infants. However, one not unreasonable guess might be that it reflects the limited number of infants available to that agency during the 1930–1940 decade. Were this to have been the situation, that fact

Table 6–4 / *Correlations between adoptive couples' expressed age preference* [a] *and other selected independent variables*

VARIABLES	CORRELATIONS
Placing agency:	
Catholic Home Bureau	−20 *
Chapin Nursery/Spence Alumnae	13
Free Synagogue Committee	18
State Charities Aid	−11
Characteristics of the adoptee:	
Sex (*female;* MALE)	12
Age at placement in adoptive home (*under 4 months;* 36 MONTHS OR OVER)	35 **
Number of preadoptive placements (*one preadoptive placement;* EIGHT OR MORE PLACEMENTS)	13
Characteristics of the adoptive parents:	
Children in family prior to adoptee (*none;* ONE OR MORE)	15
Children in family after adoptee (*none;* ONE OR MORE)	−01
Motivation to adopt (*high for one or both parents;* LESS THAN HIGH FOR ONE OR BOTH PARENTS)	−03
Presence or absence of infertility (*not infertile;* ALL OTHER RESPONSES)	−18
Strength of effort to overcome infertility (*all other responses;* STRONG EFFORT)	−13
Sex preference: girl (*girl desired;* ALL OTHER RESPONSES)	04
Sex preference: boy (*boy desired;* ALL OTHER RESPONSES)	−00
Age of adoptive father at application (*20–24 years;* 50 YEARS OR OVER)	10
Age of adoptive mother at application (*20–24 years;* 50 YEARS OR OVER)	03
Socioeconomic status (SES) (*low;* HIGH)	−16

* Significant: $p < .05$. ** Significant: $p < .01$.
[a] Direction: *infant or baby;* ALL OTHER RESPONSES.

could have been communicated to applying couples either directly or indirectly, and it would have resulted in their modifying their expressed age preferences in order to obtain a more available older child as soon as possible.

PARENTAL AGE AT APPLICATION

The only significant correlation which this variable appeared to have with any other antecedent variable relates to the age of the woman at the time the couple applied to the agency for adoption. The older she was at that point, the fewer children, all told, she and her husband were apt to have had over the subsequent years. This, of course, is a logical and quite readily explainable relationship. The older adoptive applicant would have had fewer child-bearing years ahead of her had she been able to conceive following the adoption. Furthermore, she and her husband, probably her senior in age, would likely have been considered by the agency increasingly less eligible to receive additional adopted children as the years passed.

The findings of a research study ought not be confined exclusively to the identification of significant correlations among variables. Oftentime, equally meaningful is the *failure* of significant relationships to appear where one would expect them. Our data disclosed one such finding in connection with the variable under discussion. Current placement standards and practice in many adoption agencies led us to anticipate at least a moderate correlation between the age of adoptive applicants and the age of the children placed with them.

The assumption of many adoption workers is that older parents are generally not as able as younger ones to cope with the manifold incessant physical needs of an infant and an active young baby. Moreover, the Child Welfare League of America has stressed the desirability of reducing as far as possible any glaring discrepancy between the relative ages of adoptive parents and their children as compared with the age relationship obtaining among the general population of parents and their biological children.[8] Consequently, many agencies will tend not to place an infant with, say, a couple older than forty years of age. Rather, assuming that such applicants were qualified in all other respects, they would most likely be offered an older child more comparable in age to the average biological offspring of forty-year-old parents.

Had such an agency policy guided the placement of the adoptees in our sample, we would have found a positive, and most likely significant, correlation between the ages of both members of the adoptive couple at application and the age of the adoptee placed with them. As it was, however, the actual correlation coefficients between these two variables not only hover close to zero; they carry negative rather than the positive signs which might have been logically expected.[9] This means simply that the relative ages of the applicant couples and the children placed with them did not systematically enter into or influence the agencies' choice of adoptees for specific couples.

SOCIOECONOMIC STATUS (SES) [10]

It is apparent from Table 6–5 that in this study the socioeconomic status of our adoptive families is important in shedding light upon several aspects of the adoption experience. At least two allusions have already been made in this chapter to the linkage between this variable and other independent variables examined in our study. To recapitulate briefly, we have seen: (1) that lower SES families were significantly more likely to have received older rather than younger children for adoption; and (2) that in higher SES families the cause of the adoptive couple's infertility was more apt not to have been determined at the time of application. We also discovered—but have not thus far explained—that less than high motivation to adopt was more characteristic of one or both partners in high than in low SES couples ($r = .21$).

Another correlation, only touched on in passing, was that between socioeconomic status and the identity of the placing agency. This relationship was significant in the case of only two of our four participating agencies, but highly so. We see in Table 6–5 a quite strong tendency for Catholic Home Bureau families to be at the lower end of the socioeconomic scale and a somewhat weaker but still statistically significant tendency for the Free Synagogue Committee families to be located at the higher end of the SES continuum. Families who adopted through Chapin Nursery/Spence Alumnae were also apt to be in the upper income brackets, but the correlation does not quite attain significance. Finally, there exists virtually no relationship between adoption through State Charities Aid and the SES of families who obtained their children from that agency.

Table 6–5 / Correlations between adoptive parents'
socioeconomic status (SES) [a] *and other selected*
independent variables

VARIABLES	CORRELATIONS
Placing agency:	
Catholic Home Bureau	49 **
Chapin Nursery/Spence Alumnae	−16
Free Synagogue Committee	−29 **
State Charities Aid	−04
Characteristics of the adoptee:	
Sex (*female;* MALE)	−18
Age at placement in adoptive home (*under 4 months;* 36 MONTHS OR OVER)	−42 **
Number of preadoptive placements (*one preadoptive placement;* EIGHT OR MORE PLACEMENTS)	−17
Characteristics of the adoptive parents:	
Children in family prior to adoptee (*none;* ONE OR MORE)	20 *
Children in family after adoptee (*none;* ONE OR MORE)	07
Motivation to adopt (*high for one or both parents;* LESS THAN HIGH FOR ONE OR BOTH PARENTS)	21 *
Presence or absence of infertility (*not infertile;* ALL OTHER RESPONSES)	07
Strength of effort to overcome infertility (*all other responses;* STRONG EFFORT)	02
Sex preference: girl (*girl desired;* ALL OTHER RESPONSES)	−19
Sex preference: boy (*boy desired;* ALL OTHER RESPONSES)	09
Preference for age of child (*infant or baby;* ALL OTHER RESPONSES)	−16
Age of adoptive father at application (*20–24 years;* 50 YEARS OR OVER)	22 *
Age of adoptive mother at application (*20–24 years;* 50 YEARS OR OVER)	15

* Significant: $p < .05$ ** Significant: $p < .01$.
[a] Direction: *low status score;* HIGH STATUS SCORE.

Reference to Table 6–5 also reveals that the older the prospective adoptive father at the time of the adoption application, the higher tended to be his socioeconomic level. This finding intuitively makes sense: older age is logically related to achievement with respect to at least two of the three components of our SES index, viz., income level and level of education. Less easily explainable is the positive relationship between the adoptive father's socioconomic status and the number of adopted or biological children already likely to have been present in the home at the time the couple applied for the adoptee who became the subject of our inquiry. This is not a function of the age of the adoptive applicants, since that variable was found not to be significantly correlated with the number of previous children in the home; nor was the fact of having adopted through any one of the four agencies. Indeed, there is nothing in our data which affords a basis for interpreting this finding.

We note, finally, that socioeconomic level tends also to be negatively correlated with the expressed preference for a girl adoptee. Upper class couples were more apt than lower class couples to have voiced such a preference, the relevant correlation coming quite close to statistical signficance (viz., $r = -.19$). Once again, however, this relationship turns out to be largely the result of underlying correlations between each of the two variables and adoptive placement by Catholic Home Bureau. When we computed the partial correlation between SES and expressed preference for a girl, controlling for adoption through Catholic Home Bureau, the resulting coefficient was clearly not significant ($r_{12.3} = -.08$).

Summary

In this chapter, we have examined the significant interrelationships among the two principal groups of background variables in our study: the characteristics of the adoptees at placement, and the characteristics of their adoptive parents. With regard to the former variables, we saw that the sex of the adoptees on whom we focused was related to the presence or absence of other children already in the home at the time of placement. We noted, too, a moderately pronounced relationship between adoption through two of the participating agencies in the study and the likelihood that the adoptees placed by them were at the older or younger end of their first three-year age span.

We observed also a strong negative correlation between the child's age at placement and the socioeconomic level of his adoptive parents, and we suggested a partial explanation of this relationship. Not surprisingly, we found that the older the child when placed for adoption, the greater the number of preadoptive placements he was likely to have experienced. However, we were not able to account for the fact that children with a greater number of such prior placements were more apt to have been adopted by childless couples than by couples with one or more children in their families. Finally, reference was made to a finding that one of the participating agencies was associated with adoptees who had undergone fewer preadoptive placements, while another agency had worked with adoptees having a history of more such prior placements.

We then considered a number of adoptive parent characteristics which were significantly linked to other independent variables. Among these findings perhaps three are most noteworthy. We were struck first of all by the *absence* of any meaningful correlation between the age of applicant couples and the age of the children placed with them. Where, on the basis of current placement standards, we would have anticipated a strong positive correlation between these variables, we found virtually none at all. On the other hand, we saw that the adoptive couple's socioeconomic status *was* strongly related to a number of other variables. Finally, we noted that families adopting through one of the four agencies participating in the study tended to depart from the age- and sex-preference patterns prevailing among the total sample. Such couples were significantly likely *not* to request infants or very young babies and *not* to express a preference for girl adoptees over boy adoptees. The reasons behind these findings were not apparent in our data.

seven / Revelation
of adoptive status

THE QUESTIONS of whether, when, and how to tell adoptees of their adoptive status have long been crucial issues both to adoptive parents and to the adoption agencies who place children with them. Moreover, these have been and currently still are controversial questions not fully resolved in adoption practice theory. For many years agencies encouraged new adoptive parents to tell their children "the adoption story" at the earliest feasible point in their lives. Shapiro surveyed some 270 agencies in this regard and noted:

> . . . most agencies specifically direct adoptive parents to inform the child early before he hears about his adoption from others. "Awareness of need to inform child a must" and "we do not accept if couple refuses" were comments frequently made. Agencies believe that adoptive parents reveal important attitudes on acceptance of adoption in discussions about telling the child. Their ability to be relaxed about it is essential. It is an important factor in determining a couple's readiness to adopt.[1]

118

Telling the adoptee as early as possible about his status has in the past generally received widespread support in professional circles on the grounds that telling the child at an early age would spare him the severe emotional trauma of learning this fact inadvertently from other sources.[2] Ideally, the development of a youngster's self-concept would include the fact that he was adopted. This would alleviate the severe turmoil and conflict that would arise if he were faced suddenly with having to incorporate this fact into a new self-conception at a later age.

However, more recently, less firm prescriptions have been suggested, and parents are being urged to take into account their own degree of comfort in making decisions about when and how to tell their youngsters about their adoptive backgrounds. For example, Bernard, after considerable experience as a psychiatric consultant to an adoption agency, has suggested:

> When parents feel comfortable and sure enough of themselves, they do not need to overdo or underdo on this score. They neither force the topic on the child, inopportunely, nor discourage his further questioning by closing the issue after it has been dealt with "once and for all."

> Agencies avoid suggesting any single set formula for how best to tell the child that he is adopted. They realize that the particular wording is far less important than the feelings and attitudes behind it, which somehow always come through. The agency helps primarily in the crucial preplacement tasks of coming to terms with infertility and adoption, but sometimes later as well when these problems are prone to flare up again to some extent as the time of telling approaches.[3]

Other writers in the adoption field have also voiced reservations about some of the assumptions underlying the advice often given in support of early revelations. Peller's comments are illustrative of this point of view:

> It is my conviction that adoption should be discussed with the child after his social orbit has widened, *after* he has met other children and their parents, that is, in his early school years. Probably all latency children toy with the idea that these parents who care and provide for them and who say NO to some of their most ardent wishes are not their real parents. . . . The only difference is that the adopted child's fantasy is supported by reality. . . . It seems that in these years a child can learn about his adoption with less upset than earlier and later in his life.[4]

Schechter, in reporting his concern about the prevalence of emotional disturbance among adopted children, expresses a similar point of view:

> A major question suggested is referable to the timing and period of telling the child that he is adopted. The Oedipal period is a time when ambivalence is still very evident. This is the time when children fantasy a great deal, and, frustrated by the parents, imagine better parents who could love them and cherish them more. . . . children who have these feelings can see the bad side of their parents contrasted with the good, permissive, and giving side of the same parent. The adoptive child has a chance, however, of splitting the image of his parents and attributing the good elements to one set and the bad to the other. . . . the material presented suggests that the immature ego cannot cope with the knowledge of the rejection by its original parents, representing a severe narcissistic injury. The child tends to react to this information by character change or symptom formation. It is, therefore, recommended that the thorough investigation of the child and his environment should be accomplished to determine the method and timing of giving the information of his adoptive status.[5]

In supporting Schechter's observations, Toussieng points up the severe emotional dilemmas also faced by the adoptive parents, and he calls attention to the fact that a number of studies have suggested that "major unconscious emotional conflicts in one or both parents often are involved in sterility."[6] Kirk has criticized many adoption agencies for failing to be sensitive to the dilemma implicit in the apparent social work emphasis upon recommending complete candor with the child about his adoption and about his birth status. He feels that agencies too often err in insisting that adoptive parents tell the child he is adopted without at the same time helping them to anticipate the pangs of pain that are invariably aroused by the awareness that this information is potentially disruptive to the adoptive child and his family.[7]

As can be seen from the points of view cited above, the revelation phenomenon is quite obviously an aspect of adoption which holds great professional interest and around which there are many unresolved questions. It therefore seemed useful for us to go into some detail with the adoptive parents we interviewed about their manner of handling revelation with their children and to secure as many details about this as possible. We did not anticipate, of course, that our findings would serve to resolve these thorny issues. Rather, we thought they would serve to add to the background of information available about revelation.

The parents were therefore asked to recall at what age their children had *first* been informed about their adoptive status, the circumstances under which this had occurred, the amount of information that had been divulged to them, and the adoptee's response to this new knowledge. The interviewers also inquired into the manner in which the parents had treated the subject of adoption subsequent to the initial revelation, the frequency with which it had been discussed over the years, the nature and amount of information that had been imparted to the adoptees regarding their biological parents, the willingness and ability of the children to talk about this subject, and the extent to which they had requested or sought information beyond that which the adoptive parents knew or were willing to divulge to them.

The adoptive parents' tendency to have revealed or to have withheld knowledge of the child's adoptive status from friends, neighbors, business associates, the adoptee's teachers, the family minister, physician, dentist, and casual acquaintances was also explored. Finally, the adoptive parents were asked about aspects of their children's adoptive status which had created problems for them as parents as well as for the adoptees. The remainder of this chapter will be devoted to presenting the findings resulting from this exploration.

The initial revelation

SOURCE OF INITIAL REVELATION

For the most part, the adoptees first learned of their adopted status from their adoptive parents. Table 7–1 reveals that this was true for 83 percent of all sample families and for approximately the same proportion of families in each of the three outcome groups. In only slightly more than one out of ten families, for the sample as a whole, did the adoptee discover he was adopted from some source other than his adoptive parents. In this respect, the three outcome groups do show some minor variations: somewhat more of the children in the middle-range outcome group learned of their adoption from nonparent sources than was true of adoptees in the other two outcome categories. There is no basis for explaining why Group II families should exceed the others in this regard.

It is noteworthy that in four of the one hundred families studied, adoptive parents reported that the adoptees had *never* been told they had been adopted. Two of these families fell in the low-problem group and one each in the remaining two outcome groups. While it would be foolhardy to generalize from four cases, it is nevertheless of interest that the failure to be apprised of their adoptive status is not apparently linked with major difficulties in subsequent life adjustments. In examining our data, we noted that three of the four families who did not divulge to their children their adopted status had adopted from Catholic Home Bureau; the other, from the State Charities Aid. This finding seems fairly consonant with a pattern which emerged in our data and is noted in the next chapter,[8] viz., that the parents of the adoptees in the low-problem group tended to be somewhat protective of their children and less ready to accept some of the normal risks entailed in child rearing—for example, separation experiences. As was shown in Table 5–2, adoptees placed by Catholic Home Bureau and State Charities Aid comprised more than half (58 percent) of the membership of the low-problem outcome group. What aspect of raising an adopted child could be riskier in the minds of protective parents than to tell the child that they were not his original parents? The chance of possibly alienating him and losing his love would seem to constitute a real threat for these parents.

What were the reasons offered by these four sets of parents for

Table 7–1 / Source of initial revelation

	GROUP I	GROUP II	GROUP III	TOTAL
Adoptive parents	82%	82%	85%	83%
Adoptee never told he was adopted	6	3	3	4
Disparate response	3	—	3	2
Other source	9	15	9	11
Total cases	(33)	(34)	(33)	(100)

withholding from their children the fact that they were adopted? The following are brief summaries of the parents' explanations. As can be seen by the reader, in only one case were the parents absolutely sure that the adoptee was completely uninformed about his adoptive status.

CASE NO. 24. Mrs. C. maintained that they had never directly told the adoptee that he was adopted and that even at the time of the research interview, she doubted whether he fully appreciated or consciously knew that he was adopted. She had always found herself unable to tell him of his background and had given herself various reasons for delaying doing so. Initially, she had thought he was too young to learn about adoption and then subsequently, in the face of other family problems, she had felt that it was not desirable to add this information to an already tense family situation. She did note that when the adoptee was less than five years of age, a playmate mentioned to him that his mother was not his real mother. However, the adoptee did not seem to consider this to be a true fact and therefore the matter was not raised again. There had been absolutely no discussion of adoption since that incident although Mrs. C. maintained that if the child were to raise the question with her, she would tell him the truth. She did express, however, her considerable fear and reluctance to divulge this information, commenting that she had never thought of the adoptee as anything but her own child. She was fearful that "something will change" if she were to divulge to him his adopted status.

CASE NO. 49. Mr. and Mrs. S. had never told either of their adopted children about their adoptive status. As far as they knew, to the day of the research interview the adoptees did not know they were adopted. The parents' justification for not having given such information was that both of their children had come into their home while toddlers and had revealed considerable insecurity stemming from experiences they had before coming into the home. The child who was the subject of the research interview had come to them severely malnourished and with a swollen belly. He had been extremely fearful of physical harm by adults and it had taken many years before he ceased being a "coward" according to Mrs. S. It was her reasoning that knowing they had been adopted might have subjected the boys to ridicule or taunts from others. The parents felt that the children had been too vulnerable to be subjected to this. The parents explained their ability to keep the facts of adoption secret as having been due to the cooperation of other persons. Even though immediate members of both families were aware of the children's backgrounds, they have not revealed this information in a way that would violate the family secret. Mr. and Mrs. S. noted that both families knew how to be "clams," and they had no fear that the information would be revealed. However, should the children find out in the future, the parents felt that this would not be any great catastrophe as they were now older and could cope with it. Nevertheless, they had no intention of revealing this information themselves unless forced to do so.

CASE NO. 61. The revelation of the adoptee's adoptive status was not made in any way until she was thirteen years of age, and even then this was not revealed *in toto*. Prior to the child's thirteenth birthday, at which time her adoptive mother died, Mr. and Mrs. R. had told her nothing about being adopted. The father explained this in terms of the child having been extremely happy and very much a part of the family in her feelings and relationships. He questioned the purpose of making such a happy youngster unhappy by telling her that she was adopted. He feared that this information would have made the adoptee feel that she had no one who was really hers and thus deprive her of a source of great security and comfort. In the parents' way of thinking, there was nothing more grievous than to unnecessarily make a happy child sad. Mr. R. and his wife had done some thinking about talking the matter over with the adoptee at some undetermined point in the future, but it had not been clear to them what they were going to tell her and at what point. At the mother's death, however, the maternal aunt had begun to talk to the child about her being adopted. The father at this point had denied the validity of the aunt's story, and the child had seemed to be very ready to accept this version. She had never again raised questions about this matter and had not seemed to be the least bit disturbed about it.

CASE NO. 66. Mr. B., the widowed father of the adoptee, told the interviewer that neither of his adopted children had been told that he was adopted. The reason for this was that the adoptive mother had been opposed to this; she had felt that it was not in the interest of the children. The grown-ups in the family had agreed not to discuss the matter of adoption with any outsiders. To the day of the research interview, there had been no discussion with the adoptees about this subject. At the same time, Mr. B. was willing to admit that it was hard for him to believe that his two children did not know that they were adopted. Yet, he had seen no sign of this. To some extent, he regretted not having told them, because he had always feared that they might learn this in a painful way. However, he was not inclined at this late date to open up discussion about the subject.

TIMING OF INITIAL REVELATION

In more than four out of every ten families, the adoptive parents reported that their children had "always" known they were adopted. "Always" was defined as a situation where there had been no identifiable point in time when the adoptive status had been revealed to the adoptee. Typically, the adoptive parents had spoken of adoption "from the beginning," usually before the adoptee had been able to understand any words, let alone comprehend the meaning of "adoption." In other words, these adoptive parents had seemingly taken to heart and acted upon the advice apparently given by most of the agencies at that time to use the word adoption as soon as possible so that the adoptee would become familiar with it and consider it as something natural and normal. An interesting finding is the absence of any notable trend in this matter of revelation with respect to our outcome groupings. The intergroup differences in the first line of Table 7-2 are obviously slight.

Considering those families where the adoptee had been apprised of his status at specific ages, we note that for both the entire sample and for two of the three outcome groups, approximately equal proportions (20 to 25 percent) of the adoptive parents had first told their children they were adopted when the latter were below age six and an equal proportion when they were six or older. Outcome Group III appears in Table 7-2 to be the exception to this tendency, with only about half as many high-problem adoptees falling in the older revelation group as in the younger. This is a misleading impression, however, because two sets of Group III parents, coded as having given disparate responses to this question, actually agreed that their children had been over age six at the time of initial revelation; they disagreed only on the specific age. When these two families are added to the "six and over" category, the Group III distribution conforms with those of the other two outcome groups.

The same lack of strong difference among outcome groups is seen when we combine the "below six" revelation families with those where the adoptees were reported to have "always" known they were adopted, forming a composite group of *early* revelation families. Two-

Table 7-2 / Age at which adoptee first informed he was adopted

	GROUP I	GROUP II	GROUP III	TOTAL
Adoptee "always" [a] knew he was adopted	49%	44%	40%	44%
Informed at a specific age:				
Below age 2	—	6	—	2
Age 2 and 3	6	6	9	7
Age 4 and 5	12	12	12	12
Age 6 and 7	15	12	6	11
Age 8 and 9	6	—	—	2
Age 10 and 11	—	—	3	1
Age 12 and over	3	8	3	5
Adoptee never told he was adopted	6	3	3	4
Disparate response	3	—	18	7
Parent did not know when adoptee first informed	—	—	3	1
Other/Unable to determine	—	9	3	4
Total cases	(33)	(34)	(33)	(100)

[a] "Always" defined as no identifiable point in time when this information was revealed to the adoptee. Adoptive parents spoke to him of adoption "from the beginning."

thirds of the families of low-problem and middle-range adoptees were characterized by early telling, as were three-fifths of the families of high-problem adoptees, this difference not being significant.

In view of the apparent tendency of agencies to emphasize the need for early revelation, we expected to find that where late revelations took place—say, at six years and older—this would be associated with a more negative type of outcome. Yet, examination of Table 7-2 reveals this not to be the case. Even when we add to the Group III figures, as described above, the two families in which the adoptive parents agreed that initial revelation had occurred after age six but did not agree on the specific age, the proportion of high-problem adoptees who had experienced *late* revelation (18 percent) remains somewhat, though not significantly, lower than the comparable proportions of middle-range and low-problem adoptees (21 and 24 percent, respectively).

We examined another important aspect of the timing of the initial revelation, viz., whether this telling had been handled by the adoptive parents according to a predetermined plan or whether it had arisen precipitously. We anticipated that in the latter event there would likely be reported a negatively charged emotional climate or a feeling of crisis which could have created problems for the adoptive parents in their handling of the event. Such a situation might also augur poorly for the adoptee's ability to accept and assimilate in a constructive way the suddenly revealed information that he was an adopted child.

Table 7–3 presents the results of our inquiry into this topic and reveals some rather striking differences among the three outcome groups. Fully one-third of the families of high-problem adoptees had had to cope with a precipitous initial revelation of adoptive status. This was true for only one-fifth of the parents of middle-range adoptees and less than one-tenth of the families of low-problem adoptees. Thus, if there are in fact potential negative consequences associated with sudden and unanticipated revelation, the adoptees in the high-problem group tended to be more disadvantaged than those in the other groups in an area of central importance to their emotional and person-

*Table 7–3 / Planned or precipitous occurrence of
initial revelation*

	GROUP I	GROUP II	GROUP III	TOTAL
Handled according to plan [a]	82%	73%	55%	69%
Arose precipitously	9	21	33	21
Adoptee never told he was adopted	6	3	3	4
Disparate response	3	—	3	2
Unable to determine or not applicable	—	3	6	4
Total cases	(33)	(34)	(33)	(100)

[a] Includes all families reporting that the adoptee "always" knew he was adopted in addition to those who had revealed adoption at a specific age and had handled the telling according to a predetermined plan.

ality development. That is, our findings suggest that the ad hoc and makeshift handling of revelation may have contributed to the subsequent adjustment problems of the adoptees with the most problematic overall adjustments.

CONTENT OF INITIAL REVELATION AND
REACTION OF ADOPTEES

Forty-five sets of parents reported that they had divulged the fact of adoption to their children when the adoptees had been at a given age rather than stating that the adoptee had always known he was adopted.[9] We queried these parents about the content of the revealed information and about the adoptees' emotional response to it, and we obtained usable responses in forty-two instances.[10] The reader should bear in mind that the following findings, summarizing these responses, reflect initial revelation which took place over a wide range of ages, from below age two to beyond age twelve.[11] This meant that the ability of these adoptees to understand and comprehend the full meaning of the information they received varied greatly, and this factor undoubtedly conditioned the nature and the amount of information supplied them by their adoptive parents.

Our data reveal that the preponderance of the parents in these forty-two families did not divulge *any* information to their children regarding the background of their biological parents. In thirty-seven instances, the adoptees were given no information concerning the marital or family status of their natural parents; in the same number of instances they were told nothing about their biological parents' personal and social characteristics; and in thirty-five instances they received no information regarding the reason why the biological parents had given them up for adoption or had abandoned them. With regard to the first category of information, only one-quarter of the thirty-seven adoptive parents were ignorant of the true facts; the remaining three-quarters purposely withheld information known to them. Approximately half of the parents who gave their children no information regarding the other two aspects of their natural parents' background did not themselves know the facts; the other half withheld, by design, facts known to them. A small proportion of the adoptive parents provided the adoptees with an untrue account of the facts in each of the three background categories—from 5 to 14 percent. Finally, and strikingly, not a single set of adoptive parents reported having given their child accurate information regarding their biological parents' marital or family status or regarding the reason why the biological parents had given the children up for placement. Only three sets of adoptive parents described accurately to their children their natural parents' personal and social characteristics.

The forty-two families were equally divided among the three outcome groups, and our data show that for the most part the adoptive parents in each group handled the giving of information about the biological parents in substantially the same manner. Relatively equal proportions provided their children with no information in any of the three categories discussed above, roughly half of these failing to divulge facts known to them. The provision of an untrue account of the facts also was reported by about the same number of parents in each outcome category. Of the three sets of adoptive parents who did share with their children an accurate picture of their natural parents' personal and social characteristics, two sets were parents of high-problem adoptees, and one set had an adoptee classified in the low-problem category.

What was the reaction of the adoptees to the content of the initial revelation? Approximately three-quarters of the forty-two sets of parents claimed that their children had not been emotionally upset or disturbed upon learning of their adoptive status—about equal proportions in each of the three outcome groups. Five sets of parents, three of Group III adoptees and two of Group II adoptees, reported that their children had been moderately or very upset upon being confronted with this revelation; a sixth couple, with an adoptee in Group III, stated that their child had been mildly upset. No parents of low-problem adoptees reported any upsetness or disturbance on the part of their children in being informed of the fact of their adoption.

Thus, for this subgroup of our adoptees who were told of their adoption at a specific age rather than "always" having been aware of it, revelation does not on the whole appear to have been a very emotionally traumatic experience—at least as far as the adoptive parents could discern or were willing to report. We should of course bear in mind that this area of the adoptive experience would likely be one of the most susceptible to repression or distorted reporting if in fact the adoptive parents had noted that their children had become severely upset upon learning—usually directly from the adoptive parents—of their adoptive status.

Subsequent handling of adoptive status

ADOPTEES' COMPREHENSION OF
MEANING OF "ADOPTION"

During the discussion of revelation, we asked the adoptive parents how old they thought the adoptees had been before they had been first really able to understand the meaning of adoption and to distinguish it from a biological relationship. Three out of ten parents were unable to give definitive answers to this question: they did not know when their children had first developed this awareness. This was true of about equal proportions of parents in each of the three outcome groups. Some 14 percent of the parents—also distributed about evenly among the outcome groups—identified the point of initial comprehension as coinciding with the time of revelation. An additional 29 percent placed the first awareness of the real meaning of adoption at some point following the initial revelation; once more, these were divided almost equally among the three adjustment groups. The ages most frequently cited for the time of initial comprehension were six through nine years.

FREQUENCY OF DISCUSSION OF ADOPTION

We considered it important to secure a picture of the extent to which the adoptive parents had sought to make adoption visible to their children over the years. We believed this would provide some additional clues about how comfortable the parents had been with the phenomenon of adoption. Exaggerated efforts on their part at either end of the continuum, i.e., to make adoption highly and constantly visible or to make it almost totally invisible, were interpreted, from our theoretical standpoint, as possibly reflective of unresolved or conflicted feelings about their "sense of entitlement" to their children. The question utilized to tap this dimension was the frequency with which the parents had over the years discussed with their children the latter's adoptive status.

We see in Table 7-4 that during all three age periods the largest group of parents for the total sample tended to cluster near the middle of the frequency range, having discussed adoption somewhat frequently or relatively infrequently. The proportion of families in these categories declines slightly as the adoptees grow older. Concomitantly, the figures show a modest rise over time in the proportion of parents who claimed to have discussed the subject of adoption very infrequently, which increases from a low of about one-fourth, when the adoptees were youngest, to a high of almost one-third when they had entered late adolescence and early adulthood. At the extreme poles, we see that 6 percent of the parents reported having discussed

Table 7-4 / Frequency with which adoptive parents discussed with adoptee his adoptive status during three age periods

	BELOW AGE 10 OUTCOME GROUP			AGE 10–17 OUTCOME GROUP			AGE 18 AND OVER OUTCOME GROUP		
	I	II	III	I	II	III	I	II	III
Very frequently	6%	9%	3%	6%	3%	—%	6%	3%	—%
Somewhat frequently	12	18	18	9	15	18	6	9	15
Relatively infrequently	21	26	25	18	35	21	21	38	18
Very infrequently	34	18	18	40	23	21	40	26	31
Never after initial revelation	3	12	3	3	12	6	3	15	6
Disparate response	12	6	18	12	3	21	12	3	18
Adoptee never told he was adopted	6	3	3	6	3	3	6	3	3
Other	6	9	3	6	6	—	6	—	—
Not covered	—	—	9	—	—	8	—	3	9
Total cases	(33)	(34)	(33)	(33)	(34)	(33)	(33)	(34)	(33)

the subject of adoption with their children very frequently when the latter were below age ten; this was true, however, of only 3 percent of the parents during the two succeeding age periods. At the other end of the spectrum there is a slight but continuous increase over the years in the proportion of families (from 6–8 percent) who claimed not to have discussed the subject with their children *at all* after the initial revelation. This rise is due to late revelation (during the ten to seventeen and eighteen and over age periods) in two families who never again subsequently discussed adoption with their children.

A comparative examination of the data in Table 7–4 for the three outcome groups reveals no striking differences in the frequency of discussion of adoption. If any tendency is at all noteworthy, it is the greater proneness of the parents of low-problem and middle-range adoptees to have discussed the topic "very infrequently" than was the case for parents of high-problem adoptees. All in all, however, we were quite surprised to find this lack of differentiation in the behavior of parents, grouped by outcome, in this patently important domain. On the face of it, our findings appear to suggest that the frequency with which the parents spoke about adoption showed little association with how the adoption turned out. This is demonstrated by the fact that even in the best outcome category at least three times as many parents reported discussing adoption "relatively infrequently" or "very infrequently" as reported having discussed it "very frequently" or "somewhat frequently."

In reflecting upon the absence of a positive association between better outcomes and more frequent discussions of adoption it seemed to us that there was a danger in oversimplifying the revelation phenomenon by being concerned with only the frequency issue. Also, there is the matter of the parent's comfort with the topic. Successful parental adjustment in this area could include two *diverse* types of behaviors. On one level, there is the parent who may be uncomfortable with the discussion of adoption. Hence, his recourse to infrequent discussion of the topic might represent the optimal behavior possible for him. In a sense this may reflect good ego functioning which could lead to better results than if he chose to overcome his discomfort through forced "overdetermined" and unnatural opening up of discussions. On the other hand, there is the parent who is quite comfortable in discussing adoption and does this frequently in a manner which connotes lack of strain or conflict. *Both* parents might succeed in creating a secure atmosphere for their children even though this is done by diverse routes.

NATURE OF INFORMATION GIVEN TO ADOPTEES

Besides the above quantitative aspects of making the adoptive status visible, we also explored the qualitative aspects of this phenomenon. We did this by inquiring into the kind of information the adoptive parents had given their children about their biological parents. This time we focused on the parents' handling of this topic *subsequent* to the initial revelation, although we used the same questions with which we had earlier explored the initial revelation in families where the children had been told of their adoption at a specific age.

Our findings, as revealed in Table 7–5, are quite similar to those presented earlier concerning the more circumscribed group. The majority of adoptees had been given no information whatever over the years about the family or marital status or the personal and social characteristics of their biological parents or about the reasons why their natural parents had abandoned them or given them up for adoption. In each of these three areas, at least half of the parents who had given their children no information at all withheld relevant facts known to them regarding their children's natural parents. This was true of approximately equal numbers of parents in each of the three outcome groups.

We see in Table 7–5 that 4 percent of the adoptive parents provided their children with false information about the marital status of their biological parents and that 8 percent gave an untrue account of the reasons why the natural parents had given up or abandoned the children. Only somewhat more than one in ten parents were either willing or able to share with their adoptees the true facts as they knew them. This applies to about equal numbers of parents in each of the three outcome groups with regard to information concerning the marital status of the biological parents. With respect to the other two aspects of the natural parents' background, we noted some variation among the adjustment groups in the proportions of parents reportedly

Table 7–5 / Nature of information regarding
biological parents revealed by total sample
of adoptive parents to adoptees over the
years following the initial revelation

	INFORMATION REGARDING CHARACTERISTICS OF BIOLOGICAL PARENTS		
	FAMILY OR MARITAL STATUS	PERSONAL AND SOCIAL CHARACTERISTICS	REASONS FOR GIVING UP OR ABANDONING ADOPTEE
No information revealed: parents did not know facts	26%	36%	26%
No information revealed: parents withheld facts	45	36	36
Some information provided: not true account of facts	4	—	8
Some information provided: accurate account of facts	13	15	12
Disparate response	5	2	7
Other	2	5	2
Not covered/Unable to determine	5	6	9
Total cases	(100)	(100)	(100)

giving their children accurate descriptions, but these differences were not significant.

Our data, in short, suggest that neither the divulging of information to the adoptees regarding their biological past nor the withholding of such information seems related to subsequent favorable or unfavorable life adjustment. Such a conclusion gains additional support from the correlation analysis to be reported on subsequently. This finding may cause surprise for those who would hold that a realistic, yet positive and sympathetic picture of an adoptee's natural parents is important to the development of a sense of self-worth in the child. Such a view fails to gain support in the above data. Of course, some degree of tentativeness must be attached to evaluating this finding. Although we have seen that substantially equal proportions of adoptees at all three outcome levels were presented with accurate information regarding the characteristics of their natural parents, we have no way of knowing whether in every case the accurate and realistic description was necessarily also a sympathetic one.

ADOPTEE CURIOSITY AND ANXIETY DUE TO
CONTENT OF REVELATION

How did the adoptees react to the manner in which their adoptive parents sought to make visible or to play down the matter of their adoptive status? We queried the adoptive parents with respect to three kinds of information: (1) the degree of curiosity and anxiety displayed by the adoptees in response to the information given them regarding their biological parents, (2) the readiness of the adoptees over the years to initiate discussion of their adoptive status and to participate in such discussions when the subject was raised by others in the family, and (3) the degree to which the adoptees showed a desire to learn more about their natural parents than their adoptive parents voluntarily revealed to them.

With regard to the first of these areas, more than half (54 percent) of the adoptees who received some information, true or false, about the characteristics of their biological parents were reported by their adoptive parents to have demonstrated either little or no curiosity about their natural parents following the revelation. Another one-fourth (26 percent) were reported to have evinced either great or moderate interest. Among the three outcome groups, low-problem and middle-range outcome adoptees tended more to express little or no curiosity, while the high-problem group was more characterized by expressions of great or moderate curiosity.

In three-quarters of the families where the adoptees had been given some information about their natural parents, the adoptive parents reported that their children had showed no noticeable anxiety as a result of learning information. This was generally equally true for adoptees in each of the three outcome categories. Only one set of parents (of a high-problem adoptee) stated that their child had revealed great anxiety, and another set of parents (of an adoptee in the problem-free group) reported having noticed "a little anxiety" in their child. We thus receive the distinct impression from our data that these adoptees were able to accept and handle with relative equanimity whatever information they received about their biological parents, regardless of its content and quantity—at least so far as the adoptive parents could discern.

Notwithstanding the above impression, almost three fifths (58 percent) of the adoptees either had never initiated discussion of their adoptive status over the years or had done this only very infrequently. The three outcome groups showed no significant differences in this regard. On the other hand, one-fourth of the adoptees were reported to have had no reluctance at all or only some reluctance to embark upon discussions of their adoptive status.[12]

Caution must be exercised in interpreting the findings just cited. The disinclination on the part of an adoptive child to initiate discussion of his adoptive status could have many diverse psychological and sociocultural roots. The phenomenon could denote unresolved conflicts including feelings of inferiority experienced by the adoptee over the fact that he was not actually born to his adoptive parents. No doubt this explanation would apply to at least some of the adoptees in this study although we cannot ascertain how many were so affected. On the other hand, failure or reluctance to raise the question of adoption might well signify the reverse state of affairs: the topic may have been introduced by the adoptive parents at an appropriate time and handled without anxiety and candidly in such a way as to have satisfied the curiosity of the adoptee. He may thus have integrated the information as part of his self-concept without undue difficulty and without resulting unresolved or ambivalent feelings. Hypothetically, the topic for such an adoptee might not be highly emotionally charged, and he would consequently have little need to allude to it over the years.

This alternative interpretation of our findings is offered precisely because it is the one offered by many adoptive parents in this study who reported that their children had either very seldom or never initiated discussion of their adoptive status. They contended that adoption was a very normal and natural part of the lives of their children, who consequently had had no reason to refer to it frequently. Obviously, we had no means for testing this contention except in those few cases where we also interviewed the adoptees themselves, but the parents' argument in many instances was persuasive and seemed to ring true after detailed probing and cross-checking with the adoptive parents throughout the interview.

This argument is also not inconsistent with another set of findings. While the characteristic pattern of the adoptees was to refrain from broaching the subject of their adoptive status, a sizable number were, according to their adoptive parents, willing to participate in discussions of this topic when it was raised by someone else in the family. More than two-fifths of the adoptees (44 percent) were reported as being either very willing or moderately willing to engage in such discussions; only 14 percent evidenced some or great reluctance to do so. This suggests the possibility that a goodly number of adoptees had integrated and were sufficiently comfortable with the knowledge of their adoptive status not to have to avoid talking about it when the topic was raised by others, even though they themselves had little need to broach the subject. Both the adoptees who were willing and those who were reluctant to participate in such discussions were fairly equally distributed among the three outcome groups.

Interestingly, one-fifth of the adoptive parents in effect side-stepped our query on this topic by declaring that the subject of their children's adoptive status had never or very seldom been brought up —either by the adoptive parents or by other members of the family. In other words, if the adoptees themselves had not broached the topic, they had been afforded little or no opportunity to express their feelings or attitudes about adoption. We wondered whether this situation was attributable more to the adoptive parents' or to the adoptees' feelings on the matter. It is noteworthy in this connection that the three outcome groups were less evenly divided in this avoidant response to our question. The heaviest concentration was in the low-problem group where more than a fourth (27 percent) of the parents stated that the subject of adoption had seldom or never been raised. This was reported by a fifth (21 percent) of the parents of middle-range and 15 percent of the parents of high-problem adoptees.

ADOPTEES' DESIRE TO LEARN ABOUT
BIOLOGICAL PARENTS

Our only substantial finding linking an aspect of revelation to subsequent life adjustment is presented in Table 7–6. Here we see that whether or not adoptees expressed a desire over the years to learn more about their natural parents than their adoptive parents knew or were voluntarily willing to divulge to them seems to distinguish among the three outcome groups. Nine out of ten low-problem adoptees were reported *not* to have indicated a desire to delve further into their biological backgrounds. This was true of almost eight in ten middle-range outcome adoptees but of less than six in ten high-problem children. Looking at the other side of the coin, almost a third of the Group III adoptees had expressed such an interest as compared with half that proportion in Group II and a negligible proportion in Group I. In other words, our data appear to indicate an association between a less favorable life adjustment on the part of the adoptee and his desire to probe more deeply into his background. We will see that this impressionistic finding is substantiated subsequently when the revelation variables are correlated with outcome data. As we indicate, however, the real implications of this finding cannot be assessed until we

Table 7–6 / Presence or absence of expressed desire by adoptees over years to learn more about biological parents than adoptive parents knew or were willing to divulge

	GROUP I	GROUP II	GROUP III	TOTAL
Adoptee did not express desire to learn more about biological parents	91%	79%	58%	76%
Adoptee did express desire to learn more about biological parents	3	15	30	16
Disparate response	—	—	6	2
Adoptee never told he was adopted	6	3	3	4
Unable to determine	—	3	3	2
Total cases	(33)	(34)	(33)	(100)

have firmer research evidence than we now possess concerning the various contradictory hypotheses which can be called upon to account for the finding.

PARENTAL HANDLING OF THE ADOPTIVE STATUS
WITH OTHERS

We sought to ascertain how prone the adoptive parents were to reveal their child's adoptive status to significant nonfamily persons in their lives. We believed that this inquiry might shed additional light on the adoptive parents' "sense of entitlement" to their child. Specifically, we wished to obtain some indication whether the adoptive parents saw themselves as being vulnerable to some kind of individious social distinction by virtue of not having been able to bear their own children; or whether, at the opposite pole, they perceived themselves as having successfully contended with a biological limitation in a socially legitimate and fully acceptable way through adoption. The principal dynamic underlying this self-perception, frequently highlighted in the professional literature, would be the parents' resolution of their feelings about their infertility.

One indicator of this, we believed, would be the degree to which they made adoption visible to others. If they tended to be secretive and to conceal this fact from most significant other persons in their lives, one might view such behavior as symptomatic of unresolved feelings of personal and sexual unworthiness stemming from the failure to conceive and bear their own child. If, on the other hand, they tended to be open and candid about their child's having been adopted, one might infer that a more healthy and salutary resolution of their feelings about infertility had occurred. Of course, excessive and unwarranted reference to their being adoptive parents could also be indicative of underlying uncertainty and discomfort concerning society's acceptance of them as adoptive parents.

We asked the parents whether they had tended to reveal or not to reveal their child's adoptive status to several categories of individuals, six of which were tabulated for purposes of analysis. These were (1) their friends, (2) their neighbors, (3) the adoptive father's business associates, (4) the parents of the adoptee's playmates, (5) the adoptee's teachers, camp counselors, etc., and (6) the family's minister, physician, and dentist.

Unfortunately the data yielded by this item are quite limited because the interviewers failed to ask the question of a substantial number of families (from 22 to 39 percent) with reference to the last four categories of individuals. We present the material only to identify whether any tentative trends are suggested. More than eight out of ten families (82 percent) had tended to disclose the fact of adoption to their friends; one-tenth had tended not to do so. More than half (56 percent) the families had told their neighbors that their child was adopted; about one-fourth (23 percent) had not. Substantially more families had shared this information with their physicians, dentists, and ministers than had withheld the knowledge from them. The balance was also in favor of revealing rather than concealing with regard to teachers, counselors, and the adoptive father's business associates, but not by as great a margin. Finally, slightly more families withheld than disclosed the adoptee's status from the parents of his playmates. Overall the impression is one of a substantial readiness to make the adoption apparent to significant others in the adoptive parents' lives. There were no marked differences among the three outcome groups in this respect.

Problems created by the adoptive status

PROBLEMS FOR THE ADOPTIVE PARENTS

Adoption in our society is an alternative to biological procreation as a way of achieving parental status. Though the model for simulation would appear to be the relationship prevailing between parents and their naturally conceived children, there are possible impediments to the degree to which a close duplication can actually be achieved. At least one investigator has reported that adoptive parenthood is viewed with curiosity, suspicion, and a certain amount of condescension by many in our society,[13] and it is regarded as an exotic phenomenon by still other more accepting and understanding individuals. Moreover, it contains within it the potentialities for unique stresses stemming from a variety of factors, e.g., the placement of children after they have become attached to foster parents or the incompatibility of a child's intellectual potential with the demands of his parents for achievement.

Consequently, we believed it important to attempt to pinpoint the nature and the severity of those problems arising over the period of two to three decades which the adoptive parents felt were directly attributable to the fact of adoption or to its concomitants. We queried them about this in an open-ended question and then categorized the responses according to four dimensions:

1. Problems in dealing with certain characteristics of the adoptee (e.g., his appearance differing from that of the adoptive parents, his having personality characteristics they found difficult to accept, their having been given a child who did not meet their preferences, etc.).

2. Problems in telling the child he was adopted and/or in answering his questions about this.

3. Problems in coping with their own feelings of strangeness about being adoptive parents (e.g., not feeling like *real* parents).

4. Problems in handling questions concerning the adoptee's birth status on forms, application blanks, and the like.

For each problem the adoptive parents acknowledged to have experienced, we asked whether this had loomed as a major or a minor difficulty and whether it had been recurring or confined to a single incident.

The majority of parents (73 percent) reported that they had *never*, at any time, experienced a problem associated with being adoptive parents or with their child's adoptive status. However, almost nine out of ten parents of low-problem adoptees (88 percent) made this statement whereas seven in ten parents of middle-range adoptees and only six in ten parents of high-problem adoptees made such a claim. In other words, the less favorable the adjustment of the adoptees the smaller the number of parents who could contend they had encountered no problems directly attributable to adoption. In one respect, of course, this finding is not surprising. We had formed the three outcome groups precisely to identify adoptees who had experienced progressively more numerous and severe adjustment problems currently and in the past. It therefore does not seem strange that successively smaller proportions of parents of adoptees in Groups II and III should report that *none* of the problems seemed related to adoption per se. At the same time, however, we were impressed by the magnitude of the Group III proportion, notwithstanding the fact that it was the smallest of the three. That more than three-fifths of the parents of our most problematic adoptees were able to report no connection between their children's adjustment difficulties and the adoptive status strikes us as being an unexpected and revealing finding.

What had been the specific nature of the problems encountered by those parents who had experienced them, and how severe had they been? Let us look first at the major problems identified. No parents had been confronted with serious problems in dealing with specific characteristics of their adopted children. Only four sets of parents had faced major difficulties connected with revelation, two each with adoptees in the middle-range and the high-problem groups. Only one couple, whose child had demonstrated a middle-range adjustment, had encountered significant problems in coping with their own feelings about being adoptive parents, and not a single set of parents recalled having met important problems relating to the adoptee's birth status on forms or applications. Three families, however, referred to major problems in two or more of the above areas; one such couple being the parents of a low-problem adoptee, two were the parents of adoptees classified as high problem.

Eleven sets of parents who claimed to have experienced no major problems did acknowledge minor problems in one or more of the listed problem areas. These families were about evenly distributed among all three outcome groups. Only three couples, two with high-problem adoptees and one with a middle-range adjustment child, reported problems of a major nature in areas other than the precoded ones. All in all, we are impressed with the degree to which the parents minimized the difficulties of parenthood attributable to the adoption aspects of that experience.

PROBLEMS ENCOUNTERED BY THE ADOPTEES

We asked the parents a comparable question concerning their children: had the adoptees experienced any problems attributable to their adoptive status, and if so, what had been the nature and severity of such problems? The parental responses are presented in Table 7–7.

We note in this table a response pattern similar to that of the adoptive parents concerning their own problems. Three-fourths of the parents reported that their children had at no time experienced difficulties or problems directly related to their being adopted. Also, the proportion of parents making such a report diminished from the most favorable to the least favorable outcome group. As we indicated earlier, such a trend might have been expected considering our use of in-

Table 7–7 / Nature and magnitude of problems experienced by adoptees and attributable directly to their adoptive status as perceived and reported by the adoptive parents

	GROUP I	GROUP II	GROUP III	TOTAL
No such problems at all	91%	85%	52%	76%
Major problem:				
In accepting or handling knowledge he was adopted	—	—	—	—
In being unhappy, conflicted, etc. re biological parents	—	—	3	1
In having feelings of being different as result of being adopted	—	—	—	—
In heterosexual relations, due to feelings of being different as result of being adopted	—	—	—	—
In 2 or more of above areas	—	—	12	4
No major problems but 1 or more minor problems in above areas	3	6	12	7
Disparate response	—	3	6	3
Problems in 1 or more areas but severity not known	—	3	—	1
Other	—	—	9	3
Not applicable: adoptee never told he was adopted	6	3	3	4
Not applicable: adoptee always psychotic	—	—	3	1
Total cases	(33)	(34)	(33)	(100)

creasing problematic adjustment as the criterion for classifying adoptees in Groups I–III. We again believe, however, that we have a noteworthy finding in the fact that more than half the parents of the high-problem adoptees saw no direct relationship between their children's adjustment difficulties and the fact that they had been adopted.

Perhaps the most interesting datum in Table 7–7 is that of only 5 percent (or a total of only five) of our entire sample of adoptive couples reported that their children had experienced one or more major problems in any of the four areas listed in the table. These five couples were parents of high-problem adoptees. This is a revealing finding because of the very few families involved. All of the adoptees in the least favorable outcome group were classified as "high problem" because of the manifold adjustment problems they had reportedly experienced over the years. Yet, in only five instances did their adoptive parents perceive and report that any major problems were clearly traceable to the children's adoptive status per se. Even if we add to this figure the four high-problem adoptees reported to have experienced one or more minor problems originating in this status, the total amounts to only nine of the thirty-three adoptees in the least favorable third of the sample.

Thus, the adoptive status has a relatively modest part in the parents' view of the etiology of their children's problems. This is a noteworthy finding which clearly merits additional research and exploration. It is consistent with other findings we have presented in this report, which indicates that the phenomenon of adoption and its concomitants in the area of child-rearing practices are not viewed by our sample of adoptive parents as a critical dimension in shaping parent behavior. Being an *adoptive* parent is but one of many and diverse considerations most of which are common to the large proportion of biological families in our society and to the raising of children in these families. Such an appraisal, if supported by additional research into adoptive family life, would be of great value in helping to place the purely adoptive aspects of adoptive family life in their proper perspective for future adoptive parents and for professional workers in the field. Clearly, of course, supplemental research would have to be undertaken to determine whether the perceptions of the other major actor in the drama—the adoptee, himself—were consonant with those of the adoptive parents. Only if this were found to be true would it be justifiable to assert that the adoptive component per se is not viewed by the persons most intimately involved as a source of major life adjustment problems.[14]

Summary

This chapter had been devoted to a consideration of how, when, and to what extent our adoptive families communicated the facts of adoption to their children and with what reaction on the part of the adoptees. Among the particularly noteworthy findings was the fact that only four sets of parents reported never having informed their children they were adopted. The remaining ninety-six families first revealed this fact to their children in a variety of ways and over a great range of ages. Of importance is the fact the subsequent adjustment of the adoptees appeared not to be related to how old they had been at the time of initial revelation. Also, during this first telling most adoptees had been given very few facts about their biological parents, and in most instances they had not appeared to be emotionally upset upon learning they were adopted.

Concerning the subsequent treatment of the subject of adoption as the adoptees were growing up, a relatively small proportion of parents had alluded to and discussed the children's adoptive status frequently or somewhat frequently, while a sizable proportion had brought the topic up either very infrequently or never again after the initial revelation. We consider this a finding of potentially great importance which warrants further investigation. Also of interest is the fact that over the years the adoptive parents continued by and large to withhold from the adoptees a true account of the personal and social characteristics of their natural parents and of the circumstances leading up to their being placed for adoption.

We noted with some surprise that the majority of adoptees who had been given some information about their biological past reportedly had evinced little or no curiosity about their true parents. An even larger proportion apparently had not revealed any noticeable anxiety concerning this material. Consonant with these findings was the fact that about three-fourths of the adoptees had displayed no desire over the years to learn more about their natural parents than their adoptive parents had been voluntarily inclined to reveal to them. A revealing finding, however, was that high-problem adoptees had been substantially more interested than the adoptees in the other two outcome groups in delving more deeply into their biological backgrounds.

In the main, the adoptive parents in our sample had tended over the years to make adoption visible to others in the community and had shared this fact with significant other nonfamily individuals in their lives. Finally, and of great importance, the large majority of parents reported that neither they nor their children had encountered any problems over the years which they could attribute directly to the fact of adoption.

*eight / Child-rearing
practices: behavioral indicators
of entitlement*

IN CHAPTER II we presented the concept of *entitlement* as one of our guiding orientations in specifying aspects of parental behavior to be covered in the research interviews. Our thinking had led us to postulate that adoptive parents are confronted with a task of identity resolution comparable to the one faced by the adoptee. A number of writers have commented upon the complex identity problems of the adopted child centering around the two sets of parents in his life. It seemed to us that, for the adoptive parent, the parallel task is to develop a feeling of entitlement to his adopted child, a conviction that the adoptee truly belongs to him.

Our assumption was that the principal obstacle to the attainment of this conviction is the adoptive parent's basic questioning about his worthiness as a parent, which is rooted in the self-doubt associated with the problem of infertility. It would seem obvious that the parent must be able to master these doubts if he is to resolve successfully his identity problem and develop a sense of rightful possession to his child. To the extent that he is unable to do this, the parent might well harbor unconscious hostility toward the adoptee as a symbol of his own inability to procreate a child of his own.

Our efforts to make use of the concept of entitlement for purposes of research investigation led us to identify three areas of parental child-rearing behavior which we believed were at least indirect indicators of successful or unsuccessful resolution of the above problem: (1) the socialization patterns employed by the adoptive parents, (2) their risk-taking behavior, and (3) their handling of the normal experiences of separation from the adoptee. In the present chapter, we will examine the findings of our study describing the performance of our one hundred sets of adoptive parents in each of these three areas.

We shall first deal with the socialization patterns they used and focus in turn upon the spheres of discipline, supervision, and control, and the fostering of a sense of independence in the adoptee. Next, we shall examine our adoptive parents' risk-taking behavior, concentrating particularly upon their readiness to use baby-sitters and the frequency with which they availed themselves of this resource. However, we shall also touch upon such other related aspects of risk-taking as the extent to which the parents curtailed their out-of-home activities after the arrival of the adoptee, and the extent to which they engaged in chronic worrying and displayed undue cautiousness regarding the adoptees' health and possible physical hazards to their well-being. Finally, we shall address ourselves to the manner in which the adoptive parents coped with normal separation experiences arising in their lives and the lives of their children, such as attendance at sleep-away camps, out-of-town secondary schools, and colleges.

Socialization patterns

We hypothesized that parents who had successfully resolved their own identity conflict to the point where they felt a deep sense of entitlement to their adopted child would be capable of employing realistic socialization procedures appropriate both in substance and severity to the situations calling for them. They would be able, in other

words, to apply techniques of discipline and control generally characteristic of their own social class without the need to be unduly lenient
or excessively severe. Contrastingly, parents who did not really feel
they had a right to the adoptee might well reveal unrealistically harsh
or permissive socialization patterns inappropriate to the behavior or
situation involved.

DISCIPLINE

Chief disciplinarian In our interviews with the parents we asked
each partner to specify which of the two had tended most frequently
to assume the role of disciplinarian. Some rather striking findings
emerged in the responses to this question and are summarized in
Table 8–1. It is apparent that the adoptive mother was clearly the
chief disciplinarian in our sample of adoptive families. She assumed
that role in more than half the families, while the adoptive
father assumed it in only one family in ten. Equal sharing of the disciplinary task was reported in only one-fourth of the families.

We note, however, some very marked differences with respect to
the principal disciplinary agent among families whose adoptees are in
the three different outcome categories. Among the families of high-
problem adoptees the adoptive mother took on the role of major disciplinarian twice as often as did her husband. Among the families of
adoptees in the other two adjustment groups, however, the mother as-

Table 8–1 / Chief disciplinarian in the family

	GROUP I	GROUP II	GROUP III	TOTAL
Adoptive father	3%	9%	18%	10%
Adoptive mother	64	53	37	51
Both adoptive parents equally	24	32	18	25
Disparate response	—	3	6	3
Other	3	3	3	3
Not covered/Unable to determine	6	—	18	8
Total cases	(33)	(34)	(33)	(100)

sumed such a role in even more pronounced fashion. In other words, the less problematic the life adjustment of the adoptee, the more apt was he to have come from a home in which his adoptive mother was reported to have been the principal disciplinarian in the family.

While the adoptive mother emerges as clearly the primary dispenser of discipline in all three outcome categories, there were some differences in the proportion of adoptive fathers in each category who did not relinquish this traditionally paternal role. Of the fathers of low-problem adoptees, 3 percent were reported to have been the chief disciplinarians. This, however, was true of 9 and 18 percent, respectively, of the fathers of middle-range and high-problem adoptees. In other words, as the adjustment of the adoptees was classified as increasingly problematic over the years, the adoptive fathers in these families appeared to be more prominent in the disciplinary capacity.

We did not inquire into the underlying reasons for these disciplinary patterns, but several feasible hypotheses readily present themselves. That the adoptive mother predominated as the chief disciplinarian in all three outcome categories seems not surprising to us. Like mothers in nonadoptive middle-class families, it seemed clear that the adoptive mothers had probably handled discipline problems more frequently simply because they were more apt to have been at home and on the scene when infractions occurred. However, although in middle-class families the mother may be called upon to cope with a greater number of instances of misbehavior, chances are that she is also apt to confine her role to the punishment of minor or middle-range misdeeds. The more serious problems may well be attended to by the father when he returns home in the evenings.

It would thus seem reasonable to conjecture that in homes where the adoptees presented few or no adjustment problems over the years, a substantial proportion of adoptive mothers (almost two-thirds) assumed the role of major disciplinarian. By contrast, in homes where adoptees tended over the years to present behavior problems, either of middle-range intensity, as was likely of the adoptees in Group II, or of a more continuous and serious nature, as was apt to have been true of adoptees in Group III, we may speculate that substantially smaller proportions of adoptive mothers were capable of adequately handling the required disciplinary tasks, and that their spouses may have tended to take on this responsibility. Furthermore, male adoptees comprised three-fifths of the children in the high-problem outcome group. Traditionally, the father is seen as the one who metes out punishment to the boys in the family, particularly as they grow older, larger, and stronger and are more able to defy attempts by the mother to discipline them.

Strictness in the disciplinary role In line with our hypothesis that behavior at either extreme of the strictness continuum might provide us with an indicator of incomplete resolution of the entitlement conflict, we asked each adoptive parent interviewed to place both himself and his spouse at some point on that continuum to represent their orientation toward discipline as the adoptee grew up. As might have been anticipated, these self-perceptions tended to concentrate in the middle of the strictness range. Almost two-thirds (64 percent) of the adoptive mothers were perceived by themselves and/or their husbands as having been "somewhat strict," "neither strict nor soft," or "somewhat soft," while about three-fifths of the adoptive fathers (58 percent) were categorized in the same way. Only four mothers and four fathers were classified as having been "very strict," but twelve adoptive fathers assessed themselves as having been "very soft" while only four adoptive mothers were placed in this extremely lenient category. Thus, as these one hundred couples rated themselves, relatively few cases appeared at the polar ends of the strictness continuum, making it no longer feasible to use this item in the supplementary analyses we had originally contemplated undertaking.

There were some but not very notable differences among the perceptions of parents of adoptees in the three outcome groups with respect to disciplinary strictness. The overall impression is one of complementarity between the two spouses whose children fell in Groups I and III. The wives in the former group tended on the whole to be classified as more strict, while their husbands were apt to be assessed as being generally more lenient. The reverse tendency characterizes the couples with adoptees in Group III: it is the husbands who appear to have been oriented toward stricter discipline and their wives who seem to have leaned toward less severity in discipline. The configuration for parents of Group II adoptees is rather inconclusive, with the complementarity between spouses not readily apparent.

Frequency of spanking In addition to the above global self-rating as disciplinarians, we obtained from the adoptive parents some specific information regarding two of the various disciplinary techniques they had used as the adoptee was growing up and the frequency with which each had been invoked. Although we had initially envisioned inquiring into a range of techniques, we ultimately concentrated this part of the interview on the use of corporal punishment in the form of severe and mild spanking. We believed that the former behavior, particularly if engaged in frequently, could be symptomatic of the hostility referred to earlier which could have its roots in the adoptive parent's unresolved identity conflicts relating to his infertility. Mild spanking, too, while fairly common in middle-class families, might also reflect the same feelings and uncertainties in the parent if resorted to very often.

We asked the parents to recall how frequently they had used each of these two disciplinary techniques focusing particularly upon the period when the adoptee had been below age ten. We considered this period to be quite important with respect to its influence upon the child. Moreover, we believed that the parents' approach to discipline during the latter half of the period, when the child was quite dependent and relatively pliant, would offer the most fruitful insights into the parents' underlying feelings of entitlement.

However, it is precisely when parents are asked to admit how frequently they departed from what many consider the norm of "good parents" by severely spanking their children to punish them that the limitations of a retrospective study should become most apparent. Not only is it likely that memory loss would be operative; defenses such as repression, denial, or outright falsification would be expected to loom large. We were therefore somewhat surprised that more than one-fourth (29 percent) of our adoptive families were willing to acknowledge that they had severely spanked their adopted child sometime during his first ten years of life and that 15 per cent admitted to having used such discipline "sometimes" or "often." More than two-fifths of the parents, however, denied that they had ever severely spanked their child.[1]

Even more interestingly, we observe from Table 8–2 that the proneness to employ severe spanking clearly distinguishes among the par-

Table 8-2 / Frequency of severe spanking when
adoptee below age 10

	GROUP I	GROUP II	GROUP III	TOTAL
Often used	—%	—%	9%	3%
Sometime used	6	15	15	12
Seldom used	12	15	15	14
Never used	52	38	40	43
Not covered/Unable to determine	30	32	21	28
Total cases	(33)	(34)	(33)	(100)

ents of adoptees in the three outcome categories. The only couples
who reported having severely spanked their children often were parents of high-problem adoptees. None of the parents of children in the
other outcome groups had used this disciplinary technique with such
frequency or were willing to admit that they had. Not unexpectedly,
the parents of low-problem adoptees reported substantially less frequent resort to severe spanking than was reported by parents of adoptees with middle-range or high-problem adjustments. Less than one-
fifth of the parents of adoptees in Group I (18 percent) had ever
severely spanked their children, while 30 percent of the parents of
Group II adoptees and 39 percent of the parents of Group III adoptees had used severe spanking at some time or another.

A comparable but somewhat less definitive picture emerged from
the findings regarding the use of mild spanking. Only five couples, all
parents of high-problem adoptees, acknowledged that they had used
such discipline often. Six families (18 percent) among the parents of
low-problem adoptees reported having often or sometimes used mild
spanking as compared with eleven (32 percent) among both the parents of middle-range and high-problem adoptees. Finally, while about
one in four parents of the best adjusted adoptees claimed never to
have resorted to even mild spanking as a disciplinary technique, such
a claim was made by only about one in ten parents of adoptees with a
middle-range adjustment and by one in five parents of the poorest adjusted adoptees.

In general, the differences among outcome groups with respect to discipline are not surprising. It seems reasonable to expect that adoptees manifesting the more serious adjustment problems over the years —particularly continuously disruptive and antisocial behavior—would provoke the use of increasingly more severe disciplinary techniques by parents seeking to modify or end such behavior. Further, to the extent that such parents were in fact contending with unconscious anger displaced upon the adoptees, the latter's continuously provocative and nonconforming behavior would likely seem only to justify the parents' hostility and encourage them to give it full vent. That such handling might well engender still additional misbehavior on the part of the adoptee and exacerbate parent-child conflict is theoretically apparent although the study provides no firm data concerning the actual prevalence and seriousness of such spiral effects.[2]

Effectiveness of parental discipline Finally, we attempted to ascertain how effective each parent considered his disciplinary efforts to have been over the years. Table 8–3 presents the resulting findings which are revealing if not totally unexpected. Only a minority of interviewed parents evaluated their discipline as having been either partly or totally ineffective. The largest single group of both mothers and fathers assessed their efforts as having been very effective. For the sam-

Table 8–3 / Parental assessment of effectiveness of discipline

	FATHER				MOTHER			
	OUTCOME GROUP				OUTCOME GROUP			
	I	II	III	TOTAL	I	II	III	TOTAL
Very effective	61%	38%	21%	40%	73%	71%	24%	56%
Somewhat effective	—	18	21	13	6	6	15	9
Somewhat ineffective	—	3	6	3	—	3	12	5
Very ineffective	—	—	15	5	—	—	28	9
Other	—	—	6	2	3	3	—	2
Not covered/Unable to determine	6	15	12	11	3	11	9	8
Parent not interviewed	33	26	19	26	15	6	12	11
Total cases	(33)	(34)	(33)	(100)	(33)	(34)	(33)	(100)

ple as a whole, however, as well as for each outcome group more wives attributed optimal effectiveness to their discipline than was true of the husbands' ratings of their efforts in this area.

An unequivocal picture emerges when we examine the data in Table 8–3 across outcome groups. The parents of the low-problem adoptees were clearly the most sanguine concerning the effectiveness of their discipline. Three-fifths of the fathers of adoptees in this category and almost three-fourths of their wives judged their disciplinary methods as having been very effective; none assessed these methods as having been at all ineffective. Adoptive fathers of middle-range outcome adoptees showed somewhat less certainty than their Group I counterparts about the results of their disciplinary efforts, although mothers of middle-range adoptees saw their efforts as having been just about as effective as were the efforts of the Group I mothers. Nevertheless, no parent of a middle-range adoptee judged his disciplinary efforts as having been very ineffective, while only 3 percent of the fathers and 3 percent of the mothers were willing to acknowledge that their efforts had been even somewhat ineffective.

By contrast, the parents of high-problem adoptees painted a substantially more negative picture. Less than one-fourth each of the mothers and fathers concluded that their discipline had been very effective, and, all told, only two-fifths of both the husbands and the wives were able to conclude that their efforts to discipline their children had been effective in any way. More strikingly, while virtually no parent in either of the other two outcome groups acknowledged that his discipline had been at all ineffective, more than one-fifth of the fathers of high-problem adoptees and almost two-fifths of their wives did express such a view.

These findings, while clear-cut, were not completely unanticipated. The fact that by definition Group III adoptees had manifested many adjustment problems throughout their lives argues for the assumption that their parents' attempts to modify or channel their behavior by means of discipline were apt to have met with limited success. However, the magnitude of the difference between Group III and the other two outcome groups with respect to this variable is striking.

SUPERVISION AND CONTROL

We explored with our adoptive parents the amount of control and supervision they had excercised over the adoptee's activities throughout the years. The results of this inquiry, summarized in Table 8–4, reveals a rather clear finding: parents of low-problem adoptees consistently reported more intense control and supervision of their children at all ages than did parents of high-problem adoptees. They also slightly exceeded parents of middle-range adoptees in the degree to which they had tended to oversee their children's activities.

The intergroup disparity is most notable for the earliest age category. Of the parents of Group I adoptees, 91 percent (as compared with 83 percent of the parents of Group II and only 69 percent of the parents of Group III adoptees) reported having exercised either much or moderate control over their youngsters' activities when the latter were below age ten. During the ensuing age period, much or moderate control was claimed by more than four-fifths of the parents of low-problem and middle-range adoptees but by less than three-fifths of the parents of high-problem adoptees. Even after the children had reached the age of eighteen, the difference in the control patterns of parents in the three outcome groups remained marked: half

Table 8–4 / Intensity of parental control and supervision for three age periods

	BELOW AGE 10 OUTCOME GROUP			AGE 10–17 OUTCOME GROUP			AGE 18 AND OVER OUTCOME GROUP		
	I	II	III	I	II	III	I	II	III
Much control	15%	17%	21%	6%	6%	9%	6%	3%	6%
Moderate control	76	65	49	76	76	49	46	47	24
Little control	9	6	21	18	6	27	39	38	49
Disparate response	—	6	3	—	6	6	—	—	—
Other	—	—	3	—	—	6	—	—	3
Not covered/ Unable to determine	—	6	3	—	6	3	6	6	6
Not applicable	—	—	—	—	—	—	3	6	12
Total cases	(33)	(34)	(33)	(33)	(34)	(33)	(33)	(34)	(33)

the parents of Groups I and II adoptees reported much or moderate control over their adoptees as contrasted with similar reports by less than one-third of the parents of adoptees classified in Group III.

Thus descriptively, more favorable adjustment by the adoptees appears linked with greater supervision and control over the growing-up years. We will, however, examine this relationship again in greater depth in a subsequent chapter when we report on the results of our analysis of the correlations between the child-rearing and the outcome variables.

By means of a companion item in the interview, we explored the realm of control somewhat further. We asked parents to indicate how frequently over the years they had found themselves unable to control their adopted children's behavior effectively. In Table 8–5 we note that the parents' responses to this item are quite consistent with the findings just discussed. Not one set of parents of low-problem adoptees related a single instance, at any age level, where they had been unable to control their child's behavior. The same was true in the earliest age category for parents of middle-range adoptees and only a small minority of these acknowledged any such instances even during the following two age periods.

We can see from the data in Table 8–5, however, that the re-

Table 8–5 / Parental inability to control effectively
adoptee's behavior during three age periods

	BELOW AGE 10 OUTCOME GROUP			AGE 10–17 OUTCOME GROUP			AGE 18 AND OVER OUTCOME GROUP		
	I	II	III	I	II	III	I	II	III
One or more instances reported	—%	—%	30%	—%	9%	42%	—%	12%	33%
No instances reported	91	82	58	88	74	49	88	71	49
Other	—	—	3	—	3	3	—	3	3
Disparate responses	—	—	6	3	—	3	3	—	6
Not covered/ Unable to determine	9	18	3	9	14	3	9	14	6
Not applicable	—	—	—	—	—	—	—	—	3
Total cases	(33)	(34)	(33)	(33)	(34)	(33)	(33)	(34)	(33)

sponses of the parents of high-problem adoptees departed sharply from this pattern. For each age period, between one-third and two-fifths of these couples admitted to one or more instances of inability to control their adopted children's behavior. In other words, Table 8–5 reveals once more a consistent relationship between adjustment outcome and the reported amount of effective control which adoptive parents were able to exercise over their children's activities.

We feel, however, that a cautionary note is appropriate at this point. Reports concerning the ability or inability of parents to control the behavior of their children would seem particularly vulnerable to the reliability and validity pitfalls of retrospective studies to which we have already alluded several times. What is at stake here is the willingness and/or the ability of parents to present to a stranger—as well as to themselves—a picture of inadequate functioning in a central aspect of the parental role. We consequently tend to wonder what may lie behind the greater candor of the parents of high-problem adoptees in admitting substantial failure in this area in contrast with the parents of low-problem adoptees who did not acknowledge *even one instance* of such failure in two or three decades of childrearing.

We have no findings which would answer this question, but we can offer at least two reasonable and possibly interrelated hypotheses. One is that the highly disparate pictures of parental functioning may be in part a manifestation of a systematic error referred to as the "halo effect." This occurs when a rater (in this instance, the adoptive parent) is asked to judge a series of characteristics of a given individual and carries over a generalized impression from one rating to the next or tries to make his ratings consistent. The obvious result would be a decrease in the validity or accuracy of the later ratings.[3]

It is possible that this process was operating when the parents of Group I and Group III adoptees responded to our several questions concerning supervision and control of their adopted children. Having already given a picture of effective discipline and much control during all three age periods, parents of the low-problem adoptees may have had the conscious or unconscious need to maintain the consistency of this image by reporting no instances of inability to control their children's behavior. A similar but reverse halo effect might account for the comparatively large proportion of parents of high-problem adoptees who acknowledged one or more instances of inability to control their adoptee's behavior. A number of them had earlier reported their ineffectiveness in discipline and their general lack of control and supervision over their children's activities.

Another influence may also have been at work tending to reinforce the halo effect. We would speculate that families in Group I, which is heavily weighted with lower SES couples, might have had a greater need to respond to questions about parenting behavior in culturally stereotyped normative ways. Being on the whole less educated and sophisticated than the predominantly higher SES Group III families, the Group I parents may have had a greater emotional investment in projecting a culturally sanctioned image of the adequate parent, one who is able effectively to control the behavior of his child at all times. The Group III parents, on the other hand, being more knowledgeable of the multiplicity of factors entering into the ultimate life adjustment of individuals may have been less threatened both as individuals and as parents by the problems encountered by their adopted children. They would therefore have needed less to repress or deny such problems and would also not have been as prone to evaluate themselves against the unrealistic stereotype of the completely effective parent. Such an hypothesis does not negate the interesting and suggestive nature of our findings: it simply puts these findings into a more realistic framework.

FOSTERING INDEPENDENCE

The third aspect of the adoptive parents' socialization patterns that we explored concerned the parents' readiness to encourage their adopted children to handle various aspects of their lives in an independent fashion, without having to rely unduly upon the parents. In Table 8–6 we note once more an apparently clear association between parental reports of having fostered such independence in the adoptees and the severity of the problems characterizing the life adjustment of these children. We see that, for the sample as a whole, approximately two-thirds of the couples asserted that they had strongly or moderately encouraged independence in their children over the years. This practice had been even more prevalent among the parents of the low-

Table 8–6 / Reported parental tendency to
encourage independence in adoptee

	GROUP I	GROUP II	GROUP III	TOTAL
Strongly encouraged	43%	26%	27%	32%
Moderately encouraged	36	44	27	36
Mildly encouraged	9	9	3	7
Discouraged	3	3	6	4
Disparate response	3	9	9	7
Other	—	3	9	4
Not covered/Unable to determine	6	6	19	10
Total cases	(33)	(34)	(33)	(100)

problem adoptees, with almost four-fifths reporting similar encouragement of their children. Less than three-fourths of the parents of the
middle-range outcome adoptees, however, reported such an orientation and only about half the parents of high-problem adoptees.

Risk-taking behavior

Our second indicator of the adoptive parents' sense of entitlement
was their behavior with respect to some of the risks normally associated with raising children in our society. We focused chiefly upon
two of the most common of these: (1) the use of temporary parental
substitutes in the form of baby-sitters, and (2) the presence or absence among adoptive parents of excessive worrying about the health
of their children and about physical hazards to their well-being. We
hypothesized that parents who had successfully resolved their doubts
about their having rightful possession of their adopted child would, in
the aggregate, have been able without undue discomfort to use baby-
sitters on appropriate occasions and would have tended not to be
chronic "worriers" concerning their children's health and safety.

Use of baby-sitters More than half our sample families reported
either frequent or fairly frequent use of baby-sitters during the first

ten years of their adopted children's lives. About one-fifth claimed never or seldom to have utilized this mode of substitute care. However, the most interesting findings contained in Table 8-7 concern the distinct differences prevailing among the three outcome groups in their readiness to use baby-sitter services. With increasingly problematic adoptee adjustment, parents appear to have made increasingly frequent use of such services. Twice as many parents of Group III as Group I adoptees reported frequent use of sitters during both age periods investigated. When the "frequent" and "fairly frequent" response categories are combined, they encompass about two-fifths of the families of low-problem adoptees, more than half the families of middle-range adoptees, and two-thirds of the families with children classified in the high-problem category.

These findings raise questions about the nature of the relationship between frequent use of baby-sitters and the problematic life adjustment of the adoptees. We shall see in a subsequent chapter dealing with the results of our correlation analysis that a substantial portion of this apparent relationship—though not all of it—can be explained by two interrelated variables, viz., the adoptive parents' social class and the agency through which they adopted. We did not collect data in our study which can account for the residual relationship. We are led

Table 8-7 / Frequency of use of baby-sitters during two age periods

	CHILD BELOW AGE 5				CHILD AGED 5–10			
	OUTCOME GROUP				OUTCOME GROUP			
	I	II	III	TOTAL	I	II	III	TOTAL
Frequently used	15%	17%	30%	21%	15%	17%	30%	21%
Fairly frequently used	31	35	37	34	28	32	34	31
Seldom used	18	15	12	15	21	15	12	16
Never used	15	12	12	13	15	12	12	13
Disparate response	3	—	—	1	3	—	—	1
Other	6	6	3	5	6	9	6	7
Not covered/Unable to determine	12	15	6	11	12	15	6	11
Total cases	(33)	(34)	(33)	(100)	(33)	(34)	(33)	(100)

to wonder, however, whether part of it may not possibly be due to an especial vulnerability on the part of adopted children to the adverse effects of separation from their adoptive parents, however transient, entailed in the frequent use of parent substitutes. We ask ourselves: having sustained the permanent loss of their natural parents—the ultimate in separation—and having endured one or more changes in mother-figure during successive preadoptive placements, could not these adopted children have experienced renewed feelings of loss or abandonment if their adoptive parents too frequently left them in the care of other persons? To answer this question it would be essential to define "too frequently" and to identify the nature of the relationship which the other caretakers had with the adoptees. To do this is beyond the scope and the data of the present study, but we suggest that this topic may merit further investigation.

Other aspects of risk-taking As part of our inquiry into the use of baby-sitters, we asked the adoptive parents a closely related question concerning the degree to which they had curtailed their desired out-of-the-home activities because of an unwillingness to use substitute care for their adopted children. More than half the parents (53 percent) claimed not to have restricted their activities at all for this cause and, interestingly, these parents were divided almost exactly evenly among all three outcome groups. Approximately one-fourth of the families (23 percent) recalled some curtailment of desired activities because of reluctance to resort to baby-sitters, with 14 percent reporting moderate or complete restriction of such activities. Among this latter group were six families with low-problem adoptees, five families with high-problem adoptees, and three families whose adoptees had achieved a middle-range adjustment.

With respect to whether the adoptive parents had been prone to worry excessively over the years concerning their children's health and safety, our inquiry produced no definitive findings. Only ten parents admitted to having been chronic "worriers" about physical hazards befalling their children, and six of these were parents of Group II adoptees. Only fourteen sets of parents confessed to excessive worry about their children's health, and again the heaviest concentration was among parents of adoptees falling into Group II.

Coping with normal separation experiences

Our hypothesis was that adoptive parents free of conflict about entitlement to their children would be able to arrange for and encourage appropriate experiences over the years when the adoptees would be separated from them for brief periods of time. Among the most common of these experiences in our culture are the child's attendance at sleep-away camps, his out-of-town visits to relatives or friends, and his being left at home while the parents travel on vacation. In later years, additional normal opportunities for separation present themselves in the form of attendance at out-of-town secondary schools and colleges, taking summer jobs away from home, and establishing independent residence out of town or within the home town while still unmarried. We postulated that adoptive parents who had not adequately resolved their conscious or unconscious doubts about their children really "belonging" to them would tend unduly to restrict the number of such separation experiences for their children or oppose and eliminate them completely.

ATTENDANCE AT SLEEP-AWAY CAMP

We can see from Table 8–8 that a substantial majority of adoptees did experience once or oftener the separation involved in attending sleep-away camp; only about one-fourth were never afforded this opportunity, and it is among this group that we observe the principal finding of interest in this table. There seems some indication that the less problematical the adoptee's adjustment, the greater was the chance that he had never attended sleep-away camp. Whereas a third of the low-problem adoptees were reported never to have had this experience, this was true of about a fourth of the middle-range outcome group and only a fifth of the high-problem adoptees. Since the differences among these proportions are relatively small, however, we must consider the finding as more suggestive than definitive.

We obtained some data concerning the frequency with which

Table 8–8 / Frequency of attendance at
sleep-away camp

	GROUP I	GROUP II	GROUP III	TOTAL
Never	33%	26%	21%	27%
Once or oftener	67	62	73	67
Disparate response	—	6	—	2
Not covered	—	6	6	4
Total cases	(33)	(34)	(33)	(100)

adoptees were separated from their parents for purposes of out-of-town visits to friends or relatives or because they remained home while their adoptive parents vacationed without them. They are not presented in tabular form primarily because these topics were not covered in approximately one-fourth of the parent interviews. However, based on the data we were able to collect, we see a pattern roughly comparable to the one we have just discussed. A greater proportion of Group I adoptees had never had the experience of visiting alone out of town or being left at home with someone else while their parents were away than had been true for Group II and Group III adoptees. In fact, with respect to the latter type of separation experience, almost twice as many parents of children in Group I as of those of children in the other two groups had never gone on trips while leaving their youngsters at home.

Initially, we were somewhat perplexed by this finding because at first blush it seemed contrary to expectations. According to our hypothesis, we would have anticipated that a smaller proportion of low-problem than of the high-problem adoptees would have been denied the opportunity to attend camp away from home. Their more favorable adjustment would bespeak, at least in part, more relaxed and secure adoptive parents who would be more likely to have had a greater sense of rightful possession to their children. Such parents, we postulated, would have found it less rather than more difficult to provide the growth-producing separation experience represented by several weeks away at camp.

This apparent paradox, however, was partly resolved when we examined carefully the composition of the two polar outcome groups. As we saw in Table 4–5, the high-problem outcome group was heavily weighted with predominantly higher SES families who had adopted through the Free Synagogue Committee and Chapin Nursery/Spence Alumnae. Such families comprised two-thirds of Group III but only about two-fifths of each of the other two outcome groups. Thus, as a group, the parents of the high-problem adoptees had had greater financial access to the institutionalized means of providing their children with the kinds of separation experiences we are examining. They had been more able than their lower SES counterparts in Groups I and II to afford to send their children to sleep-away camps which are relatively expensive, to pay the necessary fare for the children to visit out-of-town relatives and friends, and to hire domestic help to remain with the children while the parents traveled on vacation. Assuming that the parents of low-problem and middle-range adoptees had been inclined to give their children these opportunities, realistically they would have been less able financially to do so.

Thus, we suggest, social class emerges as one variable which helps to illuminate the above otherwise puzzling findings. Undoubtedly, there are others which we have been unable to isolate on the basis of data collected in this study.

ATTENDANCE AT OUT-OF-TOWN COLLEGE

Finally we explored with the adoptive parents another common source of separation as children reach their late teens and early twenties, viz., attendance at a college away from the family's home town. Table 8–9 presents the findings of this inquiry, and the reader will note that it is arranged somewhat differently from the other tables in this chapter. This is due to the fact that varying proportions of adoptees in the three outcome groups had ever attended college. It is thus self-evident that if substantially fewer high-problem adoptees had achieved this level of education than was true of their middle-range and low-problem counterparts, markedly fewer of them would have had the opportunity to attend an out-of-town college. The only meaningful basis for assessing the adoptive parents' willingness and ability to permit such separation experiences is the proportion of actual college attendees who spent all or part of their college careers away from home.

Table 8-9 / College attendance and
location of college

	GROUP I	GROUP II	GROUP III	TOTAL
Attended college	63%	62%	45%	57%
Out of town	48%	53%	33%	45%
Not out of town	15	9	6	10
Not covered	—	—	6	2
Did not attend college	37	38	55	43
Total cases	(33)	(34)	(33)	(100)

When viewed in this light, Table 8-9 reveals relatively minor differences among the three outcome groups. Noticeably larger proportions of Group I and Group II adoptees had attended any college
than was the case among Group III adoptees. However, of those who
had, only small, and moderately comparable, proportions in each outcome group had failed to go out of town for this purpose. Thus, with
respect to the manner in which the adoptive parents had coped with
the phenomenon of separation, the variable of out-of-town college attendance does not really distinguish among families of adoptees with
varying degrees of problematic life adjustments.

Summary

In this chapter, we have examined three aspects of the child-rearing practices of the adoptive families we studied: (1) the patterns
they employed to socialize their adopted children, (2) the manner in
which they coped with some of the normal risks involved in raising
children in our culture, and (3) the extent to which they permitted
and fostered appropriate growth-producing separation experiences for
their youngsters. These behaviors were explored with reference to the
concept of the parents' feelings of entitlement to their adopted children and also with reference to the overall level of adjustment
achieved by these adoptees.

We observed some outcome-related differences in the parental reports of practices in each of the above areas of child rearing. In gen-

eral, the parents of the high-problem adoptees gave the impression of having experienced less of a sense of entitlement than did parents of adoptees in the other two outcome groups. However, we have advanced the hypothesis that part of the observed difference in behavior might be explained by differences in the predominant social class status of families in the three outcome groups.

nine | Context of adoptive family life:
interrelationships among background,
revelation, child rearing, and other
environmental variables

IN CHAPTERS IV, V, AND VI we presented findings dealing with the personal, social, and economic variables which characterized the adoptive parents and the adoptees we studied. These variables were considered to comprise the influential background which was likely to influence the course of the adoptive experience. Thus far in our report, we have sought to portray descriptively something of the nature of that experience as this was revealed to us by the adoptive parents in their interviews.

We have devoted particular attention to the parents' reports of their attitudes and behavior with respect to child-rearing practices and the revelation of the adoption story because the conceptualization underlying our study has led us to consider these aspects of adoptive family life as among the most central and revealing. They do not, however, exist in isolation. They occur within a specific personal, social, and environmental context comprised of what we have termed background and other environmental variables. The primary concern of the present chapter will therefore be an examination of the relationship of these variables to the revelation and child-rearing practices of our one hundred adoptive families. We shall also devote some attention to the noteworthy associations found to exist between certain of the adoptive parents' reported child-rearing approaches and the methods they used to cope with the thorny problems of revelation. To bring to the fore the most revealing findings and to make our discussion as pertinent and concise as possible, most of the following material will be based upon statistically significant or near significant correlations.[1]

Correlates of revelation of adoptive status

In its broadest sense, the present research is more than an investigation of how well the one hundred adoptees fared in major life-space areas; it is also a study of their adoptive parents' perceptions of the nature of adoptive family life in general and of adoptive parent-child relationships in particular. As we have indicated before, with one notable exception the manifest role requirements of adoptive parenthood do not appear in most respects to differ materially from those of biological parenthood. That one exception involves the responsibility of coping with the multiple questions concerning revelation: whether, when, and how to inform the child that he was adopted, how much information to give him about his biological background, and how visible to make the adoptive status to the adoptee as well as to the community.

That these are crucial issues for the adoptive parents and their children, with potential ramifications in all facets of their lives, is readily apparent. It is for this reason that we have chosen to focus attention in the present report upon the revelation component of our families' adoptive life experiences. Thus far, we have presented (in Chapter VII) the parents' descriptions of how they actually handled the various aspects of revelation, and in Chapter XIII we shall see how this handling appears to have been related to the adoptees' life adjustment. Meanwhile, in the present section of this chapter, we will look at how the parents' approach to presenting the adoption story was associated with major background variables, specific child-rearing practices, and certain environmental influences.

BACKGROUND CORRELATES OF REVELATION [2]

Socioeconomic status   Our correlation analysis disclosed that, by and large, our measure of the families' socioeconomic status was not strongly related to the manner in which they coped with revelation. Only two aspects of this phenomenon were significantly associated with this measure: the timing of the initial revelation, and the extent to which the adoptee felt free to initiate discussion of his status with family members. We see in Table 9–1 that the higher the adoptive family's socioeconomic status, the more likely was the adoptee to have "always" known he was adopted or to have been informed of this at an early age. In addition, he was more apt to have had few or no reservations about broaching the subject of his adoption within the family circle as he grew up.

Though admittedly scanty, these findings suggest a more relaxed or casual attitude concerning the fact of adoption on the part of the upper-class families as compared with the approach of their working-class counterparts. This would appear in harmony with findings to be discussed presently concerning a comparable social class difference in a number of other areas of child rearing.

Placing agency   Three fairly pronounced and quite distinctive agency-related patterns of approaching revelation emerged from our correlation analysis. Catholic Home Bureau families were generally inclined to underplay the adoptive status and showed a marked tendency to discuss this topic very infrequently with the adoptee over the years. Our Catholic families also displayed some propensity to withhold from the adoptees all information about their biological parents or to provide a fictitious account of the latter's characteristics. Finally, the adoptees in these families tended not to have "always" known they were adopted, and the initial revelation when it came was apt to have been handled according to plan by the adoptive parents rather than to have occurred in precipitous fashion.

Table 9-1 / Correlation [a] *of socioeconomic status*
(SES) [b] *with revelation variables*

VARIABLE	CORRELATION
Source of initial revelation (*adoptive parents;* ALL OTHER RESPONSES) [c]	—04
Handling of revelation (*adoptee "always" knew;* ALL OTHER RESPONSES)	—23 *
Timing of initial revelation (*precipitous;* ALL OTHER RESPONSES)	11
Age when adoptee informed of adoption (*below age 6;* AGE 6 OR OLDER)	—20 *
Frequency of discussion of adoption (adoptee below age 10) (*never discussed at all;* DISCUSSED VERY FREQUENTLY)	08
Frequency of discussion of adoption (adoptee age 10–17) (*never discussed at all;* DISCUSSED VERY FREQUENTLY)	09
Frequency of discussion of adoption (adoptee age 18 and older) (*never discussed at all;* DISCUSSED VERY FREQUENTLY)	12
Information given adoptee about biological parents (*no information given at all;* FULL, ACCURATE INFORMATION GIVEN)	12
Adoptee's reservations about initiating discussion of adoption (*no or only some reservations;* NEVER INITIATED DISCUSSION)	—23 *
Adoptee's desire for more information about biological parents (*all other responses;* SHOWED DESIRE FOR MORE INFORMATION)	—04
Adoptive parents' tendency to reveal adoption to others (*tended to reveal to no one;* TENDED TO REVEAL TO MANY OTHERS)	10

* Significant: $p < .05$.
[a] Decimal points omitted for this and all following tables.
[b] Direction of scoring: high score = high SES.
[c] For this and all other tables in the present chapter, the direction of each variable is presented parenthetically immediately following the variable name. The low pole is given first in italicized form; then the high pole in capital letters.

In short, the Catholic parents appeared to have tended to shelter their children from too sharp an awareness of their preadoptive background by "killing off" the biological parents, by postponing initial revelation, and by avoiding discussion of adoption over the years. They were prone, in other words, to de-emphasize that aspect of their children's lives which could potentially engender anxiety or conflict and to simulate as much as possible the "normal" reassuring biological parent-child relationship. In the face of such an orientation, it is not

Table 9-2 / Correlation of agency [a] source of adoption with revelation variables

VARIABLE	CATHOLIC HOME BUREAU	CHAPIN NURSERY/ SPENCE ALUMNAE	FREE SYNAGOGUE COMMITTEE	STATE CHARITIES AID
Source of initial revelation (*adoptive parents;* ALL OTHER RESPONSES)	00	06	−06	00
Handling of revelation (*adoptee "always" knew;* ALL OTHER RESPONSES)	−10	13	−10	08
Timing of initial revelation (*precipitous;* ALL OTHER RESPONSES)	−10	07	12	−10
Age when adoptee informed of adoption (*below age 6;* AGE 6 OR OLDER)	−03	18	−23*	08
Frequency of discussion of adoption; adoptee below age 10 (*never discussed at all;* DISCUSSED VERY FREQUENTLY)	19	−21*	15	−12
Frequency of discussion of adoption; adoptee age 10–17 (*never discussed at all;* DISCUSSED VERY FREQUENTLY)	20*	−17	08	−11
Frequency of discussion of adoption; adoptee age 18 and over (*never discussed at all;* DISCUSSED VERY FREQUENTLY)	23*	−20*	02	−05
Information given adoptee about biological parents (*no information given at all,* FULL, ACCURATE INFORMATION GIVEN)	12	−36**	27**	−03
Adoptee's reservations about initiating discussion of adoption (*no or only some reservations;* NEVER INITIATED DISCUSSION)	−18	−01	12	07
Adoptee's desire for more information about biological parents (*all other responses;* SHOWED DESIRE FOR MORE INFORMATION)	10	04	−13	−02
Adoptive parents' tendency to reveal adoption to others (*tended to reveal to no one;* TENDED TO REVEAL TO MANY OTHERS)	−05	−12	19	−02

surprising that the adoptees in such families reportedly tended, as is indicated in Table 9–2, to be quite loath to initiate discussion about adoption with family members and to demonstrate little or no desire for more information about their natural parents than the adoptive parents knew or were willing to tell them.

A quite contrasting pattern was revealed by families adopting through Chapin Nursery/Spence Alumnae. The parents in these families seemed to have assumed a nonprotective stance with respect to revelation and to their children's reaction to their nonbiological status. They tended to highlight adoption and to make it very visible to the adoptee as well as to the community at large. Thus, we see in Table 9–2 that couples adopting through Chapin Nursery/Spence Alumnae evidenced a moderately strong tendency to inform the adoptee of his status at an early age, to discuss this subject frequently with the adoptee over the years, and to provide full and accurate information about the adoptee's biological background. As might be anticipated in the light of this orientation, there was some tendency for the adoptee "always" to have known he was adopted and for the adoptive parents to make adoption visible to members of the community.

Couples adopting through the Free Synagogue Committee resembled more the Catholic Home Bureau than the Chapin Nursery/Spence Alumnae families in their approach to revelation. We see from Table 9–2 that the Free Synagogue Committee parents were very likely to have withheld from their adopted children most information about the natural parents' characteristics or to have furnished them with a contrived account of these traits. They were also apt to have postponed the initial revelation until the adoptee was older so that he tended not to have "always" known he was adopted. They were markedly inclined to have refrained from disclosing the adoptive status to the community, and they evidenced some reluctance to discuss the topic of adoption with their children over the years though their avoidance of this subject was not nearly as pronounced as that of the Catholic agency parents. Finally, the families adopting through the Free Synagogue Committee displayed some tendency to have first presented the facts of adoption to their children in a precipitous rather than in a planned way, a characteristic rather weakly associated in our findings with lower socioeconomic status.

The families who adopted children through State Charities Aid manifested a tendency to pursue a middle course with respect to their handling of revelation. This is evident in the lack of statistically significant or even moderately pronounced correlation coefficients in the last column of Table 9–2.

Characteristics of the adoptee It is noteworthy that in only two instances did any of the adoptee characteristics included in our correlation analysis prove significantly associated with some aspect of revelation. We found, first, that the older the adoptee *at the time of our study,* the more likely were the adoptive parents not to have disclosed the fact of adoption to friends, neighbors, and other nonfamily individuals in the community ($r = -.21$). This finding was somewhat surprising because the age of the adoptee *at placement* showed virtually no association whatsoever with the parental pattern of revelation to others ($r = -.00$). We must therefore conclude that the present finding reflects the influence of other as yet unidentified variables.

The age of the adoptee at placement was significantly related to the frequency with which the adoptive parents were apt to have discussed the subject of adoption with him from the age of eighteen on. The older the child when he came to the adoptive home, the less frequent these discussions were likely to be ($r = -.20$). Interestingly, the comparable correlations for the two earlier age periods, viz., below age ten and age ten to seventeen, did not approach statistical significance ($r = -.07$ and $-.11$, respectively).

In other words, the proneness of the parents to discuss adoption with the younger child did not seem to be dependent upon the latter's age when placed, although the directions of the above correlation coefficients indicate that even in the earlier years there was some tendency for the later-placed child to be exposed to less discussion of his adoptive status than his earlier-placed counterpart. However, it was only after the adoptee had reached young adulthood that his age at placement showed a marked connection with the frequency of such discussions.

These data may in part represent the influence of the revelation patterns of our Catholic Home Bureau families who (a) tended to adopt older children, (b) tended to be protective with respect to revelation, and (c) as also shown in Table 9–2, displayed a parallel tendency toward less frequent allusion to adoption as the adoptees grew older. Our findings may also partly reflect the normal course which revelation takes in homes where the adoptees are placed in a somewhat older age. Such children are likely to be more aware or conscious of their status upon first entering the adoptive home. We can speculate that the adoptive parents may therefore feel less need to dwell upon this topic over the years and particularly after the adoptee has begun to strike out on his own as a young adult.

No aspect of the handling of adoption was shown by our correlation analysis to be significantly related to either the adoptee's sex or to the number of preadoptive placements experienced. However, we discovered that these background variables did show a modest degree of association with a few of the revelation variables we explored in the study. The interested reader is invited to examine these associations by referring to Table 2 in the matrices available from the Child Welfare League.

CHARACTERISTICS OF THE ADOPTIVE PARENTS
AND THE ADOPTIVE HOME

Siblings The presence of one or more other children in the family *before* the adoptee was placed correlated fairly strongly with three aspects of the initial revelation of adoption. Adoptees entering such a home tended to have been first informed they were adopted at an early age ($r = -.20$) or "always" to have known this fact ($r = -.18$), and the initial revelation was quite likely to have been coped with in a planned way rather than to have been broached precipitously ($r = .19$). These three findings tend to be internally consistent and quite reasonable when viewed in the perspective of the adoptive parents' seeking to prepare the other children for the adoptee's impending arrival. Such a preparatory process would inevitably have brought the fact of adoption out into the open and would have tended to present it as a positive and desirable occurrence divested of the need for secrecy. In this kind of climate, the adoptive status might easily have been alluded to and talked about by the other children and the parents almost from the time of the adoptee's placement so that he would have become aware of this status at a very early age and in a gradual and relaxed rather than in a precipitous manner.

Infertility status of couple and motivation to adopt We found that neither the strength of the couple's reported motivation to adopt nor whether they had been found infertile was associated to any appreciable degree with the way they handled revelation of adoptive status. On the other hand, the strength of the couple's effort to overcome their infertility through medical help was significantly correlated with two revelation variables. Where couples reported having made a strong effort to remedy their infertile status, initial revelation of adoption tended to have been precipitous ($r = -.20$). Yet over the years, the adoptee in such a family appeared to have been quite free to initiate discussion of his adoptive status with his parents and showed few or no reservations in this regard ($r = -.23$).

These two findings may not be as contradictory as they might first seem to appear. Years of intensive but unsuccessful effort by couples to overcome their infertility might well have led them to work out for themselves the implications of this limitation and to have made peace with their inability to procreate their own children. Such an attitude could have resulted in greater feelings of entitlement to their child once they adopted him. This in turn could have caused them to be more relaxed and secure in their relationship with him while creating an environment in which the adoptee was free to broach the subject of his adoptive status whenever he was inclined to do so. At the same time, some of our questionnaire data, not presented in this report, appear to indicate that security in the adoptive mother-child relationship was associated with precipitousness in the initial revelation.

Age and sex preferences Whether a couple did or did not request an infant or baby when applying for adoption was not correlated significantly with any of the revelation variables we explored. By contrast, the expressed sex preference of couples upon application was disclosed by our analysis to be moderately associated with at least four aspects of their approach to initial revelation and their subsequent handling of this topic.

The reader may observe in Table 9-3 that where an applying couple initially voiced a desire for a girl, the adoptee tended to learn for the first time she was adopted from some source *other* than her adoptive parents ($r = -.19$). Our data, however, provide no clue as to why

Table 9–3 / Correlation of reported sex preference of adoptive parents at application with revelation variables

VARIABLE	PREFERRED GIRL [a]	PREFERRED BOY [a]
Source of initial revelation (*adoptive parents;* ALL OTHER RESPONSES)	−19	09
Handling of revelation (*adoptee "always" knew;* ALL OTHER RESPONSES)	−11	−04
Timing of initial revelation (*precipitous;* ALL OTHER RESPONSES)	17	03
Age when adoptee informed of adoption (*below age 6;* AGE 6 OR OLDER)	−12	−13
Frequency of discussion of adoption; adoptee below age 10 (*never discussed at all;* DISCUSSED VERY FREQUENTLY)	01	20 *
Frequency of discussion of adoption; adoptee age 10–17 (*never discussed at all;* DISCUSSED VERY FREQUENTLY)	03	11
Frequency of discussion of adoption; adoptee age 18 and over (*never discussed at all;* DISCUSSED VERY FREQUENTLY)	−01	15
Information given adoptee about biological parents (*no information given at all;* FULL, ACCURATE INFORMATION GIVEN)	15	−07
Adoptee's reservations about initiating discussion of adoption (*no or only some reservations;* NEVER INITIATED DISCUSSION)	07	−30 **
Adoptee's desire for more information about biological parents (*all other responses;* SHOWED DESIRE FOR MORE INFORMATION)	−12	19
Adoptive parents' tendency to reveal adoption to others (*tended to reveal to no one;* TENDED TO REVEAL TO MANY OTHERS)	07	05

* Significant: $p < .05$. ** Significant: $p < .01$.
[a] Dichotomized: *preferred girl/boy;* ALL OTHER RESPONSES

this should have been so or why the same circumstance did not also prevail in families who expressed a preference for boys.

With respect to these latter families, the data of Table 9–3 reveal that where prospective adoptive parents asked for a male child, the adoptee was apt to have been very reluctant to initiate discussion of the subject of adoption within the family circle. He was also quite likely not to have sought more information about his biological background than his adoptive parents were willing to share voluntarily with him. Finally, reference to the adoptive status by the parents in these families was apt to have been infrequent throughout the years but particularly during the adoptee's early childhood.

Age of adoptive parents at application Our data indicate that the age of neither partner in the applicant couple correlated significantly with the subsequent handling of revelation. However, this age variable was associated at a near significant level with the source of the initial revelation of adoption to the child. The older the prospective adoptive parents at application, the more likely [3] was the adoptee to have first learned he was adopted from some source other than his parents. This finding is *not* a function of older applicants receiving older children who would consequently be more likely to be aware of their adoptive status at the time of placement.

As can be discerned from Table 1 in Chapter VI, the age of the adoptee when entering the home was almost totally unrelated to the age of either adoptive parent at the point of application. Rather, we would hazard the assumption that the dynamics underlying the present finding may relate to the greater numbers of years of denial of a child experienced by older couples prior to deciding to adopt. Once their wish for a child was fulfilled, such couples may have been fearful, more so than couples who had not been deprived for so long, of the potential negative consequences of telling the adoptee that he had not been born to them. They may, for example, have feared that such information might alienate this long-awaited child. They may consequently have postponed revelation longer than younger adoptive couples, with the consequence that the adoptee had more opportunity to inadvertently discover his adoptive status from someone other than his adoptive parents.

CHILD-REARING CORRELATES OF REVELATION

Socialization practices—discipline We found that for the most part the various aspects of discipline which we explored in our study were not strongly correlated with the handling of revelation. In only three instances were discipline variables associated with revelation variables at a significant or near significant level. Where parents reportedly tended to use severe spanking often or sometimes as a disciplinary measure, they were also likely to have discussed adoption frequently with the adoptee when he was below ten years of age ($r = .20$), and the child was also apt to have been told of his adoptive status at an early age ($r = -.19$). These data cannot be interpreted easily because, as reported in Chapter VIII, only about one-fourth of the parents acknowledged having resorted to severe spanking and because the spanking variable is not significantly related to any background variable or to any of the maternal attitudinal factors discussed in the previous chapter. The most we can say is that a tendency toward severe spanking seems somewhat associated with a proneness to make the adoptive status visible to the adoptee.

We also discovered that where the mother was perceived as having been "soft" in her discipline, the adoptee was apt to have expressed a desire to know more about his natural parents ($r = -.18$). Just why is not immediately apparent from our data. Maternal strictness is not significantly correlated with either SES or the agency of placement, hypothetically two of the more likely "explanatory" variables.

Supervision and control A single noteworthy relationship between parental supervision and control practices and the handling of revelation was disclosed in our analyses. Where parents tended to exercise strong control over their children's activities, they also tended to furnish little or no accurate information to the adoptee concerning his biological parents. This tendency to "bury" the natural parents was more strongly associated with strict control of the adoptee during the 10- to 17-year-old period ($r = -.25$), but it was also related to a similar control orientation when the adoptee was below age 10 ($r = -.19$). This finding is generally consonant with data stemming from the parental questionnaires which indicate that in families where accurate information about the natural parents was withheld from the adoptees, mothers tended not to evidence attitudes favoring the promoting of autonomy in their children. The tendency to exercise close supervision and strong control over children's activities throughout their childhood and early adolescence would clearly be indicative of an underlying attitude opposing the development of autonomy in these children.

Fostering independence in the adoptee We were interested to note the general direction of the significant correlations between parental encouragement of independence in the adoptee and the handling of revelation, as revealed in Table 9–4. There we see that parents who strongly fostered such independence were apt to have reported that the adoptee had "always" known of his adoptive status and that he had been relatively free to initiate discussion of that topic with members of the adoptive family. Adoptive children in such families were also likely to have been given accurate information regarding the major characteristics of their biological parents. These data seem to indicate a certain consistency on the part of the adoptive parents in the direction of promoting a sense of autonomy and independence in their children. This, in turn, may suggest an integrity on the part of these parents in the way they handled the variegated aspects of child rearing, including those specifically related to adoption.

RISK-TAKING BEHAVIOR: USE OF
PARENTAL SUBSTITUTES

The consistency in child-rearing practices just alluded to is also evidenced by the revelation correlates of the adoptive parents' use of parental substitutes as baby-sitters when the adoptees were young. Where parents tended to use sitters frequently when the adoptee was below age ten, they were also quite prone to have made the adoptive status visible "from the beginning," so that the adoptee was likely either to have "always" known he was adopted ($r = -.29$) or to have been first apprised of this fact at an early age ($r = -.18$). Such parents were also apt to have handled the initial revelation according to plan rather than precipitously ($r = .14$), and in these families the adoptees tended to have been free to initiate discussion of their adoptive status with family members over the years ($r = -.14$). Such an approach to dealing with the facts of adoption can be seen as an indicator of security in the adoptive parent role and of a constructive resolution of the "sense of entitlement" conflict referred to in earlier chapters. This type of role performance would seem to us to be consonant with the freedom of adoptive parents to make frequent use of baby-sitters when their children were young.

Table 9–4 / Correlation of reported fostering of
independence in adoptee [a] with
revelation variables

VARIABLE	CORRELATION
Source of initial revelation (*adoptive parents;* ALL OTHER RESPONSES)	−17
Handling of revelation (*adoptee "always" knew;* ALL OTHER RESPONSES)	−25 *
Timing of initial revelation (*precipitous;* ALL OTHER RESPONSES)	14
Age when adoptee informed of adoption (*below age 6;* AGE 6 OR OLDER)	−12
Frequency of discussion of adoption; adoptee below age 10 (*never discussed at all;* DISCUSSED VERY FREQUENTLY)	10
Frequency of discussion of adoption; adoptee age 10–17 (*never discussed at all;* VERY FREQUENTLY)	06
Information given adoptee about biological parents (*no information given at all;* FULL, ACCURATE INFORMATION GIVEN)	22 *
Adoptee's reservations about initiating discussion of adoption (*no or only some reservation;* NEVER INITIATED DISCUSSION)	−20 *
Adoptee's desire for more information about biological parents (*all other responses;* SHOWED DESIRE FOR MORE INFORMATION)	−02
Adoptive parents' tendency to reveal adoption to others (*tended to reveal to no one;* TENDED TO REVEAL TO MANY OTHERS)	09

* Significant: $p < .05$
[a] Dichotomized: *all other responses;* ADOPTIVE PARENTS STRONGLY FOSTERED INDEPENDENCE

AFFORDING THE ADOPTEE SEPARATION
EXPERIENCES

Very much in harmony with the picture thus far delineated are the
two significant correlations we found between the adoptive parents'
handling of the initial revelation and their willingness over the years
to permit the adoptees the normal kinds of separation experiences
from the nuclear family characteristic of other families. Where the
adoptee was afforded ample experiences of this sort, his parents were
quite apt to have begun referring to the adoptive status very soon
after his placement so that the child "always" knew he was adopted

($r = -.29$) or was first informed of this fact at an early age ($r = -.21$). These associations seem to offer further confirmation for the conclusion that the revelation behavior of our group of adoptive parents was not a phenomenon isolated from other parent orientations but rather a reflection of an overall approach to child rearing.

OTHER ENVIRONMENTAL CORRELATES

OF REVELATION

In the main, the manner in which the adoptive parents handled the telling of the "adoption story" was unrelated to the various factors which we have termed environmental influences. Only three correlations attained statistical significance. Homes in which the adoptee had great reservations about initiating discussion of his adoptive status were likely also to be homes characterized by a heavy investment in religious activity ($r = .28$) and by the absence of nonrelated persons living with the adoptive family ($r = -.25$). We suspect that these findings reflect the influence of the Catholic Home Bureau families who, we shall see later in this chapter, tended to manifest both environmental characteristics more strongly than families adopting through the other three agencies. And we have already noted that in these families the adoptee evinced a marked reluctance to initiate discussions about his adoptive status.

Where adoptive parents perceived the adoptee's temperament to be very similar to their own, they tended to make the adoptive status more visible to various persons in the community at large ($r = .20$). This finding seems to make sense on an intuitive basis. The parents' perception that their adopted child's temperament was quite similar to theirs can be viewed as an indicator of a positive parental identification with the adoptee and a feeling that he "belonged" to or "fitted in" with the family. Couples with such an attitude would be apt to feel more entitled to their child and more secure in the adoptive parent role; thus they tend to be freer and more comfortable in acknowledging to others the nonbiological nature of their relationship with the adoptee.

Earlier in Chapter VIII we presented our conception of child-rearing behavior as an indirect indicator of the adoptive parents' success in resolving their infertility-rooted doubts about their worthiness as parents and in developing a sense of rightful possession or entitlement to their adopted children. In that chapter, findings concerning three aspects of our families' child-rearing practices were presented descriptively and related to a threefold, broad-gauged index of income. Before devoting our attention to the outcome correlates of these practices (in Chapter XIV) we shall at this point consider how the child-rearing variables incorporated in our study were associated with the principal background variables and with specific environmental influences. We have already discussed in the first section of this chapter the noteworthy relationships between various child-rearing practices and the manner in which the parents approached and handled the revelation of adoptive status.

BACKGROUND CORRELATES OF
CHILD-REARING PRACTICES

Socioeconomic status   We were able to discern a fairly clear pattern of relationships between the adoptive families' social class standing and their overall orientation to child rearing. This can be seen upon examination of the data in Table 9–5 where the reader will note that two child-rearing practices are very strongly correlated with SES and that several others are associated at a near significant level. In general, these relationships are quite consistently in the direction which the reader might have anticipated as a result of findings thus far presented in this and the preceding chapters.

A case in point is the pronounced and highly significant correlation between social class and the use of parental substitutes [4] which, according to our conceptualization, is a major indicator of the adoptive parents' ability to accept some of the normal risks involved in raising children in our culture. We note in Table 9–5 that the higher the adoptive family's socioeconomic status, the more frequently had the parents tended to employ parental substitutes throughout the first ten years of the adoptee's life. This is not a surprising finding. By definition, higher SES families were financially better able to afford the cost of substitute parental care than were their lower class counterparts. This fairly obvious point takes on additional meaning when we

Table 9–5 / Correlation of socioeconomic status (SES) [a] *with child-rearing variables*

VARIABLE	CORRELATION
Spanking practices (*never;* SEVERE)	07
Parent most frequent disciplinarian (*mother;* ALL OTHER RESPONSES)	16
Strictness of adoptive father (*very soft;* VERY STRICT)	−08
Strictness of adoptive mother (*very soft;* VERY STRICT)	13
Intensity of control of adoptee; below age 10 (*little control,* MUCH CONTROL)	−17
Intensity of control of adoptee; age 10–17 (*little control,* MUCH CONTROL)	−16
Fostering independence in adoptee (*strongly encouraged;* ALL OTHER RESPONSES)	17
Adoptee's desire for independence; below age 10 (*little or no push;* STRONG PUSH)	10
Adoptee's desire for independence; age 10–17 (*little or no push;* STRONG PUSH)	07
Use of parental substitutes; adoptee below age 5 (*never;* FREQUENTLY)	63 **
Use of parental substitutes; adoptee age 5–10 (*never;* FREQUENTLY)	64 **
Separation experiences afforded adoptee (*never;* MUCH SEPARATION)	40 **

** Significant: $p < .01$.
[a] Direction of scoring: high score = high SES

learn that where nonrelated persons such as maids, housekeepers, and governesses were reported to have lived in the adoptive home throughout the adoptee's growing up years, such families were also prone to report more frequent use made of parent substitutes.[5] And, as the reader might expect, the presence of such nonrelated persons in the home is highly correlated ($r = .45$) with upper class status. In other words, due to their more financially affluent status, these families tended to employ live-in domestic help who, among their other duties, acted as built-in baby-sitters when the adoptees were young. Such a resource would have been financially available to the higher class families to a greater extent than to their lower class counterparts.

The last line of Table 9–5 discloses that social class status also looms large as a factor in the adoptive parents' provision of separation experiences for their children. In our parent interviews, we explored this aspect of child rearing with reference to the frequency with which the adoptee had been afforded three principal types of opportunity for separation from the nuclear family. For purposes of correlation analysis, however, we combined both the frequency and the variety dimensions into a single variable ranging from no experience at all with any kind of separation to experience with two or more types of separation. We see that this variable is associated with SES in a direction undoubtedly anticipated by the readers; the higher the socioeconomic standing of the adoptive family, the more likely was the adoptee to have been afforded ample separation experiences. We noted, in addition, a strong positive relationship between the presence of nonrelated persons, i.e., maids or housekeepers, living in the home and the likelihood that the adoptee had been provided such separation experiences ($r = .32$).

From a purely monetary standpoint, these findings make intuitive sense in much the same way as our previous finding that upper class families tended to make frequent use of parental substitutes. The more well-to-do families obviously had greater financial access than did their less affluent counterparts to the institutionalized means of providing their children with the kinds of separation experiences we examined in our study. They were better able to finance sending their children to sleep-away camps and to afford the cost of having them travel away from home, just as they were more able to pay for babysitter services or for live-in domestic help to care for the children while the parents vacationed alone. Monetary considerations aside, however, the pronounced correlation between SES and separation experiences for the adoptee is quite in keeping with the three near-significant correlations in Table 9–5 which indicate that higher SES families had some tendency to exercise less stringent control over their children's activities throughout the growing-up years and also to foster these children's independence.

Finally, the influence of social class with respect to the separation experiences afforded the adoptees was further dramatically underscored in our analysis of the correlation between such experiences and adoption through Catholic Home Bureau. We found that children placed in these homes tended to have experienced few or no instances of normal separation. When we controlled for socioeconomic status,

Table 9-6 / Correlation of adoption through each of four agencies [a] *with child-rearing variables*

VARIABLE	CATHOLIC HOME BUREAU	CHAPIN NURSERY/ SPENCE ALUMNAE	FREE SYNAGOGUE COMMITTEE	STATE CHARITIES AID
Spanking practices (*never*; SEVERE)	−03	13	05	−15
Parent most frequent disciplinarian (*mother*; ALL OTHER RESPONSES)	−01	−01	01	04
Strictness of adoptive father (*very soft*; VERY STRICT)	01	−04	09	−06
Strictness of adoptive mother (*very soft*; VERY STRICT)	−02	−07	09	01
Intensity of control of adoptee; below age 10 (*little control*, MUCH CONTROL)	−22*	07	12	03
Intensity of control of adoptee; age 10–17 (*little control*, MUCH CONTROL)	−22*	07	12	02
Fostering independence in adoptee (*strongly encouraged*; ALL OTHER RESPONSES)	03	−10	13	−06
Adoptee's desire for independence; below age 10 (*little or no push*; STRONG PUSH)	09	−10	02	−01
Adoptee's desire for independence; age 10–17 (*little or no push*; STRONG PUSH)	02	−11	05	05
Use of parental substitutes; adoptee below age 5 (*never*; FREQUENTLY)	52**	−09	−36**	−07
Use of parental substitutes; adoptee age 5–10 (*never*; FREQUENTLY)	51**	−10	−37**	−05
Separation experiences afforded adoptee (*never*; MUCH SEPARATION)	20*	−11	−08	−02

* Significant: $p < .05$. ** Significant: $p < .01$.

a ... did not adopt through agency

however, we discovered that the magnitude of this relationship had been spuriously high due to the effect of social class. The original statistically significant correlation all but disappeared when this effect was removed,[6] which indicated that our initial finding was almost completely attributable to the overriding influence of the lower SES standing of the Catholic Home Bureau families.

Placing agency The patterns of child-rearing characteristics of parents according to their agency identification were not nearly as clearly defined as was the case when we examined the agency correlates of revelation of adoption. The reader may observe in the data of Table 9-6 that only three child-rearing practices were significantly associated with Catholic Home Bureau families and but a single practice with the Free Synagogue Committee families, while no such variables were significantly correlated with adoption through either Chapin Nursery/Spence Alumnae or State Charities Aid.

With reference to the Catholic families, we found that they reportedly had been prone to exert intensive control over their children from early childhood through adolescence, had been very likely to make little or no use of parent substitutes during the two age periods studied, and had tended to provide their children with few or no separation experiences. This constellation of findings is quite in line with the generally traditional attitudes of Catholic Home Bureau mothers toward child rearing expressed in their questionnaires [7] and provides support for the conclusion that these families tended to display a rather protective orientation in the upbringing of their adoptive children. Interestingly, we discovered by means of partial correlation analysis that this orientation, as it applied to the infrequent use of parental substitutes, was not primarily a function of the Catholic families' working class status [8] or of their strong investment in religious activity.[9] Nor were the intensive control patterns a reflection of SES to any appreciable degree.[10] Only the reluctance of these families to afford ample normal separation experiences for their children was, as we have already seen,[11] largely attributable to the influence of their socioeconomic level. Incidentally, we note in Table 9-6 that, contrary to the prevailing tendency among the Catholic families, the Jewish families were inclined to have made frequent use of baby-sitters or other parent substitutes.

Characteristics of the adoptee We were interested to note that, in the main, the adoptee characteristics included in our correlational analysis were not strongly associated with the nature of the child-rearing practices to which the adoptees were exposed. For example, the child's sex was significantly related only to the perceived disciplinary posture of the adoptive father, who was seen as having tended toward greater strictness when the adoptee was male ($r = .25$). The adoptee's sex and the perceived severity of the adoptive mother's discipline were not comparably significantly correlated ($r = -.05$).

We may speculate that these findings may be partly explained by the observation that when the boys grow older they become more able to defy the mother's attempts to discipline them, whereas when the children are younger the mother tends to assume the responsibility for disciplining both sexes equally. With specific reference to the present group of adoptive families, a previous finding may also shed some light upon the father's perceived stricter disciplinary role vis-à-vis male adoptees. We noted in Chapter IV that this sex comprised three-fifths of the adoptees in the high-problem outcome group. It seems reasonable to assume that in many instances such problem behavior may have evoked some type of discipline or punishment, principally on the part of the adoptive father, because of the sex of the children involved. This might well have led these fathers to perceive themselves as having been strict disciplinarians with reference to the adopted males.

The adoptee's preadoptive placement history was also significantly correlated with the perceived disciplinary stance of both adoptive parents. The more temporary placements experienced by the adoptee before coming to his permanent adoptive home, the more likely were the adoptive father ($r = -.23$), and the adoptive mother ($r = -.20$) to perceive themselves as having leaned toward a "soft" disciplinary approach. Our data shed no light upon the reason for such a tendency, and hypothesizing in this area seems particularly hazardous and inadvisable in view of the limited nature of our basic data regarding the quality of and the circumstances surrounding the preadoptive placements of our group of adoptees.

The age of the adoptee at placement in the adoptive home is seen in Table 9–7 to be significantly associated with two child-rearing variables and to be correlated just short of significance with a third such

Table 9-7 / Correlation of age of adoptee at placement [a] with child-rearing variables

VARIABLE	CORRELATION
Spanking practices (*never;* SEVERE)	02
Parent most frequent disciplinarian (*mother;* ALL OTHER RESPONSES)	−06
Strictness of adoptive father (*very soft;* VERY STRICT)	05
Strictness of adoptive mother (*very soft;* VERY STRICT)	01
Intensity of control of adoptee; below age 10 (*little control,* MUCH CONTROL)	21 *
Intensity of control of adoptee; age 10–17 (*little control,* MUCH CONTROL)	30 **
Fostering independence in adoptee (*strongly encouraged;* ALL OTHER RESPONSES)	03
Adoptee's desire for independence; below age 10 (*little or no push;* STRONG PUSH)	−08
Adoptee's desire for independence; age 10–17 (*little or no push;* STRONG PUSH)	−00
Use of parental substitutes; adoptee below age 5 (*never;* FREQUENTLY)	−43 **
Use of parental substitutes; adoptee age 5–10 (*never;* FREQUENTLY)	−43 **
Separation experiences afforded adoptee (*never;* MUCH SEPARATION)	−18

* Significant: $p < .05$. ** Significant: $p < .01$
[a] Direction of variable: low score = younger age

variable. The data show that the younger the child when placed, the more apt he was to have been subjected to less rigorous control and supervision as he grew up, frequently left in the care of baby-sitters or other types of parental substitutes, and afforded ample opportunity to experience normal separation from his adoptive parents. This constellation of findings seems internally consistent.

CHARACTERISTICS OF THE ADOPTIVE PARENTS
AND THE ADOPTIVE HOME

We discovered a paucity of strong and statistically significant correlations between reported child-rearing practices and the variables characterizing the adoptive home and the adoptive parents at the time of placement.[12] This appears to signify that at least for our group of adoptive families these background variables did not play a prominent role in the parental approach to their children's upbringing.

The composition of the adoptive family prior to the adoptee's placement, however, is one of the two background variables which are correlated significantly or near significantly with a child-raising practice. Where the adoptee was placed in a home already containing one or more biological or adoptive children, he was more likely to have been exposed to greater frequency of separation experiences over the years ($r = .22$). We suggest that this association may in part reflect the greater relaxation and security in the parent role so often manifested by couples in the rearing of their second and subsequent children. It may also be somewhat linked to the SES variable in that upper class families were more apt than working class families to have already included one or two children at the time the adoptee came into the home ($r = .20$), and we have seen earlier that higher SES families tended to have arranged more separation for their children.

Our data also revealed a noteworthy association between the reported strength of adoptive parents' motivation to adopt and whether or not they tended to encourage independence in their child ($r = .19$). Where one or both partners of the couple reported having been less than highly motivated to embark upon adoption in the first place, these families were also inclined to promote strongly independence in the adoptees. Subsequent partial correlation analysis revealed that this correlation was not attributable to the influence of the families' socioeconomic status,[13] and none of our other data provide us with a basis for explaining it.

Before turning to a consideration of the environmental correlates of our families' child-rearing practices, we think the reader would be interested in the general thrust of the intercorrelations among the child-rearing variables themselves. As might be anticipated from the findings thus far presented in this chapter, we discerned a rather clear consistency in the adoptive parents' reported approach to the various aspects of raising the adoptees. We noted, for instance, that parents who strongly encouraged independence in their children were likely also to have been less intrusive and controlling of their children's activities, particularly during the youngsters' pre- and early adolescence ($r = -.21$ for the 10- to 17-year age period). They tended, too, to have afforded the adoptees ample opportunity to attend sleep-away camps, to travel alone away from home, etc. ($r = .26$).

In turn, parents who saw to it that their children had enjoyed such normal separation experiences were strongly prone to have made frequent use of baby-sitters or other parent substitutes throughout the adoptee's early childhood ($r = .49$ and $.50$ for the two age periods studied), and they were also likely to have reported that the adoptee had exhibited a strong push for independence, both in his early years ($r = .29$) and as he reached adolescence ($r = .25$). Not surprisingly, similar reports of the adoptee evidencing a desire for independence tended to come from parents who reported having fostered such independence ($r = .38$ and $.30$ for the two age periods). This last finding is probably largely a manifestation of the "halo effect" which indicates that the parents were striving for consistency in their answers, but it may also partly reflect the adoptees' positive response to a home environment which tended to value and to promote the development of independence in children.

This configuration of interrelated child-rearing practices tends to provide support for the conclusion that there seemed to be some consistency or integrity in the way our group of adoptive parents approached and coped with *all* aspects of child rearing. Parents who tended to promote independence and autonomy in their children were also apt not to have been protective in their orientation to other facets of their child-rearing role.

Other environmental correlates of child-rearing practices

The variables covering environmental influences are rather clearly associated with the child-rearing practices of our adoptive families. Five of the nine environmental factors investigated in our research were significantly correlated with one or more aspects of child rearing.

ADOPTIVE MOTHER'S DAYTIME ABSENCE FROM
THE HOME

Our data disclosed that where the adoptive mother had tended to be out of the home when the adoptee was below ten years of age, the family had also been prone to make frequent use of baby-sitters or other parental substitutes during those years ($r = .26$ and $.27$, respectively, for the two age periods studied). This finding is not unexpected for several reasons. First, it seems patently reasonable that in families where the mother was apt to be away from home frequently while the adoptee was quite young, she would arrange for the child to be cared for by someone else during that time. Secondly, the mother's daytime absence is strongly correlated ($r = .44$) with the presence of nonrelated persons living in the home, which in turn is even more strongly associated with the frequent use of parental substitutes during both the preschool years ($r = .52$) and the elementary school years ($r = .53$). This suggests that the substitute caretakers utilized by such mothers tended to be live-in domestic help such as housekeepers or governesses. Finally, the tendency to be out of the home during the day was characteristic of upper class adoptive mothers ($r = .20$), and we have already seen that higher SES families were very apt to have had nonrelated persons living in the home.

What our data seem to reveal, in other words, is an SES-related phenomenon, viz., that among our group of adoptive families, higher rather than the lower class mothers tended to be out of the home during the day as the adoptees were growing up. This would seem to be in accord with a finding in the sociological literature that women of upper socioeconomic status tend to have more diversified out-of-the-home social contacts than do working class women.[14] It also suggests that the primary reason for the mother's absence was not likely connected with the economic need for her to supplement the family income.[15] Our more well-to-do mother could permit herself to be away during the day because she was able to afford live-in help who acted, among their other capacities, as parental substitutes in caring for and supervising the adoptees, at least during their first ten years of life.

NONRELATED PERSONS LIVING IN
ADOPTIVE HOME

We have already speculated upon the meaning of the strong correlation between the presence of nonrelated persons in the home and the use of parental substitutes. Our data also indicate that in families where the adoptee was left in the care of such persons, he was also apt to have been afforded ample opportunities to experience normal separation from the nuclear family ($r = .32$). This finding seems again to be a function of social class status: both the presence of nonrelated persons in the home and the provision of much separation experience are significantly correlated with higher socioeconomic level.

Our analysis revealed that where nonrelated persons lived in the adoptive home, the adoptive mother tended to be seen as having been a strict disciplinarian ($r = .21$). We suspect that this association, too, may be a reflection of social class differences. One bit of evidence suggestive of such an assumption is the positive correlation we found linking higher socioeconomic status with the perceived greater strictness of the adoptive mother. While this association is not statistically significant ($r = .13$), it seems sufficiently pronounced to permit the speculation that it may be related to the above finding. In other words, we have already observed that high SES is strongly correlated with the presence of nonrelated persons in the adoptive home, and now we see that it is also related to strict maternal discipline. Hence, the socioeconomic factor may help to explain why the other two variables are also related.

ADOPTIVE FAMILY'S CHANGES IN RESIDENCE

This variable is significantly correlated with but a single child-rearing practice, viz., the number and variety of normal separation experiences afforded the adoptee over the years. Families which tended to provide such experiences were also apt to be families which had undergone fewer changes in residence following the adoptee's placement ($r = -.20$). This could conceivably reflect a generally more stable family situation in which both the parents and the adoptee could be more receptive to the prospect of the adoptee leaving the family home for short periods of time.

ADOPTIVE FAMILY'S INVESTMENT
IN RELIGIOUS ACTIVITY

We observed a consistent pattern in the child-rearing correlates of the extent of our adoptive families' involvement in religious observances and practices. Families reporting great investment in such activities tended to have made infrequent use of parental substitutes throughout the adoptee's childhood,[16] to have exercised intense control and supervision over their children's activities,[17] and not to have fostered independence in these children.[18]

Several other interrelated associations in our data suggest that this constellation of findings is primarily a function of lower socioeconomic status generally and of adoption through Catholic Home Bureau, specifically. We noted, first of all, a comparable patterning of child-rearing correlates of lower SES and also discovered that lower social class is strongly correlated with pronounced religiosity ($r = -.37$). We have furthermore called attention several times to the marked working class status of Catholic Home Bureau families as a group, and earlier in this chapter we discerned among these families a generally protective orientation toward the upbringing of children which included the same reluctance to use baby-sitters and the same propensity toward rigorous control of children's activities that we have seen above to characterize highly religious families. Finally, we discovered that the Catholic Home Bureau families reported having been strongly involved in religious activities as the adoptee grew up ($r = -.43$), the only one of the four agency groups to report this tendency in significant fashion.

Summary

We have examined in this chapter what we have referred to as the context of adoptive family life for the one hundred sets of parents and adoptees who were the focus of our study. This context consists

of the interrelationships among the personal and demographic characteristics of the families, their manner of dealing with revelation of
adoptive status, their child-rearing practices, and certain other environmental influences which we had reason to believe might have
helped shape the nature of the adoptive experience. The basic data
concerning these variables were obtained in face-to-face interviews
with the adoptive parents.

A number of thought-provoking findings stemming from our correlation analysis of these data were identified in this chapter. It was
shown, for example, that differences in social class status tended to
underlie different overall orientations to child rearing but were not
generally strongly related to the way in which families coped with
revelation. Contrastingly, we observed some pronounced and distinctive agency-related patterns of approaching the problems of revelation
while at the same time noticing that adoption through each of the
four participating agencies did not figure prominently in the parents'
child-rearing practices. The background characteristics of the adoptees were seen not to be strongly or pervasively associated with either
the revelation or the child-rearing variables. Some of the attributes of
the adoptive homes and certain of the adopting couples' characteristics and preferences at the point of adoptive application were found
to be linked to their manner of handling the revelation of adoptive
status, but there was a paucity of significant correlations between
these background variables and the parents' reported child-rearing
practices. Finally, while several of the environmental factors we investigated appeared to have played a role with reference to the child-
rearing orientations of our adoptive families, such factors were in the
main unrelated to the way in which these families had coped with the
telling of the adoption story.

We were impressed throughout this chapter by the high degree of
consistency revealed by the adoptive parents in their overall orientation to the various aspects of their children's upbringing. This was
particularly apparent in the marked similarity of their approaches to
the problems of revelation and to the numerous child-rearing tasks we
explored with them.

ten / Adoptee's life situation
at follow-up

IN PREVIOUS CHAPTERS, we have described, on the basis of parental reports, the adoptee's development from the time of his placement in the adoptive home through the years of his childhood. We have also described the pertinent family environmental conditions and attitudes that surrounded him as he grew up. We now turn to a description of the adoptee as he appeared to the parents in his adult status at the time of the follow-up visit. What kind of a person was he? Under what conditions did he live? Had he married? What kind of educational background had he achieved? What was the nature of his current relationship with his parents? What impairments did he appear to suffer from? These and other questions relating to the adoptee's adjustment constitute the focus of this descriptive chapter.

RESIDENCE AND FREQUENCY OF CONTACT

Almost a fifth of the adoptees were still living with their parents at the time of the follow-up interviews. These were, by and large, those who were in their early twenties and had not yet married. Slightly more than half of the adoptees had left the abode of their parents but were living within fifty miles of them. Another fourth of the sample was living at a distance more than fifty miles from their parents. Five adoptees were out of town, either in college or in the armed forces. In one case, it was impossible to determine where the adoptee was located because of a history of aimless wandering from one community to the other.

In Table 10–1 we have presented the adoptees' residential locations according to their identification within the three types of outcome groupings. While the differences are not striking, it is nevertheless of interest to note that the low-problem adoptees showed the smallest proportion remaining at home (12 percent) while those in the middle-range and in the high-problem categories showed almost twice as many (21 and 24 percent, respectively) still within the parental home. At the same time, twice the proportion of low-problem adoptees (36 percent) were living more than fifty miles from their parents than was the case for those in the middle-range and high-problem categories (18 percent each). On the basis of this information, one is tempted to conjecture that adoptees who were relatively secure in their family relationships, as the low-problem adoptees apparently were, felt greater freedom to leave home and go some distance from their parents. One is encouraged to pursue such an explanation from Pollak's model for describing a family with healthy

*Table 10–1 / Adoptee's residence at time of
follow-up interview*

	GROUP I	GROUP II	GROUP III	TOTAL
Same residence as adoptive parents	12%	20%	24%	19%
Living within 50 miles of parents	49	53	52	51
Living more than 50 miles from parents	36	18	18	24
Child in college or armed forces, out of town	3	9	3	5
Unable to determine	—	—	3	1
Total cases	(33)	(34)	(33)	(100)

emotional relationships.[1] He has made the point that families that are comparatively healthy would find it easier to separate from their children than those suffering disordered relationships.

Among the families of the adoptees who were still living in the parental home, all but a very few were reportedly characterized by frequent contact between the adoptees and their parents, with a daily sharing of meals, evening leisure time, weekend outings, and the like. In only one instance was the adoptee said to be out of the home a great deal, thus having infrequent contact with his parents. It is also noteworthy that two-thirds of the parents with adoptees at home expressed pleasure or satisfaction with their children's continued residence in the home. In only one family did the parents indicate minor misgiving about such an arrangement, and in two others there was strong parental feeling that the family or the adoptee would be better off if the latter were residing independently. As might be expected these three cases fell within the high-problem category.

We were interested in the extent of shared parent-adoptee visiting among the families characteristic of the adoptees living within fifty miles of their parents. These families were presumably in a geographical position to have fairly regular contact. Table 10–2 reveals the visiting pattern reported to us. It is apparent that the low-problem adoptees saw their parents very frequently: all those who resided within a fifty-mile radius of the parental home were said to have contact at least once a week. This was true to a somewhat lesser extent of the middle-range group, where almost half of the families who lived in close geographical proximity were reported to have regular contact. Among the high-problem adoptee group, only a third were described as being in frequent contact with their parents. By and large, therefore, for adoptees and families living within easy traveling distance of each other, there seems to be a noteworthy association between the kind of overall adjustment made by the adoptees and the frequency of their contact with their adoptive parents. With respect to the frequency of correspondence, however, the data showed almost equally frequent parent-adoptee correspondence among the middle-range group of adoptees as among the low-problem group. However, the high-problem adoptees again showed decidedly less frequent contact in their pattern of correspondence with their parents.

Table 10–2 / Frequency of contact between adoptee and parents

	GROUP I	GROUP II	GROUP III	TOTAL
Very often; at least once a week	49%	29%	18%	32%
Somewhat often; at least once a month	—	15	12	9
Not frequently; less than once a month	—	3	12	5
Not applicable; child living at home	12	21	25	19
Not applicable; child living more than 50 miles away (or at college or in armed forces)	39	26	21	29
Disparate parent response	—	—	6	2
Other	—	6	3	3
Not covered	—	—	3	1
Total cases	(33)	(34)	(33)	(100)

Partial explanation of the infrequent contact reported by some families was offered by the parents of almost a third of the adoptees in the middle-range grouping and almost half of those in the high-problem category: these families were said to be faced with circumstances that served to limit the amount of visiting between child and parents. There was a substantial group, however, where no such circumstances reportedly stood in the way of mutual visiting and where nevertheless parent-adoptee contact was infrequent.

We interviewed the parents about the *direction* of the visiting between them and their children. Did the parents or the adoptees always tend to do the visiting, or was there shared visiting back and forth between the respective homes? The pattern among families of low-problem adoptees appeared to be one of equal visiting by both generations. Among the families of middle-range adoptees, there was a greater tendency for the adoptee to visit his parents more often, while among families of high-problem adoptees the predominant pattern was for the adoptee to visit his parents rather than for them to visit him.

The parents were also queried about their satisfaction with the frequency of visitation and correspondence. While no decided sense of dissatisfaction came through among the parents of adoptees in any of the three outcome groups, there was a somewhat greater tendency for dissatisfaction to be expressed by the parents of the adoptees in the high-problem group.

MUTUALITY OF INTERESTS

One measure of the nature of the relationship that prevailed between the adoptee and his parents in his current adult status was the matter of whether he shared common interests with them in the areas of recreation, cultural pursuits, and civic activities. It was our judgment that shared interests represented one measure of family cohesion that had relevance for an evaluation of the adoptive experience. Thus, with respect to recreational interests, a third of the adoptees were said to enjoy interests very similar to those of their parents and another fifth were said to enjoy somewhat similar interests. For a fourth of the sample, the adoptee and his parents were said not to enjoy the same interests or to have very divergent recreational outlets.

In Table 10–3 we present the frequency distribution of the reports of the parents with respect to this issue. As might be predicted, there

Table 10–3 / Degree to which the parents and adoptees currently enjoy common recreational interests

	GROUP I	GROUP II	GROUP III	TOTAL
Enjoy very similar interests	55%	29%	18%	34%
Enjoy somewhat similar interests	18	26	18	21
Tend not to enjoy same interests	9	12	21	14
Tend to enjoy very divergent interests	—	6	21	9
Disparate response	3	—	3	2
Other	—	3	12	5
Not covered	15	15	6	12
Unable to determine	—	9	—	3
Total cases	(33)	(34)	(33)	(100)

was much greater tendency for the parents of the adoptees in the low-problem grouping to report that they enjoyed interests very similar to those of their children than was true of parents with youngsters in the middle-range and high-problem categories. Of the Group III adoptees, 42 percent were said not to enjoy the same interests of their parents, while this was true for only 18 percent of those in Group II and 9 percent of the Group I adoptees.

A similar pattern prevailed with respect to intellectual and cultural interests. The distributions are set forth in Table 10–4. Thus, 55 percent of the low-problem adoptees were said to enjoy interests very similar to those of their parents as compared with 29 percent of those in the middle-range outcome group, and only 15 percent of the high-problem adoptees. From these reports, we have confirmed the commonsense impression that the more disordered the adjustment of the adopted children, the more frequently the parents would report that their life-styles differed markedly from them. We should note, at the same time, that most parents did not specifically construe the adoptee's divergent interests as reflecting a "growing away" process. Such an interpretation was reported by only one parent in Group I, three in Group II, and five in Group III.

Table 10–4 / Degree to which the parents and adoptees enjoy common intellectual-cultural interests

	GROUP I	GROUP II	GROUP III	TOTAL
Enjoy very similar interests	55%	29%	15%	33%
Enjoy somewhat similar interests	18	23	9	17
Tend not to enjoy same interests	9	9	21	13
Tend to enjoy very divergent interests	—	9	15	8
Disparate response	3	—	6	3
Other	3	3	13	6
Not covered	9	15	21	15
Unable to determine	3	12	—	5
Total cases	(33)	(34)	(33)	(100)

CLOSENESS BETWEEN ADOPTEES AND PARENTS

We interviewed the parents about the closeness of their current relationship with their children. Their responses, tabulated in Table 10–5 demonstrated what might have been expected, namely, a strong association between the tendency to report closeness and the location of the adoptees within the three outcome groups.[2] Thus, nine out of ten parents of low-problem adoptees told us they were very close to their children while such reports were made by seven out of ten parents of middle-range adoptees and by only one-third of the parents whose children were classified as showing highly problematic adjustments. Almost a third of the parents in this latter grouping had relationships with their children which were described as being either casual or somewhat or very distant. There was also a fair number of families in this outcome group where the two parents presented divergent pictures of the nature of their current relationships with the adoptees.

The differences in reported family closeness is a suggestive finding, but the reader should bear in mind that, for almost two-thirds of all the families, the prevailing relationship with the adoptee was described as being "very close," while for another 12 percent a "somewhat close" relationship was said to obtain. By and large, then,

Table 10–5 / Current closeness between adoptees and parents

	GROUP I	GROUP II	GROUP III	TOTAL
Very close	91%	67%	34%	64%
Somewhat close	9	15	12	12
Casual—neither close nor distant	—	6	6	4
Somewhat distant	—	—	9	3
Very distant	—	3	18	7
Disparate response	—	9	15	8
Not covered/Unable to determine	—	—	6	2
Total cases	(33)	(34)	(33)	(100)

it would seem that these parents were enjoying intimate interaction with their adopted children.

As a way of further amplifying the above information, the parents were asked if there were any factors that had served to cause a rift between themselves and the adoptees. Only thirteen of the hundred families reported that such a situation had developed. None of these rifts had occurred in the families of the low-problem adoptees, but the proportion of families of the high-problem adoptees reporting such rifts (27 percent) was twice as high as the comparable proportion among families of their middle-range counterparts (12 percent). For the study sample as a whole, 81 percent of the families reported no such rift-producing situations.

We also inquired about the extent to which both parents and adoptees made a mutual effort to maintain the closeness of their relationship. In 71 percent of the families, parents reported that they and their children invested equally in the parent-adoptee relationship. Ten sets of parents told us that they currently invested more than did their children in maintaining the relationship, while an additional five families reported that the adoptee invested somewhat more in the relationship. In the main, it was the families with adoptees in the high-problem category whose parents reported investing more in the relationship than their children.

One aspect of the current relationship within the adoptive family is the adoptee's tendency to confide in his parents. The data in Table 10–6, showing the results of our inquiry into this topic, show quite evident differentiation by outcome category. Whereas more than nine-tenths of the low-problem adoptees were reported to confide some or a great deal in their parents, this was true of three-fourths of the middle-range outcome adoptees and of less than half their counterparts in the high-problem adjustment group. On the other hand, 39 percent of this last group were said to confide rarely or not at all in their adoptive parents while only 21 and 3 percent, respectively, of the middle-range and low-problem adoptees were described in this manner. Thus, the degree to which an adoptee tended to confide in his parents was strongly reflective of his overall adjustment in a variety of life-space areas.

We also asked the parents about the extent to which they con-

Table 10–6 / Degree to which adoptee currently confides in his parents

	GROUP I	GROUP II	GROUP III	TOTAL
Confides a great deal	61%	21%	18%	33%
Confides some	33	55	28	39
Hardly confides	3	12	15	10
Does not confide	—	9	24	11
Disparate response	—	3	6	3
Other	—	—	6	2
Not covered	3	—	3	2
Total cases	(33)	(34)	(33)	(100)

fided in their children about their own life problems and situations. While, for the entire sample, there was less of a tendency for parents to confide in their children in contrast to the latter confiding in them, there was, nevertheless, a stronger tendency for this to occur in the families of low-problem adoptees: 55 percent in such families as against 18 percent in the families in each of the other two outcome groups. One-third of the parents of high-problem adoptees reported there was no confiding at all in the adoptees about matters of personal concern to the parents. This reinforces the picture we have already developed of the lack of closeness and interaction in the family situations of the high-problem adoptees.

CONFLICT BETWEEN THE ADOPTEES
AND THEIR PARENTS

In studying the adjustment of the adopted child over the years, we recognized that we might encounter family situations where considerable conflict had prevailed between the adoptees and their parents during the growing-up years. This might conceivably have diminished as the adoptee matured; families often find smoother sailing once they have passed through the turbulence of the earlier childhood years. We therefore inquired of the parents about the nature of any conflict that might have characterized their relationship with their children, both as the latter grew up and at the time of the follow-up interview. Concerning the mother-adoptee relationship at the time of our contact with the parents, almost eight out of ten families reported no noteworthy current conflict between the adoptee and his adoptive mother. In only nine families was intense or moderate conflict said to prevail, and in only three families was mild conflict reported.

In Table 10–7, we present the adoptee-mother conflict data according to the three adoptee outcome categories. Almost no conflict was reported in the families of the low-problem and middle-range outcome groups. However, among the families of the high-problem adoptees, 30 percent of the parents reported varying degrees of conflict currently prevailing between the adoptee and his mother. Thus, although there was diminished conflict reported for all categories when we contrasted the current situation with conflict reported during the adoptees' growing-up period, there was less of a tendency for this to be true among families of high-problem adoptees. For a sizable proportion of these, the painful relationships with their adoptive mothers experienced during childhood were also carried forward to the adult years.

Quite similar data were reported with respect to current conflict between the adoptees and their adoptive fathers. One-fifth of the parents of high-problem adoptees reported some adoptee-father conflict, but no such conflict was reported by the parents of adoptees in either of the other two adjustment groups.

*Table 10–7 / Current conflict between the adoptee
and his mother*

	GROUP I	GROUP II	GROUP III	TOTAL
Intense conflict	—%	3%	3%	2%
Moderate conflict	3	—	18	7
Mild conflict	—	—	9	3
No conflict to speak of	91	94	55	80
Other	—	3	3	2
Not covered	—	—	6	2
Not applicable (mother deceased)	6	—	6	4
Total cases	(33)	(34)	(33)	(100)

MARITAL STATUS OF ADOPTEES

We were informed by seventy-one sets of parents that their adopted children were currently married. Initial parental reactions to the adoptee's present spouse during the early stages of courtship had been varied. Some 23 percent of the parents reported having been strongly enthusiastic and 15 percent moderately so. Two families spoke of having assumed a neutral attitude whereas eleven told of having taken a moderately negative viewpoint. Six families reported having had strongly negative feelings. In eight situations, the two parents in the family gave disparate responses.

In Table 10–8, we present the same data according to our three outcome groupings. Greatest enthusiasm had been manifested by parents of adoptees in the low-problem category and the least enthusiasm by parents of the high-problem adoptees. However, it would appear that even among the families of the low-problem adoptees difficulties had been encountered by some parents in accepting the adoptee's spouse; 15 percent of the parents of these adoptees reported having experienced negative responses and some parents gave disparate responses. By comparison, 27 percent of the parents of high-problem

Table 10–8 / Parents' reactions to adoptee's spouse during courtship period

	GROUP I	GROUP II	GROUP III	TOTAL
Strong enthusiasm	34%	29%	6%	23%
Moderate enthusiasm	18	15	12	15
Neutral attitude	—	3	3	2
Moderately negative	12	9	12	11
Strongly negative	3	—	15	6
Disparate response	6	6	12	8
Other	3	3	3	3
Not covered	6	3	—	3
Not applicable—adoptee not married	18	32	37	29
Total cases	(33)	(34)	(33)	(100)

adoptees reported having experienced negative reactions when they first learned of their children's interest in marriage, and among 12 percent of the parents in this group the mothers and fathers gave disparate responses. It should be noted in Table 10–8 that markedly fewer of the low-problem adoptees were still unmarried at the time of our research interviews than was true of their middle-range and high-problem counterparts. Thus, if success in obtaining a spouse can be assumed to be a positive criterion of adjustment, the low-problem adoptees may be said to have performed in somewhat superior fashion.

We asked those parents who had reported an initial negative reaction to the adoptee's spouse whether their attitude had created a crisis in their relationship with their child. In most instances, the parents reported that this had not occurred. In only four cases had the parental attitude produced mild or short-lived crises, and in only two instances had severe crises developed. With respect to the parents' stance or overt action concerning the adoptees' decision to marry their current spouses, forty of the seventy-one families with currently married adoptees reported having given strong support for the marriage, and six, only mild support. Eight families had assumed a neutral position on the issue, while five had expressed mild opposition. Two families had expressed strong opposition.

We found a slight tendency for parental opposition to the adoptees' marriage to be characteristic of families with adoptees in the middle-range and high-problem categories, but this was not of a pronounced character. In only one of the seven cases where the parents had opposed the marriage had severe parent-adoptee conflict resulted because of the parental attitude, and in only two other cases had mild or moderate crises developed. More noteworthy is the fact that in only one instance was there reported any current vestige of the earlier conflict concerning the decision of the adoptee to marry the spouse.

We also inquired about the nature of the parents' current feelings toward the adoptee's spouse, and in most cases either strong or moderate fondness was reported. Only four sets of parents spoke of currently moderate or strong feelings of coolness toward the adoptees' spouses, and these parents tended to be those with children classified in the high-problem category. Also, in only one case was the adoptee's spouse said presently to harbor strong antagonism toward the parents.

Our overall impression is that in most of the families where adoptees were currently married a quite positive acceptance of the adoptee's spouse seemed to characterize the parents and vice-versa.

One last comment about the marriages of the adopted children is in order. We asked the parents about any limitations their adoptee's spouse might have had with respect to social or intellectual qualities. Sixteen families did speak of such limitations with two such cases in the low-problem group, five in the middle-range group, and nine in the high-problem group.[3] Thus, we again find an ordering of the three groups with the more negative information characteristic of the high-problem adoptees.

RELATIONSHIP WITH SIBLINGS

We were interested in determining the nature of the adoptee's relationship with his siblings, if any, at the point of follow-up. It turned out that fifty-eight of the hundred adoptees covered by our study did have one or more brothers or sisters. About half the parents in these families depicted very affectionate and warm current adoptee-sibling relationships, while about a third of the adoptees with brothers or sisters were said to be enjoying moderately affectionate relationships with them. In three instances the adoptee-sibling relationship was said to be somewhat perfunctory, and in four cases this relationship was described as a somewhat cool one. Only one family reported that a very antagonistic relationship currently existed between the adoptee and his siblings. Most of the cases where the relationship was other than affectionate involved adoptees with high-problem adjustments.

PARENTS' OVERALL VIEW OF ADOPTEE

One aspect of the parents' global view of their children's adjustment solicited by us concerned the current major limitations or liabilities, if any, which the parents perceived their children to have. Forty of the one hundred families reported seeing no major limitations in any aspect of their children's functioning, while forty-three sets of parents spoke of one or more disabling characteristics. In seven families, parents were unable to address themselves to this issue with sufficient specificity to code their responses, and seven sets of parents gave disparate responses.

In Table 10–9, the parents' views of their adoptee's limitations are presented according to our threefold outcome classification. As might well have been anticipated, the degree to which the parents viewed their children as having major limitations correlated strongly with the ranking of the adoptees within the three outcome groups. Thus, seven out of ten parents of adoptees in the low-problem category saw their child as having no major current limitations. This was true of less than five out of ten parents of middle-range outcome adoptees and of less than in one in ten parents of high-problem adoptees.

On the other hand, the low-problem grouping showed only 12 percent where the adoptee was perceived to have at least one current major limitation, while this was true of 24 percent of the adoptees in the middle-range outcome category. Most striking, of course, was the fact that 94 percent of the adoptees in the high-problem group were reported by their parents as currently evidencing one or more major limitations. The fact that the Group III adoptees were almost uniformly characterized as having major liabilities tends to confirm the basic tripartite classification of the one hundred children.[4]

We asked the parents of the adoptees who were reported to have major limitations about the degree of parental concern regarding these limitations. No parents of low-problem or middle-range adoptees

Table 10–9 / Parents' views of adoptee's current major limitations

	GROUP I	GROUP II	GROUP III	TOTAL
Has no major limitations	70%	44%	6%	40%
Has one or more major limitations	12	23	94	43
Parent unable to make judgment	6	15	—	7
Other	3	3	—	2
Unable to determine	—	3	—	1
Disparate response	9	12	—	7
Total cases	(33)	(34)	(33)	(100)

reported being very concerned or unhappy about their children's limitations, whereas 30 percent of the parents of adoptees in the high-problem category expressed great concern. Another third of the parents of adoptees in this most problematic group expressed moderate concern about their children's limitations, and this was also true of 12 percent of the parents of adoptees with middle-range outcomes.

EDUCATIONAL ACHIEVEMENT OF ADOPTEES

Having achieved adulthood, what had been the nature of the performance of the adoptees in the realm of education? One way of answering this question was to examine the various levels of education completed by the adoptees. These data are presented in Table 10–10 and reveal only slight differences in the levels of education achieved by adoptees in the low-problem and middle-range outcome groups. About a fourth of each had completed a college education and few or no adoptees in these categories had failed to complete high school. In sharp contrast, 30 percent of the high-problem adoptees had not completed their high school education. At the same time, however, it should be pointed out that a third of the adoptees with the most problematic adjustments had managed to achieve some college education, and that 12 percent of them had succeeded in graduating from college.

Table 10–10 / Highest level of education achieved by adoptees

	GROUP I	GROUP II	GROUP III	TOTAL
Some high school; did not graduate	—%	9%	30%	13%
High school graduate	40	28	18	29
Some college; did not graduate	18	24	34	25
College graduate	27	24	12	21
Postgraduate education	12	12	—	8
Disparate response	—	3	—	1
Other	3	—	6	3
Total cases	(33)	(34)	(33)	(100)

Another way of looking at the matter of educational achievement was for us to determine the degree to which the parents' aspirations for their children had been fulfilled. It had been noted in the field interviewing that some families were dissatisfied even when the adoptees had attained a seemingly high level of education. It was thus important to see whether the lack of schooling was something that made the adoptee fall short of his parents' expectations. Our findings on this score are summarized in Table 10–11. We again note much less pronounced differences between the response distributions of parents of Group I and Group II adoptees than between these distributions and that of the parents of Group III adoptees.

Whereas only one-fourth the parents of low-problem adoptees and two-fifths of the parents of middle-range adoptees reported that their children's academic performance had fallen at all short of parental aspirations, such a report was made by 78 percent of the parents of high-problem adoptees, and half this latter group stated that their aspirations for their children had been very far from fulfilled. Only 6 percent of the high-problem adoptees in this group had fulfilled their parents' hopes for them, where this was said to be the case for 50 percent of the adoptees in the middle-range outcome category and 61 percent of those in the low-problem category. The contrast is quite striking and particularly points up the negative kind of feeling tone

Table 10–11 / Degree to which adoptee's
educational achievement fulfilled
parents' aspirations

	GROUP I	GROUP II	GROUP III	TOTAL
Fell very short	—%	6%	39%	15%
Fell somewhat short	24	35	39	33
Fulfilled aspirations	61	50	6	39
Somewhat exceeded aspirations	—	3	—	1
Parents had no special hopes	6	3	3	4
Disparate response	9	3	6	6
Other	—	—	3	1
Not covered	—	—	3	1
Total cases	(33)	(34)	(33)	(100)

conveyed in the responses of the parents of the high-problem adoptees as they contemplated the generally poor achievements of their children.

We asked the parents whose children had failed to live up to their aspirations how disappointed or unhappy they currently were about this failure. Among the parents of the low-problem adoptees, one set reported still being somewhat disappointed and five spoke of being only slightly disappointed. Four families indicated that they were currently not at all disappointed about the adoptee's past failure to have lived up to what they had expected of them. Among the families of middle-range adoptees, two expressed strong disappointment and another two, some disappointment about such failures, with six families expressing no disappointment at all. The sense of disappointment was strongest among the parents of the high-problem adoptees: seven sets of these parents spoke of keen disappointment and another ten sets referred to lesser but still some disappointment.

We were also interested in determining whether the parents felt that the adoptee had performed in a manner commensurate with his potential or capabilities. With respect to grade school performance, 21 percent of the low-problem adoptees were said to have fallen somewhat short of their potential as compared with 35 percent of their middle-range and 39 percent of their high-problem counterparts. However, among adoptees in the most problematic outcome category, 30 percent were said to have fallen very short of their potential compared to only 3 percent in each of the other two outcome categories. Conversely, two-thirds of the low-problem adoptees, about half the middle-range adoptees, and only one-fifth of the high-problem adoptees were said to have fully measured up to their performance potential. Similar findings emerged with respect to the performance of the adoptees during their high school years.

VOCATIONAL ADJUSTMENT

We regarded the area of work as an important indicator of the adult adjustment of the adoptees. We were consequently interested in determining whether the adoptee's vocational adjustment reflected an orientation to the work world which would enable him to fulfill this important adult role. However, this life-space area was not particularly germane to all of the adoptees. Because 51 percent of the sample of adoptees covered by our study were female, and because a considerable number of them occupied the status of housewives who did not carry primary responsibility for income-producing work, we decided to focus attention exclusively upon the males in the matter of vocational adjustment. We also excluded from consideration four of the males who were still in college or had not yet begun their vocational activities. Thus, we were left with forty-five adoptees who could be scrutinized from the perspective of their work adjustment.

The parents were asked how satisfied they had been with the adoptee's vocational history with respect to the nature of his career choice, his general job stability, and the average salary or wages earned by him over the years. All of the parents of adoptees in the low-problem category were either very satisfied or somewhat satisfied with these aspects of their children's adjustment. Similarly, in only one instance did the parents of an adoptee in the middle-range group express dissatisfaction in this area. However, the parents of six high-problem adoptees—one-third the total in this outcome category—spoke of some or considerable dissatisfaction with their children's vocational adjustment.

There were five high-problem adoptees whose investment in developing work skills was said to be very weak or practically nonexistent. These adoptees were seen by their parents as suffering very severe work adjustment problems. No such cases were reported in the two more favorable outcome groups.

Associated with our interest in the adoptees' vocational histories was our desire to learn about the manner in which they were handling their finances, a topic applicable to adoptees of both sexes. Table 10–12 provides information about the parental perceptions of this aspect of adjustment. The reader will again note only relatively modest differences between the perceptions of the parents of low-problem and middle-range adoptees as compared with the perceptions of the parents of the high-problem adoptees. While almost nine out of ten parents of Group I adoptees and more than six out of ten parents of Group II adoptees expressed great satisfaction with the way their children were managing their finances, only one in ten parents

Table 10–12 / *Parental satisfaction with adoptee's handling of finances*

	GROUP I	GROUP II	GROUP III	TOTAL
Very satisfied	88%	62%	12%	54%
Somewhat satisfied	3	12	28	14
Somewhat dissatisfied	3	14	12	10
Very dissatisfied	—	—	24	8
Disparate response	—	—	15	5
Not covered	6	12	9	9
Total cases	(33)	(34)	(33)	(100)

of Group III adoptees told of being very satisfied with this aspect of their children's adjustment, and another three in ten were somewhat satisfied.

None of the parents of low-problem or middle-range adoptees expressed great dissatisfaction with their children's adjustment in this life-space area, and only 3 and 14 percent, respectively, told of some dissatisfaction. In contrast, more than one-third of the parents of the high-problem adoptees spoke of some or great dissatisfaction with the manner in which their children were handling their finances. It thus seems quite clear that competence in this sphere was yet another area in which the high-problem adoptees were seen by their parents as having deficiencies in functioning which set them apart from their fellow adoptees in the other two outcome categories.

This does not mean, however, that only the high-problem adoptees were perceived by their parents to require or merit financial help. While 36 percent of these adoptees received such help from their families, this was also true for 21 percent of the middle-range and 15 percent of the low-problem adoptees. There was, however, a greater tendency for the parents of the high-problem adoptees to view their children as being improvident than was true of parents of adoptees in the two less problematic outcome categories.

We provide further information about the adoptees' economic situations in Table 10–13, which summarizes the degree of parental satisfaction with their children's current standard of living. The information in this table parallels that just reported in Table 10–12, above. By

Table 10–13 / Parental satisfaction with adoptee's current standard of living

	GROUP I	GROUP II	GROUP III	TOTAL
Very satisfied	88%	61%	24%	58%
Somewhat satisfied	—	21	24	15
Somewhat dissatisfied	3	3	19	8
Very dissatisfied	—	—	15	5
Disparate response	—	—	6	2
Not covered	3	6	6	5
Unable to determine	—	3	3	2
Not applicable	6	6	3	5
Total cases	(33)	(34)	(33)	(100)

and large, the parents of adoptees in the low-problem and middle-range outcome groups were very satisfied with their children's present living standard in contrast to the parents of the high-problem adoptees, a fairly substantial proportion of whom voiced dissatisfaction with this facet of their children's adjustment. It may be seen that a third of this latter group of parents was somewhat or very dissatisfied in this regard.

OVERALL PARENTAL SATISFACTION
WITH THE EXPERIENCE

We chose to examine the outcome of the adoption experience in a more global way by ascertaining the degree to which the adoptive parents experienced general dissatisfaction, pain, or unhappiness with the experience of raising the adoptees to adulthood. In Table 10–14 we present a summary of the parents' responses to this inquiry. It seems noteworthy that no parents of low-problem or middle-range adoptees expressed considerable dissatisfaction, pain, or unhappiness with respect to adoption while such extreme feelings *were* voiced by almost two-fifths of the parents of the high-problem adoptees. Moreover, moderate dissatisfaction was rarely expressed by parents of the adoptees in the two less problematic groups, but one-fourth of the parents of adoptees in the most problematic category spoke in this vein.

Table 10–14 / *Parental dissatisfaction, pain, or*
unhappiness about adoptee as he grew up

	GROUP I	GROUP II	GROUP III	TOTAL
Considerable dissatisfaction, pain, or unhappiness	—%	—%	37%	12%
Moderate dissatisfaction, pain, or unhappiness	3	6	24	11
Mild dissatisfaction, pain, or unhappiness	—	33	9	14
No dissatisfaction, pain, or unhappiness	94	58	9	54
Disparate response	—	3	15	6
Other	3	—	3	2
Not covered	—	—	3	1
Total cases	(33)	(34)	(33)	(100)

Thus, 61 percent of the parents of high-problem adoptees reported considerable or moderate dissatisfaction, pain, or unhappiness connected with raising their adopted children. Only 9 percent of this group of parents denied having experienced such feelings. A third of the parents of adoptees in the middle-range outcome group reported experiencing mild dissatisfaction, pain, or unhappiness, while none of the parents of low-problem adoptees reported even this mild category of complaint. Thus, 94 percent of the parents of Group I adoptees reported no dissatisfaction, pain, or unhappiness as contrasted with 58 percent of parents of Group II adoptees.

We therefore note a fairly firm correlation between the classification of the adoptees among the three outcome categories and the amount of parental dissatisfaction expressed. While this correlation is partially explained by the fact that the item regarding dissatisfaction was also included in the overall scoring system used to classify the adoptees into the three outcome groups, the reader should be reminded that it was only one of many items used. In our judgment Table 10–14 provides additional confirmation of the validity of the outcome groupings.

The information provided above should not be considered an indication that the dissatisfactions reported by the parents represented an alienation from the status of adoptive parenthood. The parents were asked whether they attributed any of the reported dissatisfactions specifically to this status. It was clear from their responses that, even for the parents of the high-problem adoptees, there was little tendency to ascribe their dissatisfaction or unhappiness to adoptive parenthood. Of the parents of the high-problem adoptees, 73 percent denied that adoptive parenthood per se was the cause of the problems they encountered; only 21 percent made such a claim. None of the parents of the adoptees in either of the other two outcome groups attributed their problems to the adoptive parent role. It is impressive to find that nine out of ten families in our sample appeared to retain an enthusiasm about adoption, and in their reports they seemed in no way alienated from this social institution even when confronted with quite serious adjustment problems on the part of the adoptees.

PARENTS WITH OWN BIOLOGICAL CHILDREN

The reader may be interested in the responses of a very small group of our study parents to a question we asked in the interviews concerning the differences, if any, they had encountered in raising both an adopted child and one or more biological children. Twenty families in our sample had had such an experience. Of the seven such families whose adopted children were classified as "low-problem," none pointed to any differences in rearing their adopted and biological children. However, two out of the seven sets of parents of middle-range adoptees and biological children felt that there had been some differences, as did three of the six families who had raised both high-problem adoptees as well as biological children. The numbers of families in each of the three groups, however, are too small to permit drawing any generalizations from these data.

ACCESS TO THE ADOPTEE

One final piece of descriptive data should be of particular interest to the reader. We wished to secure permission from the adoptive parents to seek out the adoptees for research interviews in order to appraise their adjustment independently of their parents' reports.[5] Table

*Table 10–15 / Parents' response to request that
adoptee be interviewed*

	GROUP I	GROUP II	GROUP III	TOTAL
Consented with no reservation	21%	29%	37%	29%
Consented with some reservation	21	15	9	15
Did not consent but willing to reconsider	15	15	6	12
Adamantly refused	31	26	24	27
Disparate response	3	—	9	4
Other (e. g., child out-of-town or other circumstances prevented interview)	9	15	15	13
Total cases	(33)	(34)	(33)	(100)

10–15 contains information concerning the accessibility of the adoptees
for research interviewing insofar as their parents' consent was concerned. The table, surprisingly, shows no marked tendency for the
parents of adoptees in the various outcome categories to be more or
less willing to consider having their children interviewed. As a matter
of fact, a larger proportion of parents of high-problem adoptees expressed no hesitation at all in granting us permission to contact their
children than was true of parents of adoptees in the two less problematic outcome groups. Some 40 to 50 percent of the parents of adoptees in each of the three categories consented fully or with some reser-
vation to our request that they allow their children to be contacted.
Conversely, from 24 to 31 percent of parents of adoptees in all three
groups adamantly refused to give us access to their children for interviewing purposes.

Summary

In this chapter we have set forth a picture of the adjustment of the
adoptee as seen by his parents in his adult status at the time of
the follow-up interview. Similar to the findings we have reported in
prior chapters, a fairly strong association was evidenced between the
adoptee's allocation to each of the three categories of outcome and his

parents' evaluative perception of his adjustment in a variety of life-space areas. The cases in the most problematic third of the overall rank ordering appeared most impaired in personal and social functioning. Despite the serious problems of these adoptees, we can nevertheless report that the overwhelming majority of adoptive parents did not attribute any of the problems they encountered with their adopted children to the fact of their being adopted. Further, the emotional commitment of almost all the adoptive parents to their children remained strong even when extremely serious adjustment problems had afflicted the adoptees.

eleven / Measuring the outcome
of the adoptive experience

IN THE ABSENCE of a contrast group with which to compare the adoptees and their families, our best recourse was to look at the outcome of the adoptive experience with an eye to differentiations *within* the sample of the one hundred families. This is the "internal analysis" approach suggested by investigators such as Lipset, et al.[1] We therefore undertook to organize the material derived from the depth interviews with the adoptive parents in such a form as to permit us to rank order the study families with respect to a broad array of variables dealing with the adoptees' personal and social adjustment. We also identified a smaller number of variables concerned with the families' overall experiences with adoption. This approach to measurement of outcome required the codification of the parents' responses in the comprehensive codebook described in Chapter III.

Thirty-seven codebook variables were selected on the grounds of their relevance for measuring outcome. The variables pertained to the following life-space areas: (a) The adoptee's school performance; (b)

The adoptee's personality; (c) The quality of the past parent-adoptee relationship; (d) The nature of the adoptee's social relationships; (e) The adoptee's health; (f) The quality of the current relationship between the adoptee and his parents; (g) The adequacy of the adoptee's current economic adjustment; (h) The adoptee's vocational history; (i) The adoptee's heterosexual relationships; (j) The adoptee's limitations and social deviations; (k) The parents' satisfaction with the adoptive experience; (l) The adoptee's outstanding talents.

In each of the specified areas, a number of items were linked together on the basis of conceptual relevance to constitute an index of the adoptee's adjustment in that area. The number of item indicators ranged from six in the area of educational adjustment to only one indicator in the area of demonstrated talents. The index scores generated for each adoptee were subsequently summated into an Overall Adjustment Score [2] which enabled us to rank order the hundred adoptees on the basis of a single, all-inclusive measure. It was this rank ordering that was trichotomized to develop the threefold classification of adoptee adjustment—"low-problem," "middle-range," and "high-problem"—utilized in our previous descriptive chapters.

It is important for the reader to keep fresh in his mind the nature of the data we are reporting here, perhaps the most crucial of this entire report. These are data derived from the coding of information provided by the parents in the course of depth interviews. In most cases, the coding operation was facilitated by the availability of tape recordings of the interviews and, as was pointed out in Chapter III, the reliability of this coding operation was demonstrated to be substantially high.

In some life-space areas, the adoptee's adjustment was viewed in panoramic fashion from the time of his birth to the current period. Thus, if an adoptee had evidenced severe personality difficulties as a youngster, he would receive a lower index score than would another adoptee who had not revealed such difficulties even though the current personality functioning of both might be deemed the same. As discussed earlier, this is a rather severe approach to the scoring of adjustment, but we felt justified in using it because it seemed in keeping with the purpose of the study: to facilitate the development of knowledge which can serve as a guide to adoption agencies in their current practice. All things being equal, agencies would prefer to be able to place children with families where *no* aberrations in personality occur while they are growing up as well as during subsequent adulthood.

The reader might bear in mind yet another aspect of the outcome variables used in this study. We attempted to include as many objective indicators of adoptee adjustment as possible while at the same time also taking into account the subjective expectations of the adoptive parents. Thus, for example, in developing an index of the adoptee's school performance, we include items dealing with the presence or absence of school problems and the amount of schooling actually attained, as well as an item concerning the degree to which the adoptee had fulfilled his parents' aspirations for him in the academic sphere. Thus, in some cases we found that even though an adoptee had been able to complete college, his parents nevertheless revealed a strong sense of disappointment about his inability to go on to graduate or professional school. On the other hand, some families were quite content with the performance of their children even though the latter had not gone beyond high school. Obviously, social class factors could strongly influence parental aspirations in this area.

In the tables presented in this chapter, the correlations among items comprising each index are set forth for the reader. In developing index scores for correlational analysis purposes, arbitrary weights were assigned response categories within items. Where possible, an effort was made to equalize the range from low to high scores for various items in order to take into account the fact that different items contained varying numbers of possible response alternatives.

SCHOOL PERFORMANCE

In Table 11–1 we show the correlations among items included in the index developed to measure the quality of the adoptee's achievements in the area of education. Six variables were included in this index. As can be seen by the reader, the correlations among items all achieved statistical significance and in many cases were quite substantial. More important, each item included in the index correlated substantially with the overall ranking of the adoptees reflected in their Overall Adjustment Scores. The lowest correlation was the one prevailing between the amount of education an adoptee had achieved and the overall ranking ($r = .32$). The highest correlation was that obtaining between the expressed parental satisfaction with the adoptee's school performance and the summated measure ($r = .74$).

*Table 11–1 / Intercorrelations among items
included in index of adoptee adjustment
in the area of education* [a]

	Level of school performance	School problems	Parental satisfaction with school performance	Amount of education achieved	Fulfillment of parental aspirations	Achievement of perceived potential	Rank order of Overall Adjustment Scores
Level of school performance	—						
School problems	.67	—					
Parental satisfaction with school performance	.75	.75	—				
Amount of education achieved	.40	.21	.31	—			
Fulfillment of parental aspirations	.52	.55	.65	.53	—		
Achievement of perceived potential	.55	.63	.64	.32	.53	—	
Rank order of Overall Adjustment Scores	.65	.66	.74	.32	.59	.59	—

[a] *Range of possible item responses:*

Level of school performance: $1 =$ performed extremely well, to $5 =$ performed very poorly

School problems: $1 =$ no problems, or only moderate problems, to $5 =$ two or more major problems (or one major and two or more moderate problems, or four or more moderate problems)

Parental satisfaction with school performance: $1 =$ very satisfied, to $4 =$ very dissatisfied

Amount of education achieved: $5 =$ completed college, to $1 =$ some high school

Fulfillment of parental aspirations: $3 =$ fulfilled aspirations, to $1 =$ fell very short of aspirations

Achievement of perceived potential: $3 =$ measured up to potential, to $1 =$ fell very short of potential

ADOPTEE'S PERSONALITY OVER THE YEARS

We utilized three parent interview items to characterize the adoptee's adjustment with respect to his personality. The first of these concerned the adoptee's general happiness over the years. The parental responses ranged from descriptions of the adoptee as having been generally happy to those describing him as having been generally unhappy. This item correlated with the rankings developed from the Overall Adjustment Scores at a quite substantial level ($r = .54$).

A second item used in the personality adjustment index concerned the parental response to the adoptee's personality over the years, coded response alternatives ranging from "highly pleased" to "highly displeased." The item was significantly correlated with the ranking of the Overall Adjustment Scores ($r = .77$). The third item used in the index concerned the degree to which the adoptee had demonstrated overt personality problems over the years. This item

Table 11-2 / Intercorrelations among items
included in index of personality
adjustment [a]

	Happiness of adoptee	Parental response to personality	Overt personality problems	Rank order of Overall Adjustment Scores
Happiness of adoptee	—			
Parental response to personality	.63	—		
Overt personality problems	.44	.68	—	
Rank order of Overall Adjustment Scores	.54	.77	.70	—

[a] *Range of possible responses:*

Happiness of adoptee: 1 = generally happy, to 3 = generally unhappy

Parental response to adoptee's personality: 1 = highly pleased, to 5 = highly displeased

Overt personality problems: 1 = no overt problems, to 5 = one or more very severe problems, or more than two somewhat severe problems also correlated substantially with the ranked Overall Adjustment Scores ($r = .70$). In addition, all three index items correlated with each other in substantial fashion (running a range from $r = .44$ to $r = .68$).

PAST PARENT-ADOPTEE RELATIONSHIPS

In developing a comprehensive score covering the relationship that had prevailed in the past between the adoptee and his parents, we included items dealing with the general tone of the relationship, the presence and intensity of conflict. Each of these aspects was treated separately for the adoptee-mother and the adoptee-father relationships. Specifically, the index items concerned: the general emotional climate that had prevailed between each parent and the adoptee, the degree to which the adoptee had confided in each parent, the degree of the conflict that had characterized the adoptee's relationship with each parent and, finally, the intensity of any conflict that had taken place. Examination of Table 11–3 reveals that these items were intercorrelated at statistically significant levels, the correlation coefficients ranging from .27 to .82. The strength of many of these correlations is quite striking and suggests two possible explanations. One is that all the items included in the index are relevant to a central characterization of the past parent-adoptee relationship and that these correlations therefore tend to support an assumption of construct validity. A second explanation could be that the strengths of the correlations may perhaps reflect a weakness of post hoc recollections of the parents of past relationships, viz., that the distinction between items dealing with this area may tend to be blurred due to the passage of so many years.

Examination of the association between each of the eight individual items and the ranking of the Overall Adjustment Scores showed them to be quite strong. The correlations ran from .54 to .67.

SOCIAL RELATIONS

One aspect of the adoptee's lifetime adjustment of interest to us was the degree to which his social relationships and overall social situ-

Table 11–3 / Intercorrelations among items included in index of past parent-adoptee relationships ᵃ

	General climate: father and adoptee	General climate: mother and adoptee	Adoptee confiding in mother	Adoptee confiding in father	Conflict between adoptee and father	Conflict between adoptee and mother	Severity of conflict: adoptee and father	Severity of conflict: adoptee and mother	Rank order of Overall Adjustment Score
General climate: father and adoptee	—								
General climate: mother and adoptee	.68	—							
Adoptee confiding in mother	.44	.57	—						
Adoptee confiding in father	.54	.36	.60	—					
Conflict between adoptee and father	.72	.62	.37	.38	—				
Conflict between adoptee and mother	.56	.75	.37	.27	.74	—			
Severity of conflict: adoptee and father	.65	.58	.32	.40	.80	.68	—		
Severity of conflict: adoptee and mother	.52	.69	.32	.24	.73	.82	.82	—	
Rank order of Overall Adjustment Score	.58	.62	.67	.57	.60	.54	.62	.57	—

ᵃ *Range of possible responses:*

General climate between father and adoptee: 1—very happy, to 4—very unhappy
General climate between mother and adoptee: 1—very happy, to 4—very unhappy
Adoptee confiding in mother: 1—very frequently, to 4—never
Adoptee confiding in father: 1—very frequently, to 4—never
Conflict between adoptee and father: 4—very infrequent, to 1—very frequent
Conflict between adoptee and mother: 4—very infrequent, to 1—very frequent
Severity of conflict between adoptee and father: 4—no conflict, to 1—very severe
Severity of conflict between adoptee and mother: 4—no conflict, to 1—very severe

ation had represented a positive factor in his life. To develop an index score in this area we used four items culled from the interviews with the parents. The first item was based upon the adoptee's reported gregariousness, with coded responses ranging from "very gregarious" to "not gregarious at all." This item was strongly correlated with parental reports of the adoptee's happiness in social situations ($r = .43$), was only weakly correlated with the satisfaction expressed by the parents about the adoptee's choice of friends of the same sex ($r = .25$), and was not significantly correlated with the parental reports concerning the adoptee's leisure-time activity problems. More important, the gregariousness item did not correlate significantly with the ranking of the Overall Adjustment Score ($r = .19$), which seems to indicate that gregariousness per se was not the most potent variable in the index.

Table 11–4 / Intercorrelations among items included in index of adoptee adjustment in area of social relations [a]

	Adoptee's gregariousness	Parental satisfaction with own-sex friends	Adoptee's happiness in social situations	Adoptee's leisure-time activity problems	Rank order of Overall Adjustment Scores
Adoptee's gregariousness	—				
Parental satisfaction with adoptee's own-sex friends	.25	—			
Adoptee's happiness in social situations	.43	.76	—		
Adoptee's leisure-time activity problems	.18	.67	.52	—	
Rank order of Overall Adjustment Scores	.19	.69	.64	.54	—

[a] *Range of possible responses:*

Adoptee's gregariousness: 1 = very gregarious, to 4 = not gregarious at all

Parental satisfaction with adoptee's own-sex friends: 1 = very much satisfied, to 4 = very dissatisfied

Adoptee's happiness in social situations: 1 = very great, to 4 = none or almost none

Leisure-time activity problems: 1 = no problems in any of three age segment, to 5 = four or more problems in same age segment or across age segments.

The other items in the social relations index, however, were quite highly intercorrelated and were also strongly correlated with the ranked Overall Adjustment Scores. The range of these latter correlations ran from .54 to .69.

ADOPTEE'S HEALTH

We used two variables to characterize the adoptee's health over the the years. The first described the overall health status on a continuum ranging from "excellent" to "poor." The second variable concerned the degree to which the adoptee had suffered major illnesses and handicaps. The range ran from no such illnesses to three or more. The correlation between these two variables was .32, and the correlations with the ranking of the Overall Adjustment Scores were .19 and .30, respectively (table not presented). It will be seen subsequently that the area of health did not correlate substantially with other major areas of adjustment, although there were some relationships established between overall parent orientations to child rearing and the adoptees' general health status.

PERSONAL AND SOCIAL ADJUSTMENT
OF ADOPTEE

One aspect of the adoptee's overall adjustment that we considered important to measure was the degree to which he had showed major deviancies in his personal and social behavior. Conceptually, these instances of deviancy might have included delinquent behavior as a child, altercations with legal authorities as an adult, divorce, admission to a mental hospital, and the like. We also included in the personal and social adjustment index an item of information secured from the parents concerning the degree to which they had experienced general concern about the adequacy of the adoptee's functioning in this area of his life-space. As might be expected, this latter item correlated significantly ($r = .63$) with the deviancy item. We also found that each of the two items was substantially correlated with the ranking on the Overall Adjustment Score ($r = .77$ for parental concern about the adoptee's limitations as a person and $r = .70$ for the history of social deviances).

CURRENT PARENT-ADOPTEE RELATIONSHIP

The nature and quality of most parent-child relationships change and evolve over the course of the child's development. Consequently, in thinking about the nature of the parent-adoptee relationships in our sample of families, we anticipated that we might conceivably encounter families where the growing-up period had been characterized by much conflict between the adoptee and his parents but where a coming together had been achieved as the adoptee had grown into young adulthood. Of course, the reverse might also have obtained; the adoptee might have gotten along very well with his parents as he grew up but have developed serious conflicts with them when he attempted to disengage himself and become an autonomous person. To assure achieving both perspectives, attention was given in the research interviewing not only to the past parent-adoptee relationship but to the current status of that relationship as well. Three items of information were utilized in developing an index score for this particular area: the

Table 11–5 / Intercorrelations among items included in index of current parent-adoptee relationships [a]

	Closeness of parent-adoptee relationship	Adoptee confiding in parents	Conflict between parents and adoptee	Rank order of Overall Adjustment Scores
Closeness of parent-adoptee relationship	—			
Adoptee confiding in parents	.67	—		
Conflict between parents and adoptee	.66	.43	—	
Rank order of Overall Adjustment Scores	.59	.52	.40	—

[a] *Range of possible responses:*

Closeness of parent-adoptee relationship: 1 = very close, to 5 = very distant

Adoptee confiding in parents: 1 = great deal, to 4 = none

Conflict between parents and adoptee: 4 = no conflict to speak of, to 1 = intense conflict closeness of the present parent-adoptee relationship, the degree to which the adoptee currently confided in his parents, and the amount of conflict currently prevailing between the adoptee and his parents. As can be seen in Table 11–5, these three items were significantly correlated with each other; the coefficients ranged from .43 to .67. We also found that each of the items was significantly correlated with the ranking on the Overall Adjustment Scores.

ECONOMIC ADJUSTMENT

The degree to which the adoptee had been able to achieve economic independence from his parents and to order the economic aspects of his life so as to give evidence of basic competence in this sphere of living was seen by us as an important aspect of the overall outcome of the adoptive experience. Therefore a number of questions concerning economic adjustment were covered in the interview, and these were included in the adjustment index for this area of living. The first item represented the parents' perception of the adequacy of the adoptee's handling of his own finances and the degree to which they were satisfied with this. The second item covered the degree of parental satisfaction with the adoptee's standard of living and, closely related to this, the third item was based upon the parents' reports of the level that had been achieved by the adoptee in his living standards. The coded response alternatives in this last item ranged from "well-to-do" to "serious deprivation." As can be seen from Table 11–6, these items were highly intercorrelated, and each was also substantially correlated with the ranked Overall Adjustment Scores.

HETEROSEXUAL RELATIONS

Apart from assessing the general social situation in which the adoptee had found himself as he grew up, we had additional interest in learning about the adoptee's heterosexual adjustment over the years. To this end, the research interview included material concerning the extent of parent-adoptee conflict over heterosexual relations and was also geared to elicit evidence of parental worry about the adoptee's adjustment in this area. We anticipated encountering a wide range of concerns. One set of parents might have misgivings about the

Table 11–6 / Intercorrelations among items
included in index of adoptee economic
adjustment [a]

	Satisfaction with adoptee's handling of finances	Satisfaction with adoptee's standard of living	Level of adoptee's standard of living	Rank order of Overall Adjustment Scores
Satisfaction with adoptee's handling of finances	—			
Satisfaction with adoptee's standard of living	.79	—		
Level of adoptee's standard of living	.68	.76	—	
Rank order of Overall Adjustment Scores	.65	.59	.59	—

[a] *Range of possible responses:*

Parental satisfaction with adoptee's handling of finances: 1 = very satisfied, to 4 = very dissatisfied

Parental satisfaction with adoptee's current standard of living: 1 = very satisfied, to 4 = very dissatisfied

Level of adoptee's current standard of living: 1 = well-to-do or better, to 6 = suffers serious deprivation

adoptee's adjustment if he had been "acting out" in his behavior by being promiscuous or "going with a fast crowd." On the other hand, another adoptee's parents might be concerned about their child's heterosexual relationships because of an *absence* of any interest in such relationships or because of a basic impairment in his ability to develop relationships with the opposite sex. In the sample studied here, a number of parents were able to express their fear that their child might never marry.

In addition to the items cited above, we included in the heterosexual adjustment index any information relating to marital difficulties encountered by those adoptees who were already married. Table 11–7 sets forth the associations among these items in a correlation matrix. As can be seen, all three index items are intercorrelated at significant levels with the coefficients ranging from .40 to .59. Also, each of the

Table 11–7 / Intercorrelations among items included in index of adoptee heterosexual relations [a]

	Parental concern	Parent-adoptee conflict	Problem in adoptee's marital adjustment	Rank order of Overall Adjustment Scores
Parental concern	—			
Parent-adoptee conflict	.59	—		
Problem in adoptee's marital adjustment	.53	.40	—	
Rank order of Overall Adjustment Scores	.57	.58	.53	—

[a] *Range of possible responses:*

Parental concern with adoptee's heterosexual relationships: 1 = not concerned in any area, to 5 = great concern in two or more areas, or moderate concern in four or more areas

Parent-adoptee conflict over adoptee's heterosexual relationships: 4 = none or hardly none, to 1 = very frequent

Problems experienced by adoptee or by his parents in adoptee adjustment to married or unmarried state: 1 = no problems of any kind experienced or not mentioned, to 4 = one or more severe problems

three component index items is substantially correlated with the ranking on the Overall Adjustment Scores.

PARENTAL DISSATISFACTION WITH
ADOPTION EXPERIENCE

We included as part of our overall assessment of the outcome of the adoptive experience information revealed by the adoptive parents in their research interviews concerning their satisfaction or dissatisfaction with the adoptive experience in its totality. Index scores in this area derived from two types of information: one, the amount of dissatisfaction generally expressed by the parents and, two, the dissatisfaction specifically attributed to adoptive parenthood. The correlation between these two index items was .43. As might be expected, there was a very firm correlation between the amount of dissatisfaction expressed by the parents and the rank ordering of the Overall Adjustment Scores ($r = .77$).

RELATIONSHIP BETWEEN PROFILE AREA SCORES

Table 11–8 is probably the most important table in this chapter. It sets forth the correlations among the various rank ordering of scores developed for the adoptive parents and the adoptees in the life-space areas previously described in this chapter.[3] It also provides a picture of the relationship between each of the eleven index score rankings and the ranking achieved by families on the Overall Adjustment Scores, the measure which comes closest to representing an overall outcome variable. In addition, we have included in Table 11–8 the correlations between each of the area index score rankings and a global score developed from the research interviewers' ratings of the functioning feelings and attitudes of the parents in their roles as adoptive parents. Through a factor analysis of the ratings we found that we could combine all of the interviewers' ratings into a single Global Factor Rating Score.[4] This was seen as a type of parent adjustment measure quite distinct from though certainly directly affecting the several adoptee adjustment scores. Both parent and adoptee measures of course were generated from data derived from the depth interviews with the parents.

Examination of Table 11–8 confirms what the reader may already have suspected from the foregoing discussion of the several area indices. Just as there were very strong associations among the component items of each index, there also appear to be very strong associations among the rank ordering of the composite index scores with two exceptions. The health and talent index scores had very low correlations with rankings of index scores in the other life-space areas. We also found that the ranking of scores relating to talent showed no association with the ranking achieved by families on the Overall Adjustment Scores.[5] However, the health index scores did show a significant correlation with the rank ordered Overall Adjustment Scores ($r = .31$).

The Overall Adjustment measure was most strongly correlated with rankings of (a) the index of adoptee personality adjustment, (b)

Table 11–8 / Intercorrelations of major outcome variables (all index scores, interviewer global factor rating scores, and overall adjustment scores) [a]

	Interviewer Global Factor Rating Score	Index score: educational adjustment	Index score: personality adjustment	Index score: past parent-adoptee relationships	Index score: current parent-adoptee relationships	Index score: economic adjustment	Index score: personal and social adjustment	Index score: parental dissatisfaction with experience	Index score: outstanding talents	Index score: social relations adjustment	Index score: health status	Index score: heterosexual relations adjustment	Rank order of Overall Adjustment Scores
Interviewer global factor rating scores	—												
Index scores:													
Educational adjustment	−.55	—											
Personality adjustment	−.59	.53	—										
Past parent-adoptee relationships	−.64	.58	.59	—									
Current parent-adoptee relationships	−.64	.35	.34	.52	—								
Economic adjustment	−.47	.58	.52	.54	.41	—							
Personal and social adjustment	−.66	.68	.68	.57	.46	.62	—						

Parental dissatisfaction with experience	−.59	.64	.67	.65	.36	.51	.68	—				
Outstanding talents	.05	.02	.04	.00	−.14	−.05	−.10	.05	—			
Social relations adjustment	−.57	.38	.58	.43	.43	.25	.53	.33	.06	—		
Health status	−.10	.12	.28	.13	.08	.05	.04	.15	.01	.05	—	
Heterosexual relations adjustment	−.54	.44	.55	.58	.38	.46	.59	.49	−.12	.50	.12	—
Rank order of Overall Adjustment Scores	−.71	.75	.79	.79	.60	.69	.79	.72	.06	.62	.31	.67	—

[a] High score on interviewer Global Factor Rating Score represents healthy adoptive parent functioning. For rank ordering of index scores in each life space area and ranking of overall adjustment scores, low ranking represents less problematic adjustment.

the index of the nature of the past parent-adoptee relationship, and (c) the index of the personal and social adjustment of the adoptee with respect to the presence of deviant behavior. Each of these three index score rankings showed a correlation of .79 with the rank ordered Overall Adjustment Scores. The ranking of the educational adjustment index scores correlated at .75 with the summated measure, and the ranking of scores of the index depicting parental dissatisfaction with the adoption experience showed a correlation of .72. The ranking of the index of the adoptee's heterosexual relationships produced a correlation of .61 with the ranking Overall Adjustment Scores, and the economic adjustment rankings of the index of scores correlated at .69 with the summary measure. The scores derived from the description of the current parent-adoptee relationship also correlated significantly with the overall ranking ($r = .60$). All in all, one gets an impression that each of these profile areas might well be measuring an overall dimension of adjustment outcome.

The Global Factor Rating Scores developed from the interviewers' ratings showed a similar pattern of association. We note that this global rating score showed a correlation of .71 with the Overall Adjustment Scores indicating that the two measures—one of adoptee adjustment derived from the coded interview responses of parents and the other of adoptee parent functioning derived from the judgment of the caseworker-interviewers—showed considerable agreement. We are of course aware that the high associations may be in part due to the common dependence of both measures upon the verbal reports of the parents. Interestingly, the indices describing the adoptee's talents and his health were the only adjustment indices not correlating significantly with the Global Factor Rating Scores.

Portraying the adoptees

Thus far, we have presented a detailed and rather complex statistical treatment of our measures of adoptee adjustment. Before completing our discussion of this centrally important topic, we wish to "flesh out" the statistical "bones" of our analysis through the use of selected case summaries to portray the outcome of adoption in three of our study families. Our intent is to give the clinically oriented reader a more meaningful sense of the adoptive experience than can be conveyed by the somewhat formidable correlation matrices previously presented. We prepared the following anecdotal material by scanning the data gathered by the various research instruments used in our study. We also listened to tapes of interviews with the parents to secure a more intimate knowedge of each family and adoptee.

The following three portraitures were selected only for illustrative purposes. They are not intended to constitute a representative sampling of the range of adoptee life adjustments reported by our one hundred sets of adoptive parents. Nevertheless, we have included one case from each of the three broad outcome groupings which we identified and discussed in previous chapters, viz., the "low-problem," the "middle-range," and the "high-problem" categories. The case materials have been disguised to some extent in order to protect the confidentiality of the families, but we have tried to do this in such a way as not to distort the families' actual life experiences with adoption.

A "LOW-PROBLEM" ADOPTEE

No human being is totally free of problems, and it is the rare individual who goes through a lifetime without some occasional serious personal problem. The adoptees who showed the highest ranking in adjustment on the various criteria utilized in our outcome indices were those who were functioning quite well in a variety of life-space areas. They showed relatively few signs of problems in their social relationships, school performance, personal adjustment, family relationships, and the like. Within the overall sample of a hundred adoptees these individuals stood out as relatively the "best adjusted" of the total group. However, as a group they were not completely devoid of problems, some of which were quite significant.

ROBERT W. Mr. and Mrs. W. adopted Robert when he was six weeks old. Mrs. W. had had difficulty in carrying a child through term and after several miscarriages and considerable heartache experienced by both parents, they had adopted a child through the agency. The father was a well-established attorney who impressed the interviewer as having a deep affection for his adopted child. He also gave the impression of being "very sensible" in the way in which he discussed the rearing of children. A similar orientation was reflected in Mrs. W.'s discussion. From the parents' reports it was clear that Robert had grown to adulthood without any serious problems. Although he had been a puny, underweight infant when he came into their home, he gradually assumed a robustness which stayed with him into adulthood. One slight source of embarrassment to the parents was the fact that the adoptive mother was 5'0" and the adoptive father was 5'1" whereas the 30-year-old adoptee is 5'11". However, there was some resemblance between the W.s and their son so that it was not always readily apparent to people they encountered that he was not their own biological child. Four years after the adoption of Robert, Mrs. W. became pregnant and succeeded in carrying to full term, and a son was born to them. Robert seemed to accept his brother without too much difficulty, and the brothers grew up with much less friction between them than was characteristic of other families known to the W.s. Robert always felt extremely close to and protective of his brother. The younger one had likewise always shown a strong adulation for his older brother even to the point of pursuing a similar business career.

Robert's health was excellent over the years, with only a few of the usual childhood illnesses reported for him. From a personality standpoint, he was a most outgoing sort of child. This had been characteristic of him throughout his childhood years and he was still "the life of the party." This quality of sociability was very different from the demeanor of his parents. In school, Robert performed on an average level but presented no serious problems. He tended to clown a bit and occasionally teachers had complained about this, but this behavior had never reached serious proportions. He did encounter some difficulty in his first year of college when he became so intrigued with the social life on campus that he failed to study. His grades were poor during his freshman year, and the father was quite angry with him about this. However, in ensuing years his grades improved, and the adoptee succeeded in graduating from college without any great difficulty.

The parents were both quite candid about their sense of disappointment in Robert's decision not to follow his father in a law career. The father felt he could have been of considerable direct help to the adoptee if he had entered the same profession. However, Robert seemed to have a need to find a career of his own, and the father showed some verbal acceptance of his right to do this. He felt that his own feelings in the matter were less important than Robert's. Concerning the child's intelligence, the father was quite candid in saying that Robert was not a person of superior intellect but that he certainly had better than average ability, if he applied himself.

The parents and Robert seemed to lead quite divergent lives with respect to intellectual and cultural pursuits. For the parents, this sphere of interest was an important area of their lives, and they frequently attended concerts and plays or visited museums. Robert, on the other hand, had always showed little interest in this kind of activity and the parents had some sense that in this regard they were living in quite separate worlds. Interestingly, Robert's brother seemed to be closer to Robert in his interests than either child was to the parents. Here again, both parents stressed that they had tried very hard not to convey to Robert any sense of disappointment that he had not pursued their cultural or intellectual interests.

Over the years, the parents found Robert an extremely easy child to discipline. He was described as an amiable youngster who did not seem to need to "kick up his traces" much. Thus, they found it unnecessary to assert strong controls.

The family's handling of revelation was somewhat unusual. They had told Robert that he was adopted on only one occasion, when he was six years old, and this had been done on a planned basis. The parents maintained that they could tell from Robert's reaction that he had absorbed the information but that he didn't care to make this a common theme in their discussions; they therefore had not referred to the topic again. Robert never showed any interest in discussing his adoptive status, never asked any questions about his background, and never told any of his friends that he was adopted. Similarly, the parents revealed the information only to very close relatives and friends and did not readily divulge Robert's adoptive status to outsiders. The interviewer who interviewed these parents wondered whether Robert had sensed that discussion of adoption had been kind of a taboo subject in the family and thus had learned to avoid asking questions. However, the adoptee had not seemed to suffer from a strain as a result of this. He had told his wife he was adopted and his brother was also aware of this.

From a personality standpoint, Robert did not present any serious problems over the years. Generally, he was considered to be a happy child. The mother, however, indicated that as Robert grew up he seemed to be a slightly more tense child than his brother. However, he showed no serious problems such as speech disturbances, sleep disturbances, phobia, restlessness, excessive fears, or anxieties. Neither did he suffer from any disorders which might be considered to be of a psychosomatic nature.

As an adult, Robert has been moderately successful in the business world and has earned a quite satisfactory income. He is happily married, and the parents expressed warmth about his wife and the grandchildren. They felt he has a happy family life and is a very loving and devoted father to his children. Robert has kept in contact with his parents by telephone several times a week and has confided in them about personal matters. He has not, however, shown himself to be overly dependent upon them. The parents visit Robert and his wife on a weekly basis, but this is done by invitation. They felt that Robert does not extend these invitations only as a matter of form but rather because he actually wants them to visit, as he enjoys their company. Looking back over the thirty years of experience with Robert, both parents expressed a feeling of having been very blessed by being able to have such a child in their home, and they felt very good about his current adjustment.

A "MIDDLE-RANGE" ADOPTEE

The adoptees who fell within the middle-range grouping when the sample was rank-ordered on the basis of our eleven outcome indices displayed disparate qualities. For some, there was apparently a mixed kind of life adjustment in which there was a high level of performance in some life-space areas with marked impairment revealed in other areas of living. In other cases, it became clear that the adoptee had suffered considerable problems while growing up but had somehow managed to achieve an even keel later in life. The reader will recall that the middle-range group showed fairly marked similarity to the low-problem adoptees on some measures but at the same time were more comparable to the high-problem group on others.

SALLY R. Mr. and Mrs. R. adopted Sally when she was almost two years old. She had been cared for in a large institution, and they were struck by her forlorn appearance when they first met her. However, they were very taken with her and found her to be a very appealing child. They explained that they had not adopted any other children because the family was faced with the dependency of Mrs. R.'s mother and they felt that they could not afford a larger family because of their economic circumstances. The parents spoke in glowing terms about Sally and described her as a very good child who posed no problems in discipline throughout her childhood years. There never was an easier child! However, they did feel that as a youngster she reflected some of the difficulty that might face any child who had been in an institution. They noted that the child would do as she was told in a most docile manner. For example, if she was told to go to the bathroom, she would stay there unless she was told to come out. Their feeling had been that she was just too good.

Sally enjoyed good health all of her life and had only occasional child-hood diseases. In school, she started out as an average student, but by the time she reached high school her performance was excellent and she graduated with some honors. However, the parents always worried because Sally tended to play herself down and to express discomfort with the receipt of awards. Also, while she did well in school they noted that she seemed to get no real enjoyment out of her school experience. As a matter of fact, they were particularly concerned that she had shown such little enthusiasm for most of the things that she undertook. Despite this, Sally succeeded in graduating from college and went on to secure a master's degree in science. She was considered quite gifted by her professors and was able to obtain a creative job as a research biologist. Mr. and Mrs. R. took particular pride in Sally's high level of achievement and excellent work history. She was well respected at her place of employment and they regarded her as a credit to them in this respect.

As Sally grew up, she was only slightly gregarious and had but a few friends, and those she did have were not particularly close. Mr. and Mrs. R. both felt that the adoptee's social situation as she grew up was not a particularly happy one. Sally seemed uncomfortable with strangers and was even shy and aloof with Mr. R.'s family whose members were warm, outgoing people. They could not account for this quality in her except to say that she never seemed to be particularly comfort-able with the fact that she was adopted. She had "always" known about her adoptive status and they had tried to tell her about this in a natural way. Yet, there were several occasions on which she expressed unhappiness about it, and while she did not frequently talk about being adopted, the parents always sensed that it was something that rankled her.

With respect to Sally's personality, the parents felt she was a moder-ately happy child who was of no trouble to anyone. However, she did seem to have difficulty in communicating and in showing her feelings. Even to them, she seemed quite aloof and lacked warmth. This was a source of some hurt to the parents but they tried to overlook it. They realized that basically Sally was a very shy girl and her inability to ex-press affection was a deeply engraved part of her make-up. Also, she was a girl with a number of sensitivities. For example, she suffered from several phobias, including an inability to have anyone discuss disease or illness in front of her. Most of her leisure time was spent in reading scientific textbooks and there was little room for close involve-ment with friends.

The greatest source of pain for Mr. and Mrs. R. in contemplating Sally's life was the fact that she had married a young man who was obviously not suited for her. The adoptive parents were very unhappy when she became involved in a fairly close courtship with him, since they felt that she had had no experience with boys upon which to base her decision to marry. While they did not oppose the marriage, they nevertheless told Sally that they thought she ought to give it more thought. Unfortunately, Sally had been so anxious to get married that she went ahead with it. The result was disastrous. After several years, she came to her parents and told them of her misery in the marriage. At the time of the research interview, Sally was suing for divorce and was living with her parents. She seemed somewhat disillusioned about marriage, but the parents hoped that she had learned from the experience and that perhaps she would meet a more suitable man in the future. Meanwhile, they find her somewhat detached and even less communicative than usual. They were very thankful however that she is happy with her job and that this seemed to keep her going.

Despite the unfortunate marital situation that had afflicted Sally, Mr. and Mrs. R. felt that the adoption represented a wonderful aspect of their lives. Without Sally they would be a childless couple and this would mean that life would have little joy for them. In her quiet way, Sally is attached to them and has feeling for them even though she cannot show this openly. She is a beautiful girl and capable in many ways, even though there is an inner core to her that they have never been able to reach.

A "HIGH-PROBLEM" ADOPTEE

Among the adoptees who were classified in the most problematic outcome category, several revealed a rather high degree and quality of pathology. It would be well to keep in mind the fact that, in the absence of a contrast group of nonadopted individuals of similar backgrounds, we are not in a position to make a judgment about whether our sample was unusual with respect to the maladjustment revealed. Moreover, we do know that a major survey of the mental health of residents of one area in New York City revealed a substantially high proportion of individuals who were regarded as impaired in their personal and social functioning.[6]

ROBERT A. When Mrs. A. was asked whether there was anything in particular she would like to say about her adoptive experience, she replied, "I don't believe so except that it has been as rewarding and heartbreaking as having an own child." The A.'s adopted Bobby when their own child died at age six. Mrs. A. and her husband conceded that, in a way, it may have been unfortunate for Bobby to have come into their home because there was always the cloud hanging over the family that had been created by the death of the first child. However, they knew they had very much wanted him and they responded to him almost immediately. Mr. A. noted that perhaps as a result of the loss of the first child, they became much too oversolicitous of Bobby; they constantly lived under the fear that something might happen to him. As it turned out, Bobby was actually a healthy child, but his personal and social adjustment over the years was an unremitting source of tremendous unhappiness for his parents.

Bobby was a bed-wetter until he was eight years old. During the early period of his life, he had been cared for by a nurse who had been overly attached to him. Mrs. A. was employed part-time, and the child was left in the care of the nurse for a good part of the day from the time he came into the home at one year of age until the nurse left, when he was eight. The parents found it remarkable that he had stopped bed-wetting the night she had left. Later, friends told Mrs. A. that the nurse had babied Bobby too much. Mrs. A. thought that perhaps this earlier experience with an overstimulating nurse and with parents who had suffered the loss of an own child perhaps accounted for Bobby's horrendous academic performance over the years. He performed very poorly almost from the beginning of his entrance into school, appearing to have low motivation to learn and seeming almost totally unable to get along with friends. He was placed in a number of private schools and, while he managed to secure a high school diploma, his performance was always extremely marginal. Bobby was always fully aware of the extent to which he had failed to meet his own and his parents' expectations. Indeed, he seemed to suffer almost absolute despair about his own performance and would vacillate between empty boasting to other children about what he could do in the way of schoolwork, sports, and other activities and a kind of despondency about his actual performance.

Throughout most of Bobby's childhood, he failed to make friends because other children became easily antagonized by his bragging and his failure to follow through on his claims. During school, they also became antagonized because Bobby pretended to have a variety of sexual experiences without any apparent real foundation to his stories. At one point, the stories he told became so stimulating to the other boys that he was dropped from school for a period.

Bobby received psychiatric treatment at his own request for a period of about four months. The parents were not sure what Bobby had gained from the experience because his interviews with the psychiatrist were confidential. They thought he had showed some slight improvement for a time but then had reverted back to his old behavior. From the standpoint of his general personality, Bobby was characteristically an unhappy child constantly in conflict with himself and always a source of disappointment to his family.

On a reality basis, Bobby had experienced very few meaningful heterosexual relationships while in school. However, while working in a supermarket he became attached to a fellow employee and had sexual relations with her. The young lady became pregnant and after some consideration the young couple decided to marry. They now have two children and seem happy together, according to Mr. A. However, the parents are continuously under pressure to provide a regular economic subsidy to Bobby because of the low level of his employment. Since high school, Bobby has had a series of unskilled jobs and he is very conscious of the marked contrast between his own mode of earning a living and his father's professional status. In addition to their concern about the low level of his earnings, Mr. and Mrs. A. are also concerned because Bobby often squanders money upon things which are unnecessary, e.g., an expensive camera, putting himself in a financial situation which requires additional support from them. This particularly irritates Mr. A. who worries about the time when he will have to retire and will not be able to support Bobby. He believes Bobby's demands for financial support go well beyond what any child has a right to expect from his parents.

Despite the considerable pain and disappointment the parents have suffered from their experience with Bobby, they remain quite attached to him as a person and will go out of their way to see him fairly regularly. By contrast, they feel he is somewhat aloof from them and does not show as much desire as they to retain a sense of closeness.

Mr. and Mrs. A. feel that Bobby is very slowly emerging as a more mature person. Although he is already twenty-five, they feel that he will eventually attempt to obtain specialized training by going to college at night. The marriage constitutes a basic support for him at the present time. While his wife had been considerably deprived as a child, she is very devoted and emotionally supporting to him. Also, he seems to be responding very positively to parenthood.

The parents expressed the view that they were thankful for each day that went by without a report of some catastrophe happening to Bobby.

Summary

By way of summary, it should be pointed out that we have described here the construction of outcome measures based upon a wide array of specific behaviors and attitudes reported by the adoptive parents about their children. These have been used to develop a composite overall score based upon the summation of the index scores derived from eleven areas of adoptive experience, with particular focus upon the adjustment of the adopted child.

Generally, we can report that each index area tended to include items that were significantly correlated with each other and with the overall summary measure, the ranked Overall Adjustment Score. Similarly, we found that scores developed for each index area tended to be significantly correlated with the other index area scores with the exception of those dealing with the adoptee's health and those reflecting evidence of outstanding talent. As would be expected on the basis of what was found for the items, most of the index area scores were significantly correlated with the summary measure.

Having set forth the manner in which we constructed the outcome scores, we then offered three case summaries to illustrate the adjustment of adoptees classified in each of the three outcome groupings used in our earlier descriptive chapters.

twelve / Correlates of outcome: background variables

THE SINGLE most important question to which any follow-up study addresses itself is: How have the subjects turned out? Given their characteristics at the outset of the experience, and taking into consideration the nature and quality of that experience, what have been the results? How have the subjects fared in the various crucial and inter-related aspects of their lives? These have been the central questions for which we have sought answers. They were responsible for the decision of the financing foundation to support the investigation, they piqued the interest of the two authors, they were most instrumental in stimulating the participation and full cooperation of the four agencies involved, and they are undoubtedly of pivotal concern to the adoption field as a whole.

The conceptualization of outcome and the methods used for measuring it have been discussed in detail in the preceding chapter. In other chapters, we have descriptively presented the study's findings with respect to the three groupings of outcome based upon the rank-ordering of adoptees in various life-space areas. In this and the two succeeding chapters, we shall examine the factors that were associated with the kinds of adjustment evidenced by the adoptees. As in preceding chapters, we shall define adjustment in terms of the presence or absence of problems over the years in the adoptees' major life-space areas. However, rather than dividing the one hundred adoptees into three discrete groupings as we did in previous chapters, we shall, with the use of the statistical techniques of correlational analysis,[1] conceive adjustment as a series of continuous variables, one for each life-space area, extending from good performance in an area to problematic behavior. Utilizing this conception of outcome we will explore the degree to which independent and intervening variables are related to the measure of adjustment in each life-space area and with respect to the Rank Order of Overall Adjustment Scores, which is our most significant adjustment measure.

The interrelationships among the eleven outcome indices, the overall outcome measure, and the interviewer rating factor have already been discussed in Chapter XI. The present chapter will be concerned with the relationships between these outcome variables and the background variables which characterized both the adoptees and the adoptive parents at the inception of their lives as adoptive families. The next chapter will address itself to the relationships between the outcome measures and the manner in which the adoptive parents communicated the fact of adoption to their children. Finally, in Chapter XIV we shall examine the connections between the outcome variables and the child-rearing practices reported by the parents and other environmental influences to which the adoptees were subjected as they grew from infants to young adults.

The placing agency

In previous chapters we have seen that twenty-five couples who adopted through each of the four participating agencies could be distinguished from one another as aggregate groups with regard to (a) certain of the characteristics they had brought to the adoption experience, (b) some of the child-rearing practices they had employed, (c)

Table 12–1 / Correlations [a] of agency source of adoption [b] with outcome variables [c] and with global interviewer rating factor [a]

	CORRELATIONS			
VARIABLE	CATHOLIC HOME BUREAU	CHAPIN NURSERY/ SPENCE ALUMNAE	FREE SYNAGOGUE COMMITTEE	STATE CHARITIES AID
RANK ORDERING OF OVERALL ADJUSTMENT SCORES	09	−08	−16	15
RANKING OF INDEX SCORES RE:				
Educational adjustment	05	00	06	02
Personality adjustment	15	−11	−21 *	17
Past parent-adoptee relationships	06	−03	−24 *	21 *
Current parent-adoptee relationship	09	−11	−14	15
Economic adjustment	01	−04	−02	05
Personal and social adjustment	14	−04	−14	05
Social relations	24 *	−10	−24 *	10
Heterosexual relationships	09	−12	−27 **	30 **
Health	−11	10	−12	13
Talents	01	−04	08	−06
Parental dissatisfaction	07	−05	−13	01
GLOBAL INTERVIEWER RATING FACTOR	−14	−04	35 **	−17

* Significant: $p < .05.$ ** Significant: $p < .01.$

[a] Decimal points omitted for this and all following tables in present chapter.

[b] For purpose of correlational analysis, four contrived variables were created so that each agency was coded as follows: 0 = family adopted through agency; 1 = family did not adopt through agency.

[c] For this and all following tables in present chapter, low score = low-problem adjustment.

their method of imparting to the adoptees the knowledge that they had been adopted, and (d) the environmental influences which had been exerted upon the adoptees over the years. Looking at our data from the vantage point of correlational analysis we find also that, with regard to the adoptees' life adjustment, the four subgroups of families reveal somewhat different patterns.[2] As we can see from Table 12–1, the adoptees placed by the Free Synagogue Committee emerged with clearly more problematic outcomes than those placed by any of the other three agencies. They showed a greater tendency to have encountered personality problems over the years; to have experienced difficulties in their past and current heterosexual relationships; to have met with negative experiences in their social relationships as they grew up; and to have had more turbulent and less satisfactory relationships with their adoptive parents in the past. It is not surprising therefore that the caseworker-interviewers tended to give these families more negative ratings than were assigned to families adopting through the other three agencies.

By contrast, we observe that the adoptees placed by State Charities Aid Association and Catholic Home Bureau achieved less problematic life adjustments when contrasted with other agency families. Children placed by the former agency were likely to be freer of problems in the heterosexual sphere and to have enjoyed more positive relationships with their adoptive parents through their growing-up years as compared with all the other adoptees. They also showed some tendency to have manifested fewer personality problems over the years. In view of this constellation of findings, it is again not unexpected that State Charities Aid families were somewhat more apt to have received more positive interviewer ratings.

Catholic Home Bureau adoptees tended to show, in more distinctive fashion than those from other agencies, a strong positive adjustment in the area of social relations. Also, there were no life-space areas where these adoptees, as a group, were reported to have encountered more severe problems to a statistically significant degree than adoptees of the other three agencies. Finally, we see that the Chapin Nursery/Spence Alumnae adoptees did not, on a comparative basis, manifest either more problematic or less problematic adjustments in any outcome area. However, an examination of the correlation coefficients in that agency's column of Table 12–1 does show a slight tendency in the direction of problematic adjustment.

We examined further the above pattern of relationships between outcome and identification of the agency through which adoption was arranged by controlling for the possible effect of the adoptive couples' socioeconomic status (SES) on two of these relationships. We chose for this purpose the correlations between agency of placement and (a) the index of the adoptees' personality adjustment, and (b) the global interviewer rating factor, the only two outcome variables strongly related to SES.

The resulting partial correlations [3] reveal that the socioeconomic status of the adoptive parents exerted differential effects upon the two correlations, depending upon which relationship and which set of agency adoptive parents was involved. For Catholic Home Bureau families, the strength of both relationships was noticeably reduced, which indicates that the original correlations had to a great extent been the function of the variable of SES. The same general pattern also held for the Free Synagogue Committee families although the influence of socioeconomic factors was not as great. Nonetheless, we see that SES accounted for enough of the original correlation between adoption through that agency and the emergence of personality problems in its adoptees to raise question whether chance factors might not have accounted for the association. For Chapin Nursery/Spence Alumnae and State Charities Aid families, the effect of introducing SES as a control variable was not as clear-cut: in the agency-interviewer rating relationship both correlations were slightly strengthened while in the agency-personality adjustment relationship they were slightly weakened.

Adoptee characteristics

SEX

It appears that the sex of our adoptive subjects was only moderately related to their life adjustment over the years. In general, however, boys fared less well than did girls, particularly in the area of education.[4] The girls also showed some tendency, though not a strong one, to be freer of personality problems over the years. Admittedly, this is fairly sparse evidence of a healthier adjustment on the part of female adoptees, but the adoptive parents nevertheless appear to have had some differential reaction to their overall adoption experience related to the sex of the child they took into their homes. We found some evidence of a relationship between the adoptee being a girl and the adoptive parents expressing less dissatisfaction with their adoptive experience.

AGE AT PLACEMENT

In recent years, there has been a strong emphasis in the adoption field upon early placement of infants.[5] Stress has been placed upon the potential adverse effects of delayed permanent placement, primarily with respect to the trauma associated with multiple placements and repeated separation from the mother figure.[6] Moreover, at least one child development researcher has gone further. Yarrow [7] hypothesizes that a child may well be permanently impaired in his capacity to establish relationships if: (a) separation from the mother has occurred before the child has been able to establish a stable affectional relationship with her, and if (b) the child subsequently does not have the opportunity to experience intimate personal relationships during what Yarrow considers a critical period of from approximately six months to two years of age.

In our study, all adoptees had been placed in their adoptive homes by the age of three. Thus, although we had no basis for comparing outcomes of unusually late placement with those of early placement, we did have a fairly good spread of adoptees throughout the first three-year period of their lives, a period encompassing the critical phase identified by Yarrow. We therefore undertook to examine some of the differences in adjustment associated with placement in very early infancy as compared with placement at a somewhat later stage.

In the light of the above writings, we expected that children placed when older would be more likely to have evidenced adjustment difficulties over the years. However, our initial findings pointed in the opposite direction. The most clear-cut was the relationship between age at placement and subsequent adjustment in the area of social relationships. Where we had anticipated that placement at an older age would be associated with less favorable outcome, we found that the older the adoptee when placed, the fewer problems he was likely to have encountered in his social relationships over the years. Moreover, couples receiving older children were somewhat more apt to receive positive ratings by the interviewers. Additional evidences of a tendency toward a more low-problem adjustment by these children, while not achieving statistical significance, are to be seen in Table 12–2.

We discovered, however, that the association between social relationship adjustment and age at placement could be partly explained by the fact of adoptive placement through Catholic Home Bureau and the Free Synagogue Committee. Both were rather strongly associated with outcome in the area of social relationships, and placement through the former agency was also related to older age at placement, as we saw in Chapter VI. When we controlled for the influence of

Table 12–2 / Correlations of age of adoptee at placement [a] *with outcome variables and with global interviewer rating factor*

VARIABLE	CORRELATION
RANK ORDERING OF OVERALL ADJUSTMENT SCORES	−07
RANKING OF INDEX SCORES RE:	
Education adjustment	05
Personality adjustment	−12
Past parent-adoptee relationships	−11
Current parent-adoptee relationships	−13
Economic adjustment	−05
Personal and social adjustment	−04
Social relations	−21 *
Heterosexual relationships	−12
Health	15
Talents	00
Parental dissatisfaction	−06
GLOBAL INTERVIEWER RATING FACTOR	16

* Significant: $p < .05$. [a] Low score = early age.

adoption through each of the two agencies, the partial correlations were markedly lower than the original one and were no longer significant.[8] Controlling for adoption through Chapin Nursery/Spence Alumnae and State Charities Aid, however, did not alter the correlation materially. In other words, our initial finding could be attributed to the influence of placement through two of the four agencies. Once this influence had been taken into account, the finding was modified: for our group of adoptees there was substantively a weak relationship between age at placement and later adjustment in the sphere of social relationships.

NUMBER OF PREADOPTIVE PLACEMENTS

In a related area, we uncovered a finding which at first was surprising. Our data revealed that the number of different temporary placements experienced by the adoptees prior to their adoption seemed to bear very little relationship to their subsequent life adjustment. Only a poorer health history over the years and the absence of outstanding talents were at all related with frequent preadoptive placements and then not very strongly.[9] The reader will also recall from Chapter XI that it was precisely these two outcome profiles which proved most weakly correlated with the others in the analysis of the associations among outcome indices.

This fact serves only to underscore the apparently minimal role played by multiple preadoptive moves and placements in the subsequent overall adjustment of our one hundred adoptees. On its face, such a finding appears to conflict with the assumptions and hypotheses regarding the potential adverse effect of multiple placements cited above. However, in evaluating this finding, it is essential for the reader to recall the limited nature of our basic data concerning the preadoptive placements of our sample of adoptees. Virtually no information was available regarding the circumstances under which such placements occurred, the quality of the child's relationship with the mothering person prior to each placement, or the nature and quality of the experiences encountered by the child immediately subsequent to separation from the mothering person.

These are lacunae of considerable importance when it comes to assessing the meaning of findings relating the number of placements to subsequent adjustment. In recent years, a considerable body of literature has been developed stressing the potential confounding of the phenomena of maternal separation, maternal deprivation, and multiple mothering and their impact upon the very young child.[10] Yarrow in particular has emphasized this point and called attention to the weakness of past oversimplified formulations of the relationship between separation from the mother and its consequences.[11] He has identified at least a dozen different types of separation experiences, each of which would presumably have a different potential for adverse effects upon the child,[12] and he has underscored the importance of the very modifying factors in separation about which we had a paucity of data in our study.[13]

While these writings would seem to indicate that our findings on this topic should be viewed as suggestive rather than definitive, we believe that they do warrant some serious consideration. Notwithstanding the weakness of our data, the failure to find the theoretically predicted relationship between the number of preadoptive placements a child may have experienced and his subsequent life adjustment still constitutes a challenge to the theory. Put another way, it is noteworthy that there were children in our sample who had experienced a number of preadoptive placements and who nevertheless apparently showed good adjustments in their growing years.

Characteristics of adoptive parents and adoptive home

OTHER CHILDREN IN THE ADOPTIVE FAMILY

Our analysis revealed no significant relationships between outcome and the arrival in the home of other biological or adopted children *following* our subjects' placement. We did find, however, that there was a relationship between the adoptees' adjustment and the presence or absence of other children *already in the adoptive home* at the time the adoptees were placed.[14] Children who entered families containing one or more other children tended to fare better than did adoptees placed with childless couples. They were more apt, for example, to have performed better in school, and they were also somewhat more likely to have been freer of personal and social adjustment problems over the years. In addition, their current relationships with their adoptive parents tended to be more positive and less turbulent than the parent-adoptee relationships experienced by their counterparts in previously childless homes. Consonant with these findings, adoptive parents who had had other children prior to adopting were prone to express relatively little dissatisfaction with their adoptive experience as compared with couples whose first child was the adoptee covered in our study. Likewise, we see in Table 12-3 that the study interviewers were more apt to assign positive ratings to the families where the adoptee was not the first child in his family.

Our data provide no basis for explaining the general direction of these findings, but we can suggest one tentative hypothesis. Couples

Table 12-3 / Correlations of prior children in the adoptive home [a] *with outcome variables and with global interviewer rating factor*

VARIABLE	CORRELATION
RANK ORDERING OF OVERALL ADJUSTMENT SCORES	−15
RANKING OF INDEX SCORES RE:	
Educational adjustment	−21 *
Personality adjustment	−04
Past parent-adoptee relationships	−12
Current parent-adoptee relationships	−16
Economic adjustment	−11
Personal and social adjustment	−18
Social relations	02
Heterosexual relationships	−12
Health	−08
Talents	06
Parental dissatisfaction	−18
GLOBAL INTERVIEWER RATING FACTOR	23 *

* Significant: $p < .05$.

[a] Dichotomized for purposes of correlational analysis: $0 = $ no prior children; $1 = 1$ or more siblings.

experienced in raising one or more children had had the opportunity not afforded to childless couples "to learn the ropes" and to become more relaxed and comfortable in the complicated task of child rearing. Greater skill and less anxiety in the parent role could be expected, in general, to have created a favorable family climate, one more conducive to minimizing developmental problems than would ordinarily be found in a home previously devoid of children. In the latter family the adoptive parents would have to experience the inevitable trials and errors of raising a first child, together with the accompanying tensions and anxieties which could possibly be augmented by unresolved parental conflicts concerning their entitlement to their child. It would therefore seem reasonable to expect that adoptees placed with more experienced parents might tend to display fewer adjustment problems than would their counterparts placed with "inexperienced" parents. This is, of course, a phenomenon with which a great many parents of second and third biological children are also quite familiar.

SEX PREFERENCE

We found that our adoptive parents' reported desire for a boy or girl at the time they applied for a child yielded relatively limited insights into the subsequent adjustment of the adoptees. No significant relationships existed between the parents' expressed preference for a girl and the outcome in any of the life-space areas. Further, there were only a few noteworthy outcome correlates of expressed preference for a boy, all only moderately strong. Where adoptive couples requested male children at application, the adoptees tended to have encountered problems in their educational pursuits and were likely to be experiencing a less than satisfactory economic adjustment at the time our study got under way. Their adoptive parents were also somewhat inclined in their research interviews to express dissatisfaction with the entire adoption experience.

These findings are perhaps most easily explained by two other findings presented earlier in this report. In Chapter VI we noted a strong relationship between expressed sex preference and the sex of the child placed. This means that a couple who asked for a boy tended to get a boy. Then, in a preceding section of the present chapter, we saw that boys tended to experience a somewhat more problematic adjustment than girls, particularly with regard to their functioning in the educational sector of their life-space. Also, the adoptive parents of boys were apt to be more dissatisfied with their experience in adoption. These findings clearly parallel those just presented above. In other words, the negative outcome correlates of expressed preference for a boy reflect the fact that applicants who desired male children tended to receive them and that boys in actuality were likely to make less favorable life adjustments.

AGE PREFERENCE

Whether a prospective adoptive couple did or did not request an infant or baby at the time of application appears to have been at least somewhat predictive of how the child they received would fare in three life-space areas. Where couples had expressed a preference for a very young child, the adoptee tended to encounter problems in his heterosexual relationships over the years, to be experiencing difficulties in his relationship with his adoptive parents at the time our study took place, and to be having some trouble in his current economic adjustment. Concomitantly, the study interviewers showed some inclination to rate such families at the less positive end of the rating scale.

These findings are not totally unexpected since the age preference of adoptive applicants was moderately strongly related to the actual age of the children they received ($r = .35$), and we have seen earlier in this chapter that the adjustment of children placed at an older age tended to be somewhat less problematic than the adjustment of children adopted when younger. In that instance, we discovered that adoption through two of the four agencies helped to account in large measure for the original perplexing finding. This was not true, however, in the present instance. Controlling for the effect of placement by each of the four agencies did not appreciably affect the magnitude of any of the three original noteworthy correlations; neither did using the adoptive parents' socioeconomic status as a control variable. In other words, our findings in this area cannot be attributed to the influence of either of these background variables. We must therefore conclude that the observed associations between outcome and the adop-

Table 12-4 / Correlations of age preference of adoptive parents [a] *with outcome variables and with global interviewer rating factor*

VARIABLE	CORRELATION
RANK ORDERING OF OVERALL ADJUSTMENT SCORES	−14
RANKING OF INDEX SCORES RE:	
Educational adjustment	−14
Personality adjustment	−09
Past parent-adoptee relationships	−09
Current parent-adoptee relationships	−20 *
Economic adjustment	−19
Personal and social adjustment	−06
Social relations	−10
Heterosexual relationships	−23 *
Health	−04
Talents	01
Parental dissatisfaction	−03
GLOBAL INTERVIEWER RATING FACTOR	16

* Significant: $p < .05$.
[a] Dichotomized for purposes of correlational analysis: 0 = preference for infant and baby; 1 = all other categories of response.

tive parents' age preference at application are substantive in nature and/or that they are a function of still other unidentified independent or intervening variables.

AGE OF ADOPTIVE PARENTS AT APPLICATION

We discovered that the age of the adoptive couple at the inception of the adoption process was relatively insignificant in providing leads for understanding the adoptees' subsequent life adjustment. No important linkages exist between the age of the adoptive mother at application and adoptee outcome in any life-space area. Moreover, only two of these areas are significantly correlated with the adoptive father's age when he first applied to the agency for a child. The older he was at that time, the better the adoptee's economic adjustment tended to be at the point that our study was launched ($r = -.20$), and the less problematic his heterosexual adjustment was apt to be over the years ($r = -.20$).

Our data offer no clear explanation for either of these findings. We initially hypothesized that the first of the two might be a function of the adoptive family's socioeconomic status, but this proved not to be so.[15]

SOCIOECONOMIC STATUS (SES)
OF ADOPTIVE PARENTS

When we examine the outcome of the adoptive experiences of our study families with reference to the socioeconomic status of these families an interesting fact emerges. The life adjustment of the adoptee is only weakly related to the SES of the adoptive parents. Only two of the correlations in Table 12-5 achieve statistical significance: children raised in higher social class families tended to encounter more personality problems over the years than did their lower social class counterparts, and study interviewers were rather clearly predisposed to assign negative rather than positive ratings to higher SES families. Two additional correlations approach but do not achieve statistical significance: the social relations of higher SES adoptees were somewhat likely to be more problematical in nature, and adoptive parents of higher socioeconomic standing were more inclined than their lower SES counterparts to express dissatisfaction with their adoptive experience.

The comparative paucity of firm relationships between socioeconomic level and the adoptees' adjustment in various life-space areas is rather surprising in view of the quite strong associations between SES and our background variables noted in Chapter VI, and between SES and several child-rearing, revelation, and environmental variables discussed in Chapter IX. Moreover, the findings which do emerge are somewhat inconclusive in that they stem partly from the interaction of SES and other variables. When we controlled for the influence of adoption through Catholic Home Bureau and the Free Synagogue Committee, the strength of the relationship between SES and personality adjustment of the adoptees was somewhat diminished and the association between SES and the adoptees' social relationship adjust-

Table 12–5 / Correlations of adoptive parents'
socioeconomic status (SES) [a] with outcome
variables and with global interviewer
rating factor

VARIABLE	CORRELATION
RANK ORDERING OF OVERALL ADJUSTMENT SCORES	09
RANKING OF INDEX SCORES RE:	
Educational adjustment	01
Personality adjustment	24 *
Past parent-adoptee relationships	15
Current parent-adoptee relationships	12
Economic adjustment	01
Personal and social adjustment	12
Social relations	17
Heterosexual relationships	09
Health	−13
Talents	−13
Parental dissatisfaction	17
GLOBAL INTERVIEWER RATING FACTOR	−27 **

* Significant: $p < .05$. ** Significant: $p < .01$.
[a] High score = high SES.

ment was quite markedly reduced.[16] Accounting for the effect of
adoption through Chapin Nursery/Spence Alumnae and State Charities Aid, however, produced virtually no change in the original correlation.

When agency is used as a control variable in exploring the relationship between SES and interviewer ratings, a somewhat different
picture emerges.[17] The variable of adoption through the Free Synagogue Committee originally obscured the actual strength of the association. When the influence of that variable was removed, the magnitude of the negative relationship between SES and interviewer ratings
became much more apparent.[18] By contrast, controlling for adoption
through Catholic Home Bureau somewhat weakened this relationship
though it remained essentially a strong one. Once again, accounting
for the effect of placement by Chapin Nursery/Spence Alumnae and

State Charities Aid failed to materially alter the correlation involved. Thus, we see that placement through each of the four participating agencies differentially affected the relationship between the adoptive parents' socioeconomic status and the adoptees' adjustment in various sectors of their life space. All in all, however, we believe that the data contained in Table 12–5 leads to the conclusion that this relationship was not, in any real sense, a major one.

Summary

In this chapter, we have examined the associations between the major background variables employed in our study and the adoptees' subsequent life adjustment. In the main, our findings were not very striking, but there were some noteworthy exceptions. We saw, for example, that the agency through which the adoption took place was rather strongly linked to outcome. By contrast, we noted that the number of temporary preadoptive placements experienced by an adoptee bore very little relation to his subsequent life adjustment. We observed that adoptees placed with families already containing one or more children were likely over the years to be freer of problems in some life-space areas than were children placed with childless couples. Although sex preference of adoptive applicants was only weakly associated with adoptee outcome, their expressed desire for an infant or baby appeared to have somewhat more clear-cut implications for the eventual adjustment of the adoptee. Finally, and somewhat surprisingly in view of other findings, we discovered that the socioeconomic level of the adoptive parents was but a weak indicator of how adoptees would tend to fare in later years.

thirteen | Correlates of outcome:
revelation of adoptive status

NO FACET OF this investigation has commanded greater interest than the nature of the relationship between the adoptive parents' handling of the topic of adoptive status and the adoptees' subsequent life adjustment. As we saw in Chapter VII, there is not full consensus among those working in the field of adoption concerning the optimal timing and content of the initial revelation to the adoptee of his status. There is also controversy concerning the desirable frequency of subsequent discussion about the adoptee's nonbiological relationship to his adoptive parents. To the extent that the present study might disclose indications of a differential impact of various approaches to revelation upon the adoptee's later functioning in major life-space areas, additional evidence could be brought to bear upon consideration of the above issues.

For this reason, one of the most noteworthy findings in the analysis of our data was the paucity of statistically significant correlations between the adjustment of the adoptees and the handling of revelation by our one hundred study families. Only one aspect of such handling, viz., the adoptee's desire to learn more about his biological parents, was significantly associated with subsequent adjustment. And as we shall see, the substantive significance of even this finding is reduced by a limitation of the data upon which it is based. Other facets of the adoptive parents' handling of revelation fail, in the main, to achieve statistically significant associations with our outcome measures. However, there emerge some interesting and suggestive associations which we do not believe should be overlooked since they offer avenues for further exploration.

The initial revelation

SOURCE

In preparation of our data for correlational analysis, the responses concerning the source of the adoptees' initial information about their adoptive status were dichotomized: those indicating that the adoptee had initially been given this information by his adoptive parents were distinguished from all other responses. As we saw in Chapter VII, the former category comprised more than four-fifths (83 percent) of our study families. More important, the proportions were almost identical for all three outcome groups. In other words, initial revelation by the adoptive parents had been so prevalent among the one hundred families that this fact operated in the correlational analysis much like a constant attribute of the entire group. The result was that the "source of initial revelation" did not discriminate very well among the adoptees with respect to adjustment and consequently correlated very weakly with all our several measures of facets of that adjustment. This is apparent in Table 13–1.

ADOPTEE'S AGE

Our findings also indicate a strikingly weak association between the age at which the adoptees were first told they were adopted and the nature of their subsequent adjustment in most major life-space areas. We tested this relationship in two ways by dichotomizing the age con-

Table 13-1 / Correlation [a] of source of initial
revelation [b] with outcome variables [c] and with
global interviewer rating factor [d]

VARIABLE	CORRELATION
RANK ORDERING OF OVERALL ADJUSTMENT SCORES	−09
RANKING OF INDEX SCORES RE:	
Educational adjustment	−08
Personality adjustment	−09
Past parent-adoptee relationships	−06
Current parent-adoptee relationships	07
Economic adjustment	−04
Personal and social adjustment	−09
Social relations	06
Heterosexual relationships	02
Health	03
Talents	−12
Parental dissatisfaction	−13
GLOBAL INTERVIEWER RATING FACTOR	−08

[a] Decimal points omitted for this and all following tables in present chapter.

[b] Dichotomized for purposes of correlational analysis: 0 = learned from adoptive parents; 1 = all other responses.

[c] For this and all following tables in present chapter, low score = low-problem adjustment.

[d] For this and all following tables in present chapter, high score = positive rating.

tinuum at two different points. Our first cutting point was between those adoptees who reported to have "always"[1] known they were adopted and those not so reported. None of the resulting correlations with the outcome profiles was statistically significant,[2] although there was a moderate tendency for adoptees who had "always" known of their adoptive status to have encountered problems in their social relationships ($r = -.14$).

We also dichotomized the range of ages at initial revelation at between five and six years and classified the younger category "early" and the older category "not early" with respect to the timing of first revelation. The thinking underlying our choice of this breaking point was that by age six most children have already begun to express curiosity about where babies come from and how they are born. These questions offer the adoptive parents a natural "lead in" to the subject of adoption not as generally available to parents who choose to broach the topic when their children are younger.[3] Moreover, prior to age six the child tends to spend the greatest part of his life within the family circle whereas after that age he has begun to attend school full time and has been launched into the outside world on a somewhat more independent basis.

Once again, no significant correlations between our dichotomized age variable and any of the outcome variables emerged from the correlation analysis. As we can see in Table 13-2, however, three of these relationships did seem to have more strength than the others: revelation *at or after* age six was moderately associated with more problematic current parent-adoptee relationships ($r = 15$), with more reported health problems ($r = .14$), and also with the adoptee's

Table 13-2 / Correlation of age of adoptee at initial revelation [a] *with outcome variables and with global interviewer rating factor*

VARIABLE	CORRELATION
RANK ORDERING OF OVERALL ADJUSTMENT SCORES	−01
RANKING OF INDEX SCORES RE:	
Educational adjustment	03
Personality adjustment	−08
Past parent-adoptee relationships	03
Current parent-adoptee relationships	15
Economic adjustment	−04
Personal and social adjustment	−08
Social relations	−06
Heterosexual relationships	−00
Health	14
Talents	−15
Parental dissatisfaction	−05
GLOBAL INTERVIEWER RATING FACTOR	−08

[a] Dichotomized for purposes of correlational analysis: 0 = informed at an early age (below age 6); 1 = not informed at an early age (age 6 or older).

tendency *to* exhibit one or more outstanding talents over the years ($r = -.15$). The first of these associations is of interest because it seems consonant with the conviction underlying the advocacy by most adoption agencies of a policy of "early telling" of the adoption story. This is the conviction that the undue postponement or withholding of information regarding a matter so seemingly crucial to the adoptee might well threaten the development of a sound and mutually gratifying parent-child relationship by eroding the honesty and trust upon which it must be founded.[4]

At the same time, however, we are at a loss for a satisfactory explanation as to why such negative repercussions should be found related to only the current and not the past parent-adoptee relationship (where the relevant correlation was only $r = .03$). Our data also provide no basis for explaining the two somewhat more prominent associations between later revelation and health and talent adjustment, referred to above.

CIRCUMSTANCES

We also explored a different but very important aspect of the timing of the initial revelation which hypothetically could color its entire meaning and significance for the child. We inquired of the adoptive parents whether this event had occurred in a sudden or precipitous fashion under less than favorable circumstances or whether the disclosure of adoptive status had been under the control of the adoptive parents and had taken place at a time and in a manner planned by them. As we saw in Chapter VII, only about one-fifth (21) of our adoptive couples reported the handling of revelation to have been precipitous. Consequently, the outcome correlates of this variable tend not to be quite as revealing as they would have been had there been a more even distribution of responses to the revelation item. They are nonetheless quite suggestive. While none of the correlations achieved statistical significance, two only barely missed that level, and a third came fairly close. We see in Table 13–3 that where the adoptee's first confrontation with the fact of his adoptive status was a sudden one, occurring under presumably less favorable circumstances, parent-adoptee relationships tended to be more problematic both in the past

Table 13-3 / Correlation of the precipitousness of
the initial revelation [a] with outcome variables
and with global interviewer rating factor

VARIABLE	CORRELATION
RANK ORDERING OF OVERALL ADJUSTMENT SCORES	−16
RANKING OF INDEX SCORES RE:	
Educational adjustment	−13
Personality adjustment	−03
Past parent-adoptee relationships	−18
Current parent-adoptee relationships	−19
Economic adjustment	−07
Personal and social adjustment	−06
Social relations	−11
Heterosexual relationships	−10
Health	−11
Talents	−10
Parental dissatisfaction	−02
GLOBAL INTERVIEWER RATING FACTOR	15

[a] Dichotomized for purposes of correlational anlysis: 0 = adoptee informed precipitously; 1 = all other responses.

and currently. Moreover, the adoptee's overall life adjustment, represented by the rank ordering of the overall adjustment scores, was also apt to be a more problematic one.

Venturing to speculate about these findings, we believe that a reasonable hypothesis suggests itself. It is not difficult to visualize the shock and subsequent disillusion and resentment on the part of the adoptee who suddenly discovers—usually from some source other than his adoptive parents—a fact of such central importance to his sense of identity and self-worth. Similarly, one can easily imagine the resulting guilt and self-blame apt to be experienced by the adoptive parents in such a situation. Some undermining of the mutual respect and trust in the parent-child relationship would therefore not be an unexpected consequence, and this could well engender a climate vulnerable to strains and conflict over the years. Nor is it difficult to conceive of how the ensuing emotional turmoil and confusion in the adoptee concerning core feelings about himself could contribute to the generalized adjustment difficulties reflected in the first correlation in Table 13–3.

Subsequent handling of adoptive status

FREQUENCY OF DISCUSSION OF TOPIC

The question of how visible adoptive parents tend to make the child's adoptive status over the years is a critical one in at least two important respects. It has first of all important implications for the adoptee's image of himself, his sense of belonging in the adoptive family, and his feeling about his adoptive parents. Secondly, the visibility which adoptive parents give to their child's being adopted may reveal something about the degree to which they feel themselves to be the child's "real" parents.[5] Continual, repetitive allusion to the child's adoptive status, on one hand, or total avoidance of this undeniable fact, on the other, can both signal the presence of unresolved conflicts concerning the adoptive parents' sense of entitlement to their adopted child.

We saw in Chapter VII that the largest proportion of couples reported that discussion of adoption in the family had taken place "somewhat frequently" or "relatively frequently" but that there was some evidence of a spread of responses toward both poles of the frequency continuum. In our correlation analysis we therefore sought to determine the outcome correlates of this differential readiness to engage in on-going discussion of adoption.

As was the case in our prior analyses of revelation material, however, none of the correlations between frequency of discussion and our several outcome measures proved to be statistically significant. At the same time, some discernible trends were evident, pointing toward the general conclusion that the more frequently reference was made to the adoptee's status over the years, the more likely he was to encounter adjustment problems. Thus we find in Table 13–4 only a single datum providing any evidence of an association between more frequent discussion of adoption and *positive* outcome, viz., the near significant correlation with low-problem current parent-adoptee relationships seen in the "Below age 10" column. On the other hand, the signs of all but one of the remaining correlations in that column indicate a tendency toward problematic correlates of frequent reference to the subject of adoption.

This tendency is even more accentuated in the remaining two columns of Table 13–4, albeit without achieving statistical significance. We note that a propensity for frequent reference to the child's adoptive status after he had reached the age of ten is rather clearly linked with a more problematic outcome in several life-space areas. Adoptees in such families, for example, tended to encounter more problems in their personal and social adjustment, to meet with greater difficulties in their social relations, and to have more problematic heterosexual adjustments.

This apparent negative outcome pattern should be seen as sugges-

Table 13–4 / Correlation of frequency of discussion
of adoption [a] *during three age periods with*
outcome variables and with global
interviewer rating factor

	CORRELATIONS FOR PERIOD WHEN ADOPTEE WAS:		
VARIABLE	BELOW AGE 10	AGE 10–17	AGE 18 AND OVER
RANK ORDERING OF OVERALL ADJUSTMENT SCORES	07	13	10
RANKING OF INDEX SCORES RE:			
Educational adjustment	13	12	08
Personality adjustment	09	14	14
Past parent-adoptee relationships	00	−01	00
Current parent-adoptee relationships	−17	−08	−11
Economic adjustment	02	05	03
Personal and social adjustment	13	18	18
Social relations	04	16	16
Heterosexual relationships	10	16	15
Health	−08	−09	−14
Talents	10	15	13
Parental dissatisfaction	07	08	08
GLOBAL INTERVIEWER RATING SCALE	−10	10	02

[a] Range and direction: 5 = discussed very frequently; 0 = never discussed at all.

270 / Revelation of adoptive status

tive rather than as definitive. We lack some important information required for more unequivocal interpretation of the findings: the parents' perceptions of what constituted "frequent" discussions, for example; the circumstances under which the topic of adoption was broached; and the nature of the emotional climate in which the discussions were conducted. Nevertheless, we suggest that the leads we report here deserve further investigation.

NATURE AND AMOUNT OF INFORMATION
DIVULGED REGARDING NATURAL PARENTS

The manner in which adoptive parents deal with the subject of the adoptee's biological parents is conceivably one of the most crucial aspects of their general approach to the entire adoption phenomenon. Whether they attempt to "flesh out" with concrete information the adoptee's initially very sketchy picture of his "first" or "other" set of parents,[6] whether they tend to circumscribe this image to one of vague "shadow parents," or whether they endeavor to deny completely the very existence of the natural parents—each way of treating the topic has important implications for the adoptee's sense of identity and for the nature of his relationship with his adoptive parents.

We therefore inquired into the nature and the amount of information which the adoptees had received over the years regarding three facets of their background: (a) the family status of their natural parents, i.e., whether or not they had been married, (b) their personal and social characteristics, and (c) the reasons for their having given up or abandoned the adoptee. We saw in Chapter VII that the large preponderance of adoptive parents in our study had in fact tended in essence "to kill off" the biological parents by withholding completely from the adoptees information in all three of these areas. We saw also that the number of families in each of the outcome categories who had taken this approach was substantially the same. This fact permitted us to anticipate to some degree the findings that would likely emerge from our correlation analysis. In preparing our data for this analysis, both the degree of candor and the amount of information divulged in each of the above areas were combined into a single variable. The scoring code ranged from a low score indicating that no information had been provided the adoptee in any of the areas or that he had received only untrue information in all three areas to a high score denoting that accurate information had been imparted to him in all three areas.

As could have been foretold from our earlier descriptive material, virtually no associations of import appeared between the way the adoptee fared in his later life adjustment and the amount and accuracy of the information he had received about biological antecedents. However, one outcome measure did correlate at near significance with this information variable: in families where less information [7] was divulged to the adoptee the adoptive parents tended to perceive the current parent-adoptee relationship as being characterized by problems ($r = -.17$).[8] Moreover, such families were more likely to receive less positive interviewer ratings ($r = .16$).

The general direction of these last findings is not unexpected when viewed from the perspective of professional orientation to this phenomenon. Social workers supporting an open approach to revelation do so on the grounds that if the deep curiosity of an adopted child—either expressed or unarticulated—regarding his origins is not satisfied by his adoptive parents, his relationship with them could become contaminated by mistrust, suspiciousness, frustration, and lingering resentment. This in turn might well provide fertile ground for the problematic parent-adoptee relationships perceived by the adoptive parents. We are also mindful of the fact that parents who tended to withhold from their adoptive children such salient information might also have disposed our casework-trained interviewers to assess such behavior as evidence of ineffective role performance and lead them to assign to these families unfavorable ratings of this aspect of adoptive parent functioning.

ADOPTEES' DESIRE TO LEARN MORE
ABOUT THEIR BIOLOGICAL PARENTS

How satisfied were the adoptees with the nature and amount of information actually given them by their adoptive parents concerning their natural parents? To what extent did they express a desire, through questions or in other ways, to learn more about their biological antecedents than the adoptive parents knew or were willing to divulge to them? How far did they go in an effort to gain additional information about their forebears? We sought answers to all these questions in our interviews with the adoptive parents and have presented our findings descriptively in Chapter VII. The purpose of the present section is to examine our correlational data to determine what outcome sequelae tend to be associated with any attempts by the adoptees to fill in gaps in the information provided them by their adoptive parents.[9]

We see in Table 13–5 that adoptees who did press for more information about their background quite clearly were apt to experience more problems in a variety of life-space areas than were their fellow adoptees who did not exhibit such curiosity about their natural parents. The former tended to encounter more personal and social adjust-

Table 13–5 / Correlation of adoptee's desire to learn more about his biological parents [a] with outcome variables and with global interviewer rating factor

VARIABLE	CORRELATION
RANK ORDERING OF OVERALL ADJUSTMENT SCORES	29 **
RANKING OF INDEX SCORES RE:	
Educational adjustment	31 **
Personality adjustment	28 **
Past parent-adoptee relationships	14
Current parent-adoptee relationships	04
Economic adjustment	08
Personal and social adjustment	37 **
Social relations	17
Heterosexual relationships	19
Health	22 *
Talents	−05
Parental dissatisfaction	32 **
GLOBAL INTERVIEWER RATING FACTOR	−27 **

* Significant: $p < .05$. ** Significant: $p < .01$.

[a] Dichotomized for purposes of correlational analysis: 1 = adoptee showed desire to learn more about his biological parents; 0 = all other responses.

ment problems, to experience personality difficulties as they grew up, to perform less adequately in the educational area, to experience more problems in their heterosexual relationships, to have been less healthy physically over the years and, in general, to have displayed a more problematic life adjustment as reflected in their overall adjustment scores. It therefore seems not surprising that their adoptive parents tended to express dissatisfaction with the adoptive experience and that the research interviewers were disposed to assign less positive ratings to the families of these adoptees.

There has been relatively little research to date regarding the topic of how adoptive parents communicate the facts of adoption to their adopted children and the consequences of this revelation for the latter's adjustment.[10] We therefore have little tested knowledge with which to compare our findings. They can be interpreted in a variety of ways, depending upon which set of assumptions or which hypothesis is employed. Unfortunately, few of these assumptions or hypotheses have been subjected to any kind of rigorous research scrutiny. Such investigation is sorely needed, particularly concerning "parental themes and variations in interpreting adoption to children," [11] the nature and extent of information about biological parents included in such interpretation, and the different reactions and responses of the adoptees to that information at different points in their psychosocial development. Only after additional research evidence on these topics has been gathered will it be possible to assess realistically the implications of the findings presented in this section.

ADOPTIVE PARENTS' TENDENCY TO MAKE
ADOPTION VISIBLE TO OTHERS

We discovered that whether adoptive parents had or had not been inclined over the years to make the adoption visible to significant others in their life bore little relationship to the quality of their adopted children's later life adjustment. Only two modest correlations with our outcome variables emerged from the analysis, neither of which attained statistical significance. One was the relationship between the adoptive parents' propensity *to* divulge the fact of adoption to others and the likelihood of the adoptee being physically healthier over the years $(r = .17)$. The other modest relationship was in the opposite direction. The adoptive parents' willingness to make the adoptee's status visible to others was somewhat associated with the latter's more problematic personal and social adjustment ($r = .15$).

We can find nothing within the remaining data of the study to help us explain or interpret either of these findings. We confess to being somewhat surprised by the generally very low outcome correlates of the variable in question. Before going into the field with our research, we were inclined to conceive of the willingness or unwillingness of adoptive parents to acknowledge openly the fact of adoption to others in their social milieu as being linked to their feelings of entitlement to their adoptive children. We have suggested in Chapter II that the state of such feelings may be an important determinant of the quality of the adoptive parent-adoptee relationship which in turn plays so central a role in the adoptee's sense of identity, his self-acceptance, and in his general psychosocial functioning. We would therefore have anticipated that the adoptive parents' readiness or reluctance to make adoption visible to others would have been rather more strongly correlated with adoptee adjustment than it actually turned out to be.

We are also aware, however, that the failure of this expectation to materialize may be partly due to the limited quality of our data concerning this variable.[12] Perhaps even more important, we made no attempt to ascertain the circumstances under which the parents had told of the child's being adopted nor the quality of this telling. For example, we do not know whether a reported tendency to reveal represented only one offhand allusion to adoption made in a single social contact, several relaxed comments made at appropriate moments or constant, almost compulsive reference to the topic in a variety of social circumstances. Obviously, each of these approaches would have had quite different implications for the parents' basic underlying feelings about adoption which would in all probability have been conveyed in various ways to the adoptee.

Summary

In this chapter, we have been concerned with the possible relationships which might have existed between the adoptees' functioning and adjustment over the years and the particulars of how they were informed of their adoptive status. On the whole, these were found to be quite minimal. We discovered, for example, no significant associations between outcome and the source, the timing or the circumstances surrounding the initial revelation. Nor did the frequency with which the subject of adoption was discussed over the years or the amount and accuracy of information given the adoptees regarding their natural parents prove to be significantly correlated with how the adoptees subsequently fared. Finally, whether or not the adoptive parents had tended to make the fact of adoption visible to others was also very weakly related to the nature and quality of the adoptees' life adjustment.

In fact, the only aspect of adoption revelation explored in our study which did emerge as definitively associated with outcome was the adoptees' response to the information given them about their biological background. If this information had been insufficient to satisfy their curiosity about the subject and they had been led to ask their adoptive parents for more information—or to seek it from the placing agency—they tended strongly to experience adjustment problems in a number of major life-space areas. It did not seem possible, however, to offer a firm interpretation of this finding due to the absence of other research-based knowledge on the subject.

It seems to us that these findings add up to an important overarching conclusion: our one hundred sets of adoptive parents perceived "the telling" of the facts of adoption to have been largely unconnected with the nature of the life adjustment later made by their adopted children. That this finding stands in sharp conflict with what has long been a fundamental working assumption in the field of adoption placement argues strongly for further more controlled investigation of the subject than was possible in the present study. We suggest that only in this way will it be possible to determine whether and to what extent our findings can be generalized to other groups of adoptive parents and children.

fourteen / Correlates of outcome:
child-rearing practices
and environmental influences

WE WILL COMPLETE this final section of our report concerning the outcome of adoption among our study families by examining how the quality of the overall experience was related to two major clusters of variables. We shall consider first the associations between the adoptive parents' child-rearing practices and the reported adjustment of their adopted children. When we discussed this topic descriptively in Chapter VIII, we related various practices to a broad-gauged index of outcome consisting of a three-way classification of the one hundred families into groupings based upon the adoptees' overall adjustment scores. We saw that with respect to some child-raising practices there were quite distinct differences among the families in each outcome category while, with regard to other practices, less pronounced and sometimes negligible differences were discerned.

In the present chapter, we shall present the results of our correlation analysis which permitted us to make a somewhat more precise determination of the degree to which variations in child-rearing practices were associated with adjustment scores in each life-space area. We shall examine the outcome correlates of (a) the adoptive parents' handling of discipline, (b) their patterns of control over their children's activities and the latter's push for independence, (c) the parents' pattern of baby-sitter use, and (d) their tendency to promote or discourage normal separation experiences for the adoptees over the years. The reader will recognize from the focus of this analysis that we have been interested in relating to outcome the behavioral indicators of the basic concepts underpinning our investigation as these were delineated in Chapter II.

The second cluster of variables to which we will address ourselves in this chapter consists of what we consider to have been environmental influences upon the adoptees' life adjustment as they grew from infants to young adults. We shall discuss three of these which stand out as being clearly correlated with the adoptees' adjustment[1]: (a) the adoptive mother's daytime absence from the home, (b) the adoptive family's investment in religious activity, and (c) the adoptive parents' perception of the similarity of theirs and the adoptee's temperament.

Child-rearing practices

NATURE AND EXTENT OF DISCIPLINE

Some fairly clear findings emerged when we examined the outcome correlates of various aspects of the adoptive parents' approach to disciplining the adoptees. In Table 14–1, for example, the reader will see that in homes where the adoptive mothers were perceived as the major disciplinarians, the adoptees revealed a better overall adjustment, as indicated by their overall adjustment scores. With respect to specific life-space sectors, they tended to have demonstrated fewer problems in the educational area, were more apt to have evidenced one or more outstanding talents, were somewhat more likely to have enjoyed low-problem relationships with their adoptive parents in the past, and showed some tendency to have experienced less problematic social relations over the years. It seems understandable that in such families the adoptive parents would have been somewhat less prone to

Table 14–1 / Correlation of most frequent
disciplinarian [a] in adoptive family with
outcome variables [b] and with global
interviewer rating factor [c]

VARIABLE	CORRELATION
RANK ORDERING OF OVERALL ADJUSTMENT SCORES	19
RANKING OF INDEX SCORES RE:	
Educational adjustment	27 **
Personality adjustment	12
Past parent-adoptee relationships	18
Current parent-adoptee relationships	12
Economic adjustment	01
Personal and social adjustment	04
Social relations	18
Heterosexual relationships	13
Health	00
Talents	21 *
Parental dissatisfaction	16
GLOBAL INTERVIEWER RATING FACTOR	−16

* Significant: $p < .05$. ** Significant: $p < .01$.

[a] Dichotomized for purposes of correlation analysis: 0 = adoptive mother was major disciplinarian; 1 = all other categories of response.

[b] For this and all following tables in present chapter, low score = low-problem adjustment

[c] For this and all following tables in present chapter, high score = positive rating.

express dissatisfaction with their adoption experience and that study interviewers would have been somewhat disposed to accord these families more positive ratings.

Perhaps even more intriguing are the findings stemming from the data in Table 14–2. Here we see that the stricter the adoptive mothers perceived themselves to be, the greater was the likelihood of a low-problem adjustment on the part of their children. The adoptees in such homes were more apt *not* to have encountered problems in their social relations and to have revealed fewer limitations and deviances in their personal and social lives, and they also showed some tendency to have been freer of personality problems. In general, their overall adjustment was apt to have been a less problematic one.

A contrary finding is that a somewhat less favorable outcome for the adoptees appears to be associated with adoptive fathers who designated themselves as strict disciplinarians, although we note that only two of the pertinent correlations in Table 14–2 either achieve or approximate statistical significance. A stringent approach to discipline by the adoptive father is linked with more turbulent and less satisfying past parent-adoptee relationships and with the absence of outstanding talents. We initially hypothesized that the first of these two associations might be a function of the adoptive father's predilection toward severe spanking, but this was not supported by the relevant

Table 14–2 / Correlation of perceived strictness [a]
of adoptive father and of adoptive mother with
outcome variables and with global
interviewer rating factor

	CORRELATION	
VARIABLE	ADOPTIVE FATHER	ADOPTIVE MOTHER
RANK ORDERING OF OVERALL ADJUSTMENT SCORES	09	−18
RANKING OF INDEX SCORES RE:		
Educational adjustment	12	−13
Personality adjustment	−03	−18
Past parent-adoptee relationships	26 **	−03
Current parent-adoptee relations	04	−13
Economic adjustment	14	−08
Personal and social adjustment	−03	−20 *
Social relations	08	−21 *
Heterosexual relationships	02	−09
Health	−09	00
Talents	19	−11
Parental dissatisfaction	06	−14
GLOBAL INTERVIEWER RATING FACTOR	02	15

* Significant: $p < .05$. ** Significant: $p < .01$.

[a] Range and direction: 0 = very soft, to 4 = very strict.

partial correlation.[2] We must therefore attribute the disparate outcome patterns associated with the adoptive mother's and the adoptive
father's strict discipline to other factors which we have not been able
to identify. One of these might well be differential interpretations of
the concept "strict discipline" by each of the spouses.

We see, however, that where the adoptee was exposed to severe
spankings, regardless of who administered them, he was likely to have
experienced a somewhat more problematic adjustment in almost all
sectors of his life space. While none of the correlations in Table 14-3
achieves significance, their signs indicate an unmistakable direction.
Adoptees who were severely spanked tended to have encountered difficulties in the educational sphere, to have had more problems in their
social relations over the years, and to have experienced less satisfying
relationships with their adoptive parents in the past. In general, their
overall adjustment tended to be more problematic and the casework-

Table 14-3 / Correlation of spanking practices [a]
with outcome variables and with global
interviewer rating factor

VARIABLE	CORRELATION
RANK ORDERING OF OVERALL ADJUSTMENT SCORES	16
RANKING OF INDEX SCORES RE:	
Educational adjustment	18
Personality adjustment	04
Past parent-adoptee relationships	17
Current parent-adoptee relationships	09
Economic adjustment	17
Personal and social adjustment	13
Social relations	18
Heterosexual relationships	07
Health	−13
Talents	12
Parental dissatisfaction	09
GLOBAL INTERVIEWER RATING FACTOR	−19

[a] Range and direction: $0 =$ never spanked even mildly; to $2 =$ spanked
severely often or sometimes.

er-interviewers showed a marked inclination to assign less positive ratings to the families of such adoptees. Partial correlation analysis revealed that these findings are not a reflection of the influence of the adoptive parents' socioeconomic status.[3]

INTENSITY OF CONTROL OVER THE ADOPTEES'
ACTIVITIES AND THEIR PUSH FOR
INDEPENDENCE

Our analysis revealed that the amount of parental control and supervision exercised over the adoptees' leisure-time pursuits through the years was only rather moderately associated with a less problematic outcome. A child whose activities were subjected to close scrutiny when he was below age ten was markedly more apt over the years to have been free of problems in his social relations ($r = -.24$). However, while there was some evidence of a comparable relationship between eventual adjustment in this life-space area and intensity of control during the 10- to 17-year age period, this relationship was not nearly as well established.[4] Nor was there a very pronounced association between close surveillance over the adoptee's activities and his tendency to experience fewer personality difficulties. Finally, we found an equally modest correlation between intensive control and more positive interviewer ratings.

While these findings can obviously only be considered as tenuous and suggestive, we were nevertheless somewhat puzzled by their direction. We would have anticipated that close control would tend to be associated with more problematic rather than less problematic adjustment because in the clinical literature parental exercise of such control is so frequently linked to a more general and pervasive tendency to overprotect the child. The consequences of this tendency would not be expected to augur well for the child's subsequent life adjustment. We therefore wondered whether our findings in this area were in some way a function of either the adoptive family's socioeconomic status or the agency through which it adopted, variables which we have found so often in our study to shape or condition child-rearing practices.

Yet, when we tested this speculation, we discovered that neither

SES nor agency of placement had in fact materially influenced the strongest and only statistically significant outcome correlate of parental control, viz., the low-problem character of the adoptee's social relations.[5] We consequently had to conclude that the unexpected direction of our findings was a function of still other unidentified variables and/or that it represented a modest but substantive relationship between the intensity of parental control and less problematic outcome. That is to say, very firm control by parents may have a beneficial effect for some children even though this is seen as pathogenic behavior in some quarters.

Our analysis revealed a few significant outcome correlates of the adoptee's push for independence, and these we believe are more readily understandable. We found, for example, that the more strongly the adoptee asserted his desire for independence, the more his relationship with his adoptive parents was likely to be characterized by conflict and other problems. This problematic outcome was more firmly related to the adoptee's strong push for independence during the latency period and early teens than during early childhood, and in both instances the past parent-adoptee relationship was more adversely affected than was the present one.

We think these findings should occasion no surprise. They seem only to attest to the frequently observed struggle which so many other children in our society appear to undergo in order to liberate themselves from dependence upon their parents, particularly during their adolescence. It seems reasonable to expect that this struggle in adoptive as well as biological families could at the time cause severe strains and tensions in the parent-child relationship. However, we would also expect, as our findings seem to indicate, that these strains and conflicts would tend to dissipate to some degree with the passage of time, leaving the current parent-child relationship freer of problems.

USE OF BABY-SITTERS

An unusually clear and consistent pattern emerged when we scrutinized the outcome correlates of the adoptive parents' use of baby-sitters as temporary caretakers during the first ten years of the adoptees'

Table 14–4 / Correlation of the frequency of baby-sitter use [a] *when the adoptee was below age 5 and age 5–10 with outcome variables and with global interviewer rating factor*

	CORRELATION	
VARIABLE	ADOPTEE BELOW AGE 5	ADOPTEE AGE 5–10
RANK ORDERING OF OVERALL ADJUSTMENT SCORES	15	17
RANKING OF INDEX SCORES RE:		
Educational adjustment	07	08
Personality adjustment	25 *	26 **
Past parent-adoptee relationships	17	18
Current parent-adoptee relationships	08	−10
Economic adjustment	14	13
Personal and social adjustment	21 *	23 *
Social relations	21 *	23 *
Heterosexual relationships	18	19
Health	−12	−11
Talents	−10	−11
Parental dissatisfaction	29 **	30 **
GLOBAL INTERVIEWER RATING FACTOR	−27 **	−27 **

* Significant: $p < .05$. ** Significant: $p < .01$.

[a] Range and direction: from 0 = never used, to 3 = frequently used.

lives. The correlations in Table 14–4 present a fairly striking picture of problematic adjustment in a number of major life-space areas among those adoptees whose parents *did* tend to make use of baby-sitters. The most noteworthy of these associations indicate that the more frequently the adoptee was left in the care of sitters:

(a) the more problems he was apt to have encountered over the years in his personality development;

(b) the more problematic his personal and social adjustment was liable to have been;

(c) the less adequately he was likely to have functioned in his social relations over the years;

(d) the more difficulties he tended to have had in both his past and present heterosexual relationships;

(e) the more conflict and stress he was apt to have experienced in his past relationships with his adoptive parents; and

(f) the more problematic his overall adjustment tended to have been.

Expectedly, the adoptive parents in such families were much more likely to have expressed dissatisfaction with the entire adoption experience, and the study interviewers were more prone to have rated these families negatively.

On its face, this constellation of findings appears to be quite clear in its import. Frequent resort to the use of baby-sitters as parent-substitutes seems to be unmistakably and fairly strongly linked to a more problematic later life adjustment for the adoptees in this study. Were this conclusion to hold up under further analysis, its implications would tend to place in question the validity of one of the principal conceptual formulations presented in Chapter II of this report. There, we hypothesized that firm feelings of entitlement on the part of the adoptive parents would enable them to tolerate the normal risks entailed in child rearing in our society, among which the temporary use of substitute caretakers is one of the most common. By implication if not directly we were postulating that, all other things being equal, the ability of the adoptive parents to accept such risks would be evidence of greater relaxation and security in the parent role which in turn should presage a more favorable psychosocial adjustment for the adoptee. At least on the surface, our findings seemed to be in conflict with this formulation.

When, however, we subjected these findings to further scrutiny by means of partial correlation analysis, we found them to be not nearly as firm and unequivocal as they had first appeared. It is clear from the contents of Table 14–5 that the most impressive associations were in some degree artifacts of the adoptive families' socioeconomic status. When we controlled for the influence of SES, three of the four statistically significant correlations were reduced to nonsignificance, meaning that the resulting relationships could have been due simply to chance and did not represent substantive associations between the variables involved. Moreover, once the effect of social class status had

Table 14–5 / Zero-order and partial correlation of frequency of baby-sitter use when adoptee was below age 5 and age 5–10 with selected outcome variables and with global interviewer rating factor, controlling for SES

VARIABLE	ZERO-ORDER CORRELATION		PARTIAL CORRELATION, CONTROLLING FOR SES	
	ADOPTEE BELOW 5	ADOPTEE 5–10	ADOPTEE BELOW 5	ADOPTEE 5–10
RANK ORDERING OF OVERALL ADJUSTMENT SCORES	15	17	12	14
Personality adjustment	25 *	26 **	13	14
Past parent-adoptee relationships	17	18	10	12
Personal and social adjustment	21 *	23 *	18	19
Social relations	21 *	23 *	13	15
Heterosexual relationships	18	19	16	17
Parental dissatisfaction	29 **	30 **	24 *	25 *
GLOBAL INTERVIEWER RATING FACTOR	−27 **	−27 **	−13	−13

* Significant: $p < .05$. ** Significant: $p < .01$.

been controlled for, the *strength* of the relationship between frequent use of baby-sitters and negative outcome was attenuated in every instance.[6] At the same time it should be noted that even subsequent to this control procedure, *some* remnants of the original trend did remain. Thus, frequent use of baby-sitters continued to be associated significantly with parental dissatisfaction with the adoption experience, and the correlations with problematic personal and social adjustment and with heterosexual relationship problems, while not significant, remained strong enough to be suggestive of an association.

SEPARATION EXPERIENCES FOR THE ADOPTEES

Our analysis disclosed that there was very little relationship between outcome and the amount of normal, age-relevant separation experiences allowed the adoptees as they grew up. All but one of the outcome correlates of this child-rearing variable were extremely low, and even the single strongest correlate, viz., educational adjustment, failed substantially to achieve statistical significance. Nevertheless, the general direction of most of the correlation coefficients indicated a slight tendency for more separation to be associated with less problematic outcome.

This weak tendency would seem to be consonant with that anticipated by our conceptual formulation in Chapter II. We would, however, have hypothesized that such a relationship would prove to be more pronounced than our data indicate it actually was. This discrepancy could be due to one or more reasons. To begin with, our basic formulation might be weak and consequently our expectations not realistically founded. Secondly, we may not have been successful in conceptualizing the separation variable in a sufficiently precise manner to have elucidated the underlying dimension which was in fact related to subsequent life adjustment. Or, we may have identified such a dimension but have failed to formulate our operational indicators in such a way as actually to tap it effectively. It is also of course possible that the quality of the data we obtained through use of a topical outline may have been inadequate to reveal the presence of a latent relationship which may actually have existed.

Whatever the reasons, for our group of one hundred adoptive families we could discern no definitive linkage between the adoptees' adjustment in any life-space area and the extent to which they were permitted to be separated from their adoptive parents on presumably appropriate occasions during their growing-up years. We believe, however, that it may be worthwhile in some future research endeavor to reconceptualize the separation variable and to test its relationship with subsequent life adjustment.

Environmental influences

ADOPTIVE MOTHER'S DAYTIME ABSENCE
FROM THE HOME

One of the most clear-cut findings to emerge from our correlation analysis was the strong relationship between the adoptive mother's

Table 14–6 / Correlation of adoptive mother's
daytime absence from the home [a] *with*
outcome variables and with global
interviewer rating factor

VARIABLE	CORRELATION
RANK ORDERING OF OVERALL ADJUSTMENT SCORES	25 *
RANKING OF INDEX SCORES RE:	
Educational adjustment	19
Personality adjustment	28 **
Past parent-adoptee relationships	24 *
Current parent-adoptee relationships	30 **
Economic adjustment	20 *
Personal and social adjustment	16
Social relations	21 *
Heterosexual relationships	20 *
Health	05
Talents	−03
Parental dissatisfaction	16
GLOBAL INTERVIEWER RATING FACTOR	−30 **

* Significant: $p < .05$. ** Significant: $p < .01$.

[a] Scored as follows: 0 = adoptive mother not out of home, 1 = adoptive mother out of home for any reason: adoptive 10 years of age or older, 2 = mother out of home for any reason: adoptee below 10 years of age.

daytime absence from the home when the adoptee was young and the latter's subsequent problematic adjustment in several life-space areas. This linkage is very apparent in the data contained in Table 14–6. There we see that where the mother had, for whatever reason, tended to be away from the adoptive home during the day:

(a) the adoptee's overall life adjustment tended to have been more problematic;

(b) he was more prone to have experienced personality difficulties over the years;

(c) both his past and current relationship with his adoptive parents were likely to have been characterized by turbulence and conflict;

(d) there was a greater chance that he had met with problems over the years in his social relations;

(e) his heterosexual relationships were more apt to have been fraught with problems;

(f) his current economic adjustment tended to be less than adequate; and

(g) the likelihood was that he had encountered more difficulties in his performance in the educational sphere.

Not unexpectedly, in speaking of their experiences, the adoptive parents in these families showed some tendency to express dissatisfaction with adoption. Our casework-trained interviewers were also considerably more disposed to place such families at the less favorable end of the rating continuum.

We were thus again confronted with a constellation of consistent relationships which seemingly pointed to an inescapable conclusion. This conclusion appeared to be consonant with some of the formulations in the child development field which have emphasized the importance for the young child of continuous mothering by a single individual. Yet, we were also aware that the phenomena involved in this formulation are highly complex and have frequently been oversimplified in the past.[7] Moreover, we have noted several times both in the present and in the preceding two chapters of this report that what appeared at first to be firm relationships between outcome and various independent and other intervening variables have turned out to be substantially less firm after we controlled for the influence on the relationships of still other background variables.

Particularly influential in this respect has been the adoptive family's socioeconomic status, and in the present instance there also seemed some basis for conjecturing that SES might have contributed to making the observed correlations spuriously high or low. We have seen, for instance, in Chapter IX that adoptive mothers in higher social class families showed a greater proclivity for daytime absence from the home while the adoptee was in his young and formative years. We have also noted in Chapter XII that adoptees raised in higher SES families were somewhat more susceptible to personality and social relationship adjustment problems. Accordingly, we subjected the strongest correlations in Table 14–6 to further partial correlation analysis to ascertain how substantive the observed associations actually were.

Contrary to the results reported earlier in this chapter with respect to the outcome correlates of baby-sitter use, we discovered that SES was *not* a major determinant of the strength of the outcome correlates of the mother's daytime absence from the adoptive home. This is evidenced from the fact that the partial correlations in Table 14–7 are all only slightly lower or higher than the original zero-order correlations. Furthermore, in six of the eight instances where the original correlations were statistically significant, the partial correlations also remained significant, thereby ruling out the probability that their magnitude was the result of the overriding influence of social class.

In other words, we can conclude that the observed relationship between the adoptive mother's daytime absence from the home and the adoptee's problematic adjustment was not a function of differing

Table 14–7 / Zero-order and partial correlation of adoptive mother's daytime absence from the home with selected outcome variables and with global interviewer rating factor, controlling for SES

VARIABLE	ZERO-ORDER CORRELATION	PARTIAL CORRELATION, CONTROLLING FOR SES
RANK ORDERING OF OVERALL ADJUSTMENT SCORES	25 *	23 *
RANKING OF INDEX SCORES RE:		
Personality adjustment	28 **	25 *
Past parent-adoptee relationships	24 *	21 *
Current parent-adoptee relationships	30 **	28 **
Economic adjustment	20 *	20 *
Social relations	21 *	18
Heterosexual relationships	20 *	19
GLOBAL INTERVIEWER RATING FACTOR	−30 **	−26 **

* Significant: $p < .05$. ** Significant: $p < .01$.

social class statuses: the relationship held true for adoptees brought up in lower as well as higher class families. This in itself is a revealing finding. In eliminating from consideration the effect of SES, possibly the most influential background variable, it gives us a somewhat firmer basis for postulating that there *may* be a substantive relationship between adoptee outcome and the mother's daytime absence from the adoptive home. Of course, to be able to assert the existence of such a relationship more unequivocally, we would need to extend our partial correlation analysis, controlling for other relevant and potentially influential variables. We have not undertaken such an analysis but are inclined to believe that it may be a fruitful direction for further inquiry, particularly if it results in further confirmation of the existence of the postulated relationship. Such substantiation would likely have interesting implications in view of the markedly growing proportion of working mothers in our population.

ADOPTIVE FAMILY'S INVESTMENT
IN RELIGIOUS ACTIVITY

In Chapter IX, we devoted some attention to the associations between the adoptive family's involvement in religious activity and several child-rearing variables. We now examine our data to determine whether degree of religiosity was in any way related to how well the adoptee fared in his subsequent adjustment in various sectors of his life space.

A perusal of Table 14–8 discloses that there was in fact a moderately clear configuration of relationships between outcome and the family's earlier religious activity. The more heavily invested the family was in this sphere, the more favorable the adoptee's adjustment appears to have been. He seems clearly to have had fewer personality problems, to have encountered fewer difficulties in his social relationships, and to have enjoyed a less stressful and problematic relationship with his adoptive parents, both in the past and currently. In fact, there is evidence of some tendency for his overall adjustment to have been generally freer of problems. Once again, the interviewer ratings are consistent with this outcome pattern and tend to be more positive for the families with strong religious investment.

Table 14–8 / Correlation of adoptive family's investment in religious activity [a] with outcome variables and with global interviewer rating factor

VARIABLE	CORRELATION
RANK ORDERING OF OVERALL ADJUSTMENT SCORES	−17
RANKING OF INDEX SCORES RE:	
Educational adjustment	−05
Personality adjustment	−22 *
Past parent-adoptee relationships	−19
Current parent-adoptee relationships	−23 *
Economic adjustment	−08
Personal and social adjustment	−14
Social relations	−23 *
Heterosexual relationships	−09
Health	04
Talents	05
Parental dissatisfaction	−07
GLOBAL INTERVIEWER RATING	20 *

* Significant: $p < .05$.

[a] Range and direction: $0 =$ slightly or not at all invested, to $2 =$ heavily invested.

How can we account for these findings? Can we conclude that there existed a substantive relationship between the degree of an adoptive family's religious activity and the likely adjustment of their adopted child? In preceding sections of this chapter, we have endeavored to answer these questions by ascertaining whether other background variables, notably socioeconomic status and the agency placing the child, were able to explain some or a large portion of the observed relationships. We undertook a similar analysis in the present instance. The reader will recall that in Chapter IX we saw that heavy religious investment was strongly associated with lower SES, and that in Chapter XII we noted that such status was also linked to some likelihood of a more salutary personality adjustment and fewer problems in the sphere of social relations. We therefore speculated that SES might once again be able to account for some of the association we have just observed between low-problem outcome and the adoptive family's religious involvement.

The data contained in Table 14–9 clearly warrant such a supposition. When we controlled for the influence of SES, two of the three statistically significant original correlations were reduced to the point of nonsignificance, which indicates that they could have occurred by chance. The one relationship which remained significant was that between religious investment and positive current parent-adoptee relationships. However, the strength of all six correlation coefficients diminished, in some instances appreciably. In other words, the originally observed associations between religious activity and the various outcome measures had been spuriously strong due to the differential

Table 14–9 / Zero-order and partial correlation of adoptive family's investment in religious activity with selected outcome variables and with global interviewer rating factor, controlling for SES and for agency of placement

VARIABLE	ZERO-ORDER COR.	PARTIAL COR., CONTROLLING FOR SES	PARTIAL CORRELATION, CONTROLLING FOR PLACEMENT BY:			
			CATH. HOME BUR.	FREE SYNA- GOGUE COMM.	CHAPIN NURS./ SPENCE ALUM.	STATE CHAR. AID
RANK ORDERING OF OVERALL ADJUSTMENT	−17	−15	(not computed)			
RANKING OF INDEX SCORES RE:						
Personality adjustment	−22 *	−15	−18	−18	−21 *	−25 *
Past parent-adoptee relationships	−19	−15	(not computed)			
Current parent-adoptee relationships	−23 *	−21 *	−22 *	−21 *	−22 *	−24 *
Social relations	−23 *	−18	−15	−18	−22 *	−24 *
GLOBAL INTERVIEWER RATING FACTOR	20 *	11	(not computed)			

* Significant: $p < .05$.

strength of this association among upper and lower class families. Once the effect of this variable had been removed, we saw that, with the one exception noted above, the actual relationships were quite minimal.

When we substituted the placing agency for social class as a control variable, the results were very roughly comparable though not nearly as marked or consistent. As can be seen in Table 14–9, removing the influence of adoption through Catholic Home Bureau and the Free Synagogue Committee noticeably decreased both the magnitude and the degree of confidence we can place in two of the three strongest outcome correlates of religious investment. The third correlate, however, remained virtually unchanged. Controlling for placement through the other two agencies also altered the original associations only negligibly.

SIMILARITY OF ADOPTEE'S AND
ADOPTIVE PARENTS' TEMPERAMENT

A striking cluster of findings resulted from our correlation analysis, the meaning of which, however, is not easy to determine. We found that the adoptive parents' perception of the similarity of their own and their adopted children's temperaments were quite strongly related to the adoptees' later life adjustment. We see in Table 14–10 that the more similar to them in temperament the parents perceived their children to be, the more likely were the latter to be reported as having achieved a less problematic adjustment. This outcome pattern is quite unmistakable. We observe that such adoptees displayed a markedly more favorable overall adjustment and that they tended clearly to be freer of problems in the following life-space sectors: educational performance, personality adjustment, social relations, and physical health. Their current relationship with their adoptive parents also tended to be characterized by fewer conflicts and difficulties. Our study interviewers were substantially more inclined to assign such families higher or more positive ratings, and, understandably, the adoptive parents in such families were less apt to express dissatisfaction with their entire adoptive experience.

If this configuration of findings appears unequivocal in direction,

*Table 14–10 / Correlation of similarity of adoptee's
and adoptive parents' temperament* [a] *with outcome
variables and with global interviewer
rating factor*

VARIABLE	CORRELATION
RANK ORDERING OF OVERALL ADJUSTMENT SCORES	−35 **
RANKING OF INDEX SCORES RE:	
Educational adjustment	−28 **
Personality adjustment	−32 **
Past parent-adoptee relationships	−26 **
Current parent-adoptee relationships	−17
Economic adjustment	−15
Personal and social adjustment	−21 *
Social relations	−29 **
Heterosexual relationships	−09
Health	−29 **
Talents	−06
Parental dissatisfaction	−19
GLOBAL INTERVIEWER RATING FACTOR	32 **

* Significant: $p < .05$. ** Significant: $p < .01$.

[a] Range and direction: 0 = not at all similar to either parent, to 2 = very similar to either or both parents.

its interpretation is less so. To conclude, as we must from the evidence, that perceived similarity in temperaments is associated with less problematic adjustment is one thing; to determine more precisely the causal basis of this association is quite another. And it seems to us that such a determination would be necessary before the implications of our findings could become apparent. The principal question appears to be: which of the two variables was the chronologically antecedent one? Did the adoptive parents' perception over the years that the adoptee was "like us" in temperament result in a stronger identification with and greater acceptance of him? Such a feeling tone could well engender in the adoptee a greater sense of security which in turn could permit him to maximize his potentialities and enable him to function with a minimum of problem-producing stress and conflict.

Or, contrariwise, did the adoptive parents of low-problem children, in surveying for us their two or three decades of experience with adoption, come to the realization of just how successfully adjusted these adoptees were; with the result that their *ex post facto* perceptions of their children's temperament were colored and appeared to be similar to their own temperaments?

Regrettably, these questions can only be posed but not answered. First of all, in a retrospective study such as ours, there is no way to go back and reconstruct accurately the sequence of events and reactions which led to the perceptions enunciated by the adoptive parents. Furthermore, correlation techniques, our principal analytic tool in this inquiry, can illuminate only associations or relationships among variables; they cannot answer the questions of causality which are involved here. It must remain for the longitudinal studies now under way and those undertaken in the future to address themselves to such questions. It may be worthwhile in such inquiries to investigate further the nature of any relationship which may exist between adoptee adjustment and adoptive parents' perception of similarity in temperament and to endeavor to explicate the temporal or causal dimension of such a relationship.

Summary

We have examined in this chapter how the child-rearing practices of our adoptive parents and various other environmental factors in the adoptive home were related to the way the adoptees subsequently fared in their life adjustment. We saw that some such associations did exist but that by and large they were only moderately definitive.

In the area of child-rearing practices, we found what at first appeared to be a very consistent and striking constellation of correlations between the adoptive parents' frequent use of baby-sitters when the adoptee was young and the latter's problematic adjustment in several major life-space areas. We discovered, however, that this *apparent* relationship was spuriously high in that it was strongly influenced by the adoptive family's socioeconomic status. On the other hand, we determined that SES was *not* a major determinant of the fairly strong and widespread relationship we found between problematic adoptee adjustment and the adoptive mother's daytime absence from the home in the adoptee's tender years. We were thus led to conclude that this relationship may be a substantive one, although further analysis would be necessary before we could be more unequivocal on this score.

The adoptive family's heavy investment in religious activity at first appeared to predispose the adoptee to a less problematic life adjustment, but this relationship was subsequently seen to have been in large measure an artifact of socioeconomic status. However, we did observe a very pronounced association between low-problem functioning by the adoptee in many life-space sectors and his adoptive parents' perception that his temperament and theirs were similar. The meaning of this finding is nonetheless not clear since our study provided us no basis for unravelling the temporal or causal connections between such perception and the adoptee's life adjustment.

Postscript to chapters twelve–fourteen

In the preceding three chapters, we have examined in detail the correlates of a variety of variables with the overall outcome measure and the eleven outcome indices. In most cases, the correlation has been very much on the modest side. Some partial correlations have been presented to clarify the meaning of some of the more significant associations found. However, the reader might well ask: To what extent does all of this information gathered about the parents help to explain the variation in the adjustment of the adopted children over their life spans and currently? Does the information gathered offer any possibility of firm prediction to agencies who currently are in a position to gather such data? The reader might also wonder about the degree to which quite a few of the findings reflect a redundancy among the various background factors that were used as analytic variables.

Using the techniques of regression analysis, we decided to pool some seventeen background variables which seemed most important in our study and perform a multiple correlation analysis of the rank order of Overall Adjustment Scores, our major adjustment measure, to see what explanatory power they might have in combination. In Table 14–11, we present the results of this analysis.

The seventeen variables were entered into the regression equation in the order set forth in the table. The data reveal clearly that no single one of these variables is dominant in the sense that it has unusual explanatory power. Moreover, it is to be noted that collectively all of these variables account for a cumulative multiple R of .4432 and just under 20 per cent of the variance in the adjustment measure. This is extremely modest and suggests that over the large time span covered by the study—twenty to thirty years—the influence of forces taking place prior to and in the early stages of the adoptive experience may well have been "washed out" by the passage of time and the introduction of other influential forces.

That agencies cannot really predict with any great degree of accuracy what kinds of adults will emerge from the placements they ef-

Table 14-11 / Multiple correlation analysis of rank ordering of overall adjustment scores

STEP NUMBER	BACKGROUND VARIABLE	CUMULATIVE MULTIPLE R	CUMULATIVE MULTIPLE R²	F-TEST	ΔR²[a]	t-TEST
1	Socioeconomic status of family	.0989	.0098	0.9681	.0098	0.9839
2	Sex of child	.1851	.0343	1.7203	.0245	1.5678
3	Age of child at placement	.1852	.0343	1.1363	.0000	0.0595
4	Age of child at 1961 birthday	.2662	.0709	1.8120	.0366	1.9343
5	Strength of motivation to adopt	.2730	.0745	1.5140	.0036	0.6083
6	Infertility of couple [b]	.2838	.0806	1.3582	.0660	0.7815
7	Sex preference at time of adoption	.2848	.0811	1.1605	.0006	0.2378
8	Age preference at time of adoption	.3097	.0905	1.2070	.0148	1.2206
9	Mother's absence from the home [c]	.3209	.1030	1.1478	.0070	0.8397
10	Age when child informed of adoption	.3296	.1086	1.0846	.0057	0.7520
11	Frequency of discussion of adoption over the years	.3310	.1096	0.9844	.0009	0.3051
12	Age of adoptive mother at the time of placement	.3356	.1126	0.9200	.0030	0.5459
13	Number of prior placements experienced by child	.3356	.1126	0.8396	.0000	0.0415
14	Number of siblings in family before adoption	.3580	.1282	0.8927	.0156	1.2318
15	Catholic Home Bureau Families v. others	.3661	.1340	0.8668	.0058	0.7530
16	Free Synagogue Families v. others	.3946	.1557	0.9570	.0217	1.4611
17	Chapin Nursery/Spence Alumnae Families v. others	.4432	.1965	1.1793	.0407	2.0384

[a] ΔR² is the percent of variance explained by each variable when added.
[b] Couples who were not infertile or had prior miscarriages vs. all other categories of response.
[c] Mother's desire to which mother was out of the home for employment or other reasons while the child

fect should not be discouraging. Indeed, one would hope that a child's fate would *not* be "locked in" so early in his life situation. What the findings do suggest is that agencies might well be cautious in the use of the types of background information contained in Table 14–11 as criteria for accepting or rejecting adoptive applicant couples. All these variables, taken collectively, simply do not appear to have a determinative impact upon the life chances of the adopted child.

fifteen / In summary

IN THE PRECEDING fourteen chapters, we have presented a rather extensive array of statistical data. Confronted with the sheer volume of findings, the reader may find himself a bit overwhelmed at this juncture and may well feel the need for some sort of summary statement which would help put the various findings into proper perspective. In this concluding chapter, we will attempt such a summing up. We will first review some important and distinctive elements of our study method which were instrumental in shaping the nature and quality of our findings. At the same time, we will remind the reader of some of the constraints upon the interpretation of our findings that flow from our choice of research design. Next, we shall highlight what we believe to be the study's most salient findings and identify their potential implications for practice. In the process, we shall have occasion to allude briefly to findings in one particular area which seems to us especially to merit further rigorous research. Finally, we shall suggest what we consider to be some of the implications of our findings for the possible modification of adoption practice.

The study method

In Chapter III and in Appendix A the methods employed in the present investigation are set forth in detail so that the reader may be able to evaluate for himself the means by which we obtained the data reflected in our findings. We shall therefore now only call attention to the two major aspects of our general methodological approach and data analytic techniques which tended to be somewhat innovative, departing in certain respects from the methods employed in previous follow-up studies in adoption.

TREATMENT OF INTERVIEW DATA

Our major source of data was the face-to-face interviews with the adoptive parents. Unstructured and free-flowing in form, each interview was guided by a detailed topical outline, designated items of which had to be covered but in no predetermined order. The wealth of discursive material obtained in this manner was then converted into categorical data by means of a modified content analytic procedure. This required the interviewer to listen back to the tape recording of the interview, usually in its entirety, and to translate what the parent had actually said into the prestructured items of a comprehensive codebook.

Such a procedure involved essentially a *coding* process as distinguished from a judgment-making process in which the interviewer would have been required to make professional assessments on the basis of the interview content. The latter procedure was utilized by Witmer and her colleagues in their study of independent adoptions in Florida. In that investigation the interviewer and field director rated adoptive homes on a scale from "excellent" to "poor" on the basis of professional judgments formed by information gathered in interviews with the adoptive mother.[1] In our study, by contrast, interviewers were instructed to seek to eliminate from their coded material all professional assessment and diagnostic impressions. Entries were to be confined exclusively to the actual information furnished by the parent and to data clearly and directly inferrable from parental responses. It was from this type of coded factual material relating to the adoptee's adjustment in major life-space areas that we derived our outcome scores.

As the average two-parent interview was approximately three hours in duration, it is apparent that the taping of the interviews played an indispensable role in the above coding process. The tapes, however, served two other important purposes as well. They made possible a feasible procedure for testing the reliability of the codebook data which formed the basis for the outcome indices (detailed in Appendix A), and they also proved invaluable in orienting and training our several interviewers.

DEVELOPMENT OF OUTCOME SCORES

In approaching the task of describing the outcome of the adoptive experience, we attempted to come to grips with two important aspects of the problem of assessing the adoptees' adjustment. One basic but rather elusive aspect concerned the standards by which we would characterize the adoptee's adjustment. Whose standards should these represent? The adoptive parents'? Those of the adoptee himself? The norms of society at large? Each of these seemed relevant to us. As a result, we included in our outcome indices items which reflected both the subjective impressions and reactions of the adoptive parents and the more objective descriptions of the actual functioning of the adoptee in the various life-space areas we studied. Thus, for example, our final assessment of the adoptee's educational achievement was based upon such data as the amount of formal schooling the adoptee had completed and his level of academic performance over the years as well as upon the parents' satisfaction with such performance and the extent to which their expectations of the adoptee had been fulfilled.

A second major aspect of the assessment of outcome involved the time dimension which would enter into our evaluation. In this connection we decided to employ what could be called a panoramic approach. We developed a scoring procedure that took into account the adoptee's adjustment as he was growing up as well as his characteristics at the time of the follow-up interview with his parents. Thus, an adoptee who had had serious personality difficulties as a child tended to receive a lower overall adjustment score even if these problems had been overcome in later years. This is an obvious departure from an approach to the enumeration of morbid conditions commonly used by epidemiologists in the public health field. The latter are usually concerned with both the incidence of conditions, i.e., those newly emerging in a specified period, or their prevalence, i.e., those new and old cases currently making up all known cases in the population. They are not concerned with conditions that may have once afflicted an individual and then been overcome. In essence, the outcome measures used in our study were designed to rank highest those families where the adoptee had been spared problems during the growing-up years as well as at the time of the follow-up interview and to rank lowest those in which the adoptee had had problems in both childhood and adulthood.

LIMITATIONS OF DESIGN AND METHOD

We have called attention in this report to certain design and methodological characteristics of our research which place constraints upon the kinds of conclusions that can be drawn from its findings. For example, our investigation was conceived from the outset as a retrospective study in which the respondents were to be asked to hark back two to three decades in their accounts of what transpired in numerous sectors of their lives as adoptive families. While providing the opportunity to develop a fairly definitive picture of the adoptee's overall life adjustment this also possesses the limitation that one cannot establish clearly the extent of the validity and reliability of data collected after so long an interim.

Then, too, we would also remind the reader that the design of our study did not call for interviewing a group of families with adult biological children whose life experiences could be compared with those of our sample of adoptees. As we explained in Chapter I, we could not readily identify with any sense of validity a contrast group which could be feasibly sought out in a retrospective study of this kind. The absence of such a group in our design precludes a consideration of whether and to what degree the problematic outcomes of

adoption found among our subjects might deviate from the life difficulties one would expect to encounter among nonadopted individuals
in the general population. We recognize that this limitation of our findings may constitute a source of frustration for some readers, since it is
most natural to immediately raise the issue: did these adopted children do better or worse than those who are reared in their own biological families? We believe, however, that our findings can serve the
function of clarifying which factors seem to have a bearing upon the
course of an adoptive experience and which seem to be relatively unrelated.

Finally, the reader should be aware that, due to the difficulty in
locating study families after a 20- to 30-year hiatus, the representativeness of our work was probably somewhat impaired. This imposes
some tentativeness in considering the generalizability of our findings.
Moreover, the reader should bear in mind that these findings probably
present a somewhat biased picture of the adoptees' life experience
since they represent exclusively the perceptions of the adoptive parents and do not take into consideration the views of the adoptee side
of the parent-child role-set.

Salient findings

Before summarizing the principal findings of our research, we would
again call the reader's attention to two caveats which should be
borne in mind at all times. First, in no sense should or can these findings justifiably be interpreted as reflecting the likely outcomes of current adoption agency practice. All the one hundred adoptions studied
were consummated between twenty and thirty years before our field interviews when each of the four participating agencies was largely or
completely staffed by nonprofessional personnel. These families were
consequently exposed to a form of agency practice which we have reason
to believe was qualitatively quite different from, and much less well developed than, that found in the same agencies today. It would thus be
quite erroneous and unwarranted to assess the efficacy of present-day
agency practice in the light of either the high-problem or low-problem
adjustment evidenced by our adoptee subjects.

Secondly, we wish to emphasize that the research reported in these pages is not and was never intended to be evaluative of the quality of agency practice, either three decades ago or currently. Thus, findings relating to interagency differences should in no way be construed as constituting invidious comparisons of either the clientele or the service offered by the four participating agencies. To the contrary, throughout this report we have repeatedly pointed to evidence that at the time our study families adopted, these agencies appeared to be serving rather different client populations which were really not comparable in several important respects.

OUTCOME OF THE ADOPTIVE EXPERIENCE

Utilizing the approach to measuring outcome described above, we discovered, as might have been expected, a wide range of life adjustments among our one hundred adoptees. Many had manifested remarkably few problems throughout most of their lives and were also currently functioning in this manner. On the other hand, the reader may have been impressed with the fact that a number of adoptees had experienced a variety of quite serious problems in growing up, and that some were still contending with major adjustment difficulties at the time their parents were interviewed. Between these extremes was a group whose adjustment over the years and presently could be classified as middle range.

Our major outcome measures consisted of index scores of adoptee adjustment in eleven life-space areas derived from the codified interview material. The rank orderings of many of these discrete index scores were shown to be strongly intercorrelated. What is more, these rank orderings appeared firmly associated with the rank ordering of the Overall Adjustment Scores which were developed for each adoptee by summing the several life-space area index scores. In other words, our data indicate that there was a consistency of assessment which characterized the adoptive experience and which tended to pervade most of the major areas of the adoptee's life space.[2]

An illustration of this finding is the fact that an adoptee who tended, while growing up, to perform in poor fashion in the area of education was also likely to be reported as having exhibited difficulties with respect to personality characteristics, his relationship with his parents, his social relationships, and so forth. From a commonsense point of view, this type of finding does not provide a surprising perspective of the human personality. We must, however, also take into account the possibility that this consistency may reflect the weakness of our having depended upon the adoptive parents as our source of information rather than having used more direct measures. We recognize the possibility that a "halo effect" may have been partly responsible for some of the high associations we have found between the rank orderings of many of the outcome index scores.

CURRENT ADJUSTMENT

We have already referred to our conception of outcome as incorporating the adoptee's adjustments over his entire lifetime. We can well understand, however, that some readers would hold the functioning of the adoptees at the time of the follow-up study to be a more important consideration than the situation that prevailed while they were growing up. Admittedly, from the standpoint of the reliability of the parental reports, the accounts of the adoptees' current situations, when they were already entered upon adulthood, would presumably have more reliability than would the reports of conditions which had existed earlier. At the very least, the problem of faulty recall would not be present. The findings set forth in Chapter X are thus of special interest.

We remind our readers that our three-way classification of the adoptees' outcome—viz., "low-problem," "middle-range," and "high-problem"—showed that the first group of families was almost uniformly described as enjoying close current parent-adoptee relationships. The middle-range group closely approximated this positive condition. On the other hand, the high-problem category showed only one in three families where the present relationship between the adoptee and his parents was presently considered a close one.

A fairly similar pattern prevailed with respect to the degree to which the adoptee currently was said to confide in his parents. We also noted that the three groups were similarly characterized with respect to the degree to which parents and adoptees enjoyed common recreational interests. On the whole, however, despite varying degrees of closeness and sense of familiness, we noted that even the most problematic third of our sample contained very few families where major or moderate parent-adoptee conflict was reported presently to prevail. While such conflict was almost never reported by parents of low-problem and middle-range outcome adoptees, 55 per cent of the parents of high-problem adoptees also reported no current conflict to speak of between themselves and their children.

At the time of the follow-up, 40 per cent of the families interviewed indicated that they saw no major limitations in the adoptee with respect to his current functioning. For a somewhat larger group one or more major limitations were noted by the parents and these were—as might be expected—more characteristic of high-problem adoptees than of their counterparts with less problematic adjustment.

CORRELATES OF OUTCOME

Age at placement In looking at the relationship between the outcome scores and some of the family background variables in our study, we were impressed with our failure to establish the expected relationship between the age of the adoptees at the time they were placed and their subsequent adjustment. We found, for example, no significant association between the age variable and the rank ordered Overall Adjustment Scores. Moreover, in the main there was an absence of significant relationships between age at placement and adjustment in the various life-space areas we explored. The only area in which adjustment showed a significant association with placement age was that of the adoptees' social relationships. Contrary to expectations, the *older* the child had been upon coming into the adoptive home, the more positive was the description by his parents of his social adjustment over the years. As we pointed out in Chapter XII, however, we discovered that this finding was partially explained by the fact of adoptive placement through two of the four participating agencies.

The main import of our findings in this area, however, is to throw into question the commonly held assumption that later placements tend to be more hazardous. While we certainly would not want to discourage agencies which in recent years have emphasized the early placement of adoptees—such emphasis appears to coincide with the thinking of many child development experts—we would hope that our findings would encourage those who have been hesitant to promote the adoption of somewhat older children at least to reconsider the basis for this reluctance. The positive outcome of some of the placements we studied, and which occurred as late as three years of age, would seem heartening.

Sex of adoptee   Our finding that the male adoptees in our sample fared somewhat less well than their female counterparts in their life adjustment does not come as a surprise in view of other child development studies which report similar outcomes. Particularly in the area of education, our findings tend to confirm the somewhat less problematic nature of the adjustment of girls with respect to academic achievements and school behavior.

Number of preadoptive placements   Another one of our unanticipated findings concerned the number of placements experienced by the adoptees prior to entering their adoptive families. Our review of the professional literature had led us to believe that we would find more problematic outcomes among those who had experienced a number of such preadoptive placements in contrast with those who had had a minimum of such experience. Our data suggest that this variable had little relationship to the outcome in most of the life-space areas covered by our index scores. Only a poor health history and the absence of outstanding talents appeared characteristic of those exposed to frequent preadoptive placements. Even here the relationships were not very strong. We have previously cautioned the reader, however, to note that our definition of what constituted a "prior placement" was dependent upon a rather undependable source of information, viz., the case records of the agencies. Record-keeping at the time these children were placed can be described as less than systematic.

Family composition   Another of our findings relating to conditions prevailing at the time of adoptive placement concerned the presence of other children in the family besides those who were the focus of our research. We found no relationship between adoptee adjustment and the arrival in the home of other biological or adopted children *subsequent* to the placement of our adoptee subjects.

We did discover, however, that adoptees who entered families *already* containing one or more children tended to fare better than did the adoptees placed with childless couples. The former children appeared to have performed better in school and were also somewhat more likely to be free of personal and social adjustment problems over the years. In addition, their parents were also inclined to express relatively little dissatisfaction with the overall adoptive experience as compared with couples covered by our research whose first child was the adoptee. We have speculated that perhaps the couples who had already been parents before adopting performed better in the adoptive parent role as a consequence of their previous experience with their first children. If so, this is a factor which could have been instrumental in the more favorable adjustment of the adoptees placed in their homes.

Socioeconomic status   The social class position of the adoptive parents showed some association with our outcome measures, but in the main we were surprised that our findings were not firmer on this score in view of other studies in the mental health field which have highlighted the importance of the social class variable. When we examined the scores achieved in the various life-space areas covered by our outcome indices, we found that only one area was significantly related to the socioeconomic status (SES) of the adoptive parents. Children who grew up in higher status families tended to encounter more personality problems over the years than did their counterparts reared in lower status families. We also found, however, that our research interviewers tended to rate the higher SES families significantly more negatively than they rated the lower SES families.

At the same time, both of these relationships were disclosed to be partly attributable to the linkage of the social class variable with the identification of two of the agencies through which the adoptees had been placed. When the effect of adoption through these agencies was removed, the correlations between SES and the two outcome variables referred to above were altered and tended for the most part to be diminished in strength.

Adoptive status   We would emphasize in this summary chapter the fact that the large majority of parents—almost three-fourths—reported that they had never at any time experienced problems which they saw as having been connected with their being *adoptive* parents or as having been specifically related to their child's adoptive status. We think it particularly noteworthy that even among the least well-adjusted third of our adoptee subjects, the parents of three-fifths of them denied that the fact of adoption per se had constituted any problem for them or had been a specific source of difficulty for the adoptees.

Child-rearing practices One of the central concepts of our study was that of the adoptive parent's "sense of entitlement" to his adopted child. We saw the parent's need to develop such a feeling as being the counterpart of the adoptee's task of resolving the identity problems stemming from the two sets of parents in his life. We sought to operationalize the entitlement concept by conceiving of the parent's child-rearing practices in various areas as indirect behavioral indicators of his success in developing a sense of rightful possession to the adoptee.

One area we explored was the parent's ability to accept the risks commonly associated with raising children in our society, especially the use of temporary parental substitutes as baby-sitters. Our findings in this regard were suggestive rather than clear-cut. We discovered only a limited association between the frequent use of baby-sitters when the adoptees were young and the latter's subsequent problematic personal, social, and heterosexual adjustment. On a descriptive level, however, we were interested to note that twice as many parents of high-problem adoptees reported having made frequuent use of sitters as was true of parents of low-problem adoptees.

We also examined the indicators of a parental sense of entitlement in the area of parental socialization practices. Our efforts to scrutinize the relationship of such practices to subsequent life adjustment proved relatively unproductive. The findings revealed some rather inconclusive associations which tended to become substantially attenuated when we removed the influence of socioeconomic status. These meager results, we believe, are attributable in substantial measure to the retrospective design of the study. Research findings in the child development and family process literature attest to the limited validity and reliablility of maternal recall of parental child-rearing practices after only a few years. It is obvious that the recollections of our adoptive parents would be substantially more vulnerable to inaccuracies and inconsistencies after the passage of two to three decades, and such unreliable data would inevitably yield attenuated correlations when related to other variables.

One of the unfortunate consequences of this situation was that we were really unable to test the usefulness of the "sense of entitlement" concept. Its validation was prevented by the weakness of our retrospective child-rearing data. We believe, however, that the concept merits operationalization in a more viable research design than that utilized in the current study so that its soundness and value may be more decisively assessed.

REVELATION OF ADOPTIVE STATUS

A long-standing and basic working assumption in the field of adoption placement has been that the telling of "the adoption story" to the child is one of the central and most critical tasks confronting adoptive parents. Both the recent literature and the reexamination of practice on the part of some agencies have revealed that the optimal timing, content, and manner of handling revelation are still unresolved issues. Little question, however, seems to have been raised that the need to resolve these issues in some way is one of the primary and unique responsibilities of adoptive parenthood which sets it apart from biological parenthood and that the kind of resolution arrived at by adoptive parents may well have great implications for the adoptee's future psychosocial adjustment.

In the light of these assumptions, our findings concerning the revelation practices of our one hundred adoptive families and the bearing of these practices upon subsequent adoption outcome are rather challenging. We discovered first of all that the way parents dealt with revelation was by and large a reflection of a more basic underlying orientation to child rearing in general. Families which tended to take a sheltering approach to the general upbringing of their children— e.g., supervising closely, not encouraging the development of autonomy and independence, etc.—were also likely to de-emphasize the adoption component in their children's lives. They tended to postpone revelation, to give minimal information about the child's biological background, to decrease the visibility of the adoptive status and, in effect, to simulate a biological parent-child relationship. On the other hand, parents with a less protective orientation toward the rearing of children were likely also to be more "open" about adoption, to reveal more information about natural parents, and to acknowledge freely the nonbiological nature of their relationship with the adoptee. Revelation, in other words, tended *not* to take place as a separate and isolated parental activity but rather as an integral part of the overall task of the raising of children.

We were struck by our finding that the prevailing pattern among our group of families had been to withhold from their children most or all information concerning the latter's biological parents and the circumstances leading to adoption. Seven in ten families reported that they had coped in this manner with the problem of the content of revelation although there were distinct differences in this regard among families who had adopted through different agencies. Only 12 percent of the parents had shared with their children the true facts of adoption as they knew them.

It is important to realize that these data offer no basis for assessing the relative merits of full versus minimal revelation. Nor are we aware of any rigorous research which might shed meaningful light upon this knotty question. It may well be, however, that it is not so much what and how much is revealed to the adoptee that is the decisive factor in the impact of revelation upon him as it is with the degree of comfort or ease his parents experience with their choice of approach. We would suspect that adoptive couples could choose to divulge everything they know about the adoptee's biological background or almost nothing and carry off either posture well or poorly depending upon the amount of anxiety it entailed for them. That stance which is most congenial to their emotional-psychological make-up, i.e., which is most ego-syntonic for them, may in the last analysis also be the most positive and constructive one for the adoptee with respect to his subsequent psychosocial adjustment.

We learned with some surprise that only a single aspect of revelation was definitively associated with the nature of adoptive outcome. Adoptees who showed marked curiosity about their biological past and desired to learn more about it than their adoptive parents knew or were willing to divulge tended to manifest a more problematic adjustment in a variety of life-space areas. None of the other ostensibly important aspects of "the telling"—the timing of initial revelation, the nature and amount of material revealed, or the frequency of subsequent allusion to adoption—was appreciably correlated with outcome.

We consider this finding (as well as the foregoing data suggesting the nonparamount role of revelation in the child-rearing behavior of our adoptive couples) to be among the most important and provocative findings to emerge from our study. Because they run counter to some fundamental assumptions of adoption placement practice, we believe they are suggestive of the need for further investigation of the dynamics of revelation in adoptive families and its influence on the subsequent life adjustment of adopted children.

It would seem most desirable and useful, for example, to determine more definitively than we were able to do the nature and strength of the fears and anxieties experienced by adoptive parents as they contemplate how and what to divulge to their children about the latter's adoptive status and biological background. What does revelation really mean to such parents emotionally and psychologically at the time they are actually confronted with this delicate task as compared with their recollection of these feelings two or three decades later? To what degree do they actually carry off "the telling" as well as our group of parents seem on the whole to have done? To what extent is revelation actually full or scanty, its content factual or fictitious? Finally, what is the impact of different modes of revelation, different contents, and different timings upon the adoptee's self-concept and upon his psychosocial adjustment at various stages of development? It would seem to us that to obtain meaningful answers to these and other equally relevant questions would require a rigorously designed prospective or "longitudinal" study so that parent behavior and orientation can be tapped while the events are fresh in their minds.

Value and implications for practice

Earlier we acknowledged the design and methodological limitations of our research. We believe, however, that they do not deprive the study of real value for those engaged in adoption practice. In this exploratory excursion we have endeavored to develop as detailed a portraiture as possible of adoptive family life as experienced by a hundred families over a period of more than two decades—to our knowledge, the first such undertaking of its kind. We have also sought to relate significant aspects of adoptive life and the adoptees' adjustment to other variables known about those families. To the extent that we have succeeded in realizing our objectives, the information contained in these pages should add a meaningful dimension to the relatively limited knowledge which adoption agencies have heretofore had of the nature of adoptive family life and the long-term adjustment of adopted children. Such enhanced understanding would, it is hoped, provide practitioners with a heightened sense of perspective concerning the long-range aspects of the adoption experience and would sensitize them to the kinds of problems and vicissitudes likely to be encountered by adoptive families once the initial task of placement has been accomplished.

In addition, we come away from our research with certain ideas concerning possible changes and improvements which adoption agencies might make in the organization of their service programs and in their overall orientation to adoptive family life. While these views are admittedly subjective, they nevertheless do rest upon the unusual opportunity we have had to get close to the meaning of the adoptive experience as lived out by a hundred families.

1. AGENCIES' DISTANCE FROM THE ADOPTIVE EXPERIENCE

In the course of our study we have developed a conviction about the value in the form of an augmented knowledge base that would accrue to agencies if they undertook to maintain contact with a cross-sectional sample of adoptive families beyond the year of supervision that normally precedes the final legalization of a child's adoption through the courts. It strikes us that the range of experience adoption agencies have available to them is most narrow. This stems from their almost exclusive absorption with the task of screening applicants, preparing them for the adoptive experience, and maintaining contact during the first year of the child's placement in the home. It is an almost universal fact that agencies are deprived of contact with representative groups of families during the later stages of childhood when the concern with such matters as revelation, socialization, and other child-rearing tasks takes on a more vital aspect.

It is our view that agencies ought to go beyond their present primary role of acting as "brokers," i.e., bringing couples and babies together. Rather, we believe they should become experts on adoptive family life. Adoption agencies are the logical locations in the community where such expertise can be developed. By having regular and close on-going contact with a group of adoptive families, agencies would be in a position to become related to the full range of experiences encountered by these families rather than being restricted to an almost complete concentration upon infant-caring which is typical of their current work.

This shift to a long-range developmental perspective with respect to adoptive family life would not be taking the agencies in a direction unrelated to their programmatic interests. Even if their programs were exclusively devoted to the task of selecting suitable couples from among the applicants who apply to become adoptive parents, much could be said for broadening the knowledge base beyond that which is currently available for the agencies. Question does arise as to the basis upon which couples are being selected when our research indicates so much ambiguity about the range of experiences encountered by adoptive families in the two decades in which their children grow to adulthood.

We would suggest that agencies maintain contact with adoptive families for a much longer period than they now do by either of two methods: (1) by organizing developmental studies which call for annual interviews with adoptive families along the lines taken in the research reported here, or, (2) by organizing their contacts around non-research enterprises in which adoptive couples are invited to come separately or in groups to share with the agency staff their experiences over the preceding year. We recognize the possibility that for some families the continued presence of the agency in their lives would be seen as too great an intrusion and would be too anxiety-provoking for them to tolerate. We believe, however, that such reaction would not be the predominant one. Certainly, the very low refusal rate we encountered—despite the passage of twenty to thirty years following the last agency contact with our sample of families—would suggest that adoptive families are a hardier lot than many have assumed. It is our view that most families could easily accept the legitimacy of an agency wanting to enhance its knowledge about adoptive family life through an ongoing relationship. We are made optimistic in this regard by the success in securing the cooperation of adoptive parents now being achieved by several developmental studies presently under way.[3]

2. TROUBLED FAMILIES

Our study revealed a fairly sizable number of families in which adoptees had encountered moderate to severe difficulties while growing up. Although we are not in a position to determine whether this incidence of problems was more than we would expect to find among a comparable sample of nonadoptive families, the question does arise as to whether agencies ought to be geared to providing counseling services for adoptive families. While it is true that counseling and psychotherapeutic services are available for all children in the community without regard to adoptive status, some experimentation with organized clinical facilities for adoptive children might be attempted on two grounds: (1) Work with a sufficiently large sample of disturbed adopted children would further the knowledge base about adoptive family life. The current widespread interest in the frequency and nature of emotional problems among adopted children has reached such proportions that more profound study of these problems ought to be undertaken.[4] (2) Since the adoptive families have already had contact with the agencies, the development of clinical facilities would provide a test to determine whether it is easier for the families with children who are showing disturbances to return to a familiar source for help. While it is true that some families do return to the agency when they encounter difficulties, these in all probability represent a small minority of those who might be willing to come since the agency has likely not systematically advertised the availability of counseling services.

Concluding note

We come away from our research believing that as a social unit the adoptive family has attributes which make it both similar to and different from nonadoptive families. In terms of the biological family pattern prevailing in our society, the adoptive family is an artificially created unit. Yet, in certain respects it cannot be easily differentiated from its biologically based counterpart. It seeks to fulfill all the major functions served by the natural family with respect to the needs of both the child and the couple involved. Before the law, it is a bona fide family with all legal rights and responsibilities common to the biologically created unit, and in large segments of our society it is accepted on exactly the same terms as any other family. It tends to experience developmental processes comparable to those found in families with naturally conceived children, and it is subject to some of the same strains as well as to similar sources of individual and group gratification and self-fulfillment.

On the other hand, it seems clear that in certain quite fundamental respects the adoptive family is quite different from procreated families. The adopted child, for example, must face and resolve in some way complex identity problems with which the nonadopted child is not confronted, problems growing out of the two sets of parents in his life. The adopting couple is vulnerable to potential stresses unique to the adoptive parent role, e.g., the need to contend with the child's prior emotional attachment to former foster parents. Kirk [5] sees the adoptive couple as being disadvantaged by virtue of living in a rather unfriendly social climate and experiencing a basic role handicap and feelings of alienation with which they must strive to cope. We have proposed that adoptive parents must contend with an identity resolution problem parallel to that facing their child, namely, the need to develop a feeling of entitlement to their child, a problem with which parents who have been able to procreate need not struggle. Finally, Pollak questions whether the construct of "family" can even be rightfully applied to the parent-child unit created by adoption since such an arrangement cannot provide ". . . the essence of a normal family experience, which in the last analysis is immortality, or at least liberation from the destiny of irrevocably coming to an end in one's own generation." [6]

We are suggesting, in other words, that the adoptive family may perhaps be viewed as a rather special, or possibly exotic, species sharing some of the characteristics of the broader genus of family in our culture while being unique in other respects. It seems to us that this combination of traits should make adoptive family life a rewarding object of investigation for the serious student of the family.

appendix A / Additional notes on the study method

The sample

RESOURCES EXPLORED IN EFFORTS TO LOCATE SAMPLE FAMILIES

The principal factor exacerbating our location problem was that twenty to thirty years had elapsed since the adoptive placements had been effected. Allowing for an average of one year before the adoptions were legally consummated, there was a period of nineteen to twenty-nine years during which the adoptive families were no longer required to keep in contact with the placing agencies or to report their whereabouts. A few families did keep in touch, of course, for varying periods of time, but the majority did not. This meant that in addition to the passage of two or three decades during which these families could well have made several moves, we were also faced with the fact that most of the addresses available from the agencies were of very little value. Owing to an organizational emergency, one agency had been forced to develop a more current address file, and as a consequence sample families drawn from its roster were somewhat easier to locate. But this did not hold true for the other three agencies whose roster addresses were found to be extremely inadequate.

It was this unavailability of even moderately updated addresses which proved the most serious obstacle in our location efforts. Because of it, we could not avail ourselves of resources which other investigators had found very helpful and which might otherwise have also proved fruitful in our study. We could not, for example, check the names of sample families against the state's driver's license register or its motor vehicle registration file because this procedure required relatively current last-known addresses. For the same reason, we could not consult public lists of names and addresses maintained by such federal agencies as the Internal Revenue Service and the Passport Division of the State Department, nor could we turn for help in our search to the military services or the Veterans Administration. We also learned that the membership lists of churches, fraternal lodges, trade associations, unions, and professional organizations would be unlikely to yield useful information for want of serviceable addresses. With respect to these latter resources, moreover, the paucity of information in most of the agency case records prevented our being able to determine whether the adoptive parents had ever belonged to such organizations and if so, to which ones.

Other channels which at first blush had seemed promising turned out, upon investigation, to be quite unfruitful as location resources. A prime example was the U.S. Post Office which would not forward mail to any addressee who had moved more than three years earlier. Relatively current addresses were also required by the telephone company and by other utilities if they were to be of help in a search. To our disappointment, we learned, too, that credit bureaus could not be of help to us because national associations of credit bureaus did not maintain nationwide lists of credit users. Finally, we operated under the major handicap that no city directory existed for either New York City as a whole or for any of its five boroughs: such a resource would have been invaluable in tracing families through a series of moves over a number of years.

We had available to us one other type of resource which would doubtless have been helpful had we been able to exploit it, viz., individuals who had fulfilled a variety of collateral roles in the adoption process. One potentially fruitful resource would have been former employers and/or business associates of the adoptive fathers. Their names and business addresses were often available in the case records and had we contacted them they might well have provided valuable leads to the current whereabouts of sample families.

The four participating agencies, however, were very reluctant to use this avenue of search. They feared that a contact with such collaterals, even after a hiatus of three decades, was fraught with the potential danger of inadvertently divulging confidential information. They were particularly concerned about the possibility that the adoptees' status might be revealed to persons in whom the adoptive parents had not confided such information. While we felt confident that sufficient precautions could be taken to avoid such violations of confidentiality, we did not utilize this search procedure in view of the agencies' hesitancy about it.

Other persons who had been involved at some point in the original adoption process were friends and relatives who had acted as references for the adopting couples, attorneys who had handled the legal adoption procedures, and physicians who had examined the prospective adoptees prior to placement. All such persons would have naturally been aware of the child's adoptive status, and there would thus have been no question of an accidental breach of confidentiality.

However, practical considerations ruled out using such individuals to help track down our sample families. We found that the process of locating the current addresses and telephone numbers of these collaterals was an immensely time-consuming endeavor. Furthermore, it was subject to the very same obstacles and limitations which plagued our efforts to find current addresses for our sample families. Since time and budget limitations precluded our devoting the inordinate amount of time required to make this resource pay off, we abandoned it.

The successive winnowing out of all the above location resources left but a single one available: the telephone directories of the thirty to forty different communities within the study area. A trial search of successive *past* phone books revealed that time-consuming efforts to trace adoptive families in this manner—beginning with their last-known addresses—were not likely to yield appreciable numbers of usable present-day addresses. The result was that only the *current* issues of these phone directories were utilized to find all the 130 adoptive families whom we were finally able to locate.

LOCATION PROCEDURE

The specifics of the location procedure were as follows:

1. The search for each family began with an intensive screening of the various phone directories, starting with the directory of the community in which the family was last known to be residing. If examination of that directory proved unproductive, the search was then broadened, first to the directories of neighboring communities and progressively to directories of more remote communities, following the known population shifts during the past three decades out of New York City proper and into the outlying suburbs.

2. If a family with the appropriate name was found to be living at the same address as that last known to the agency, this family was considered to have been positively located. Moreover, if a family possessing a highly unusual last name were found listed under the first name of either of the adoptive parents, it, too, was considered located even though it was currently living at an address and/or in a community other than that last known to the agency. The first wave of searching yielded thirty-five sample families who fell into one of these two categories.

3. However, the search also produced families whose names and/or addresses differed in some detail from the information furnished by the agency but who otherwise seemed likely to be sample families. These were considered "good prospects" and tabbed for further search efforts consisting mainly of a second more detailed examination of the case record summaries which had been prepared at the outset of the study.[1] The purpose of this examination was to spot, if possible, some item of information which would correspond with the listing found in the directory and thus confirm the identity of the latter as a sample family. When such a confirmation could be made, the family was reclassified as "located." Otherwise, it was assigned to a group of direc-

tory listings which required an exploratory phone call in order to ascertain whether they were or were not sample families. This group also consisted of all the families in each directory possessing very common names identical with those of sample families.[2]

4. Each exploratory phone call was made by one of the two authors whose initial statement was as follows: "I am trying to locate the family of John and Mary Jones who formerly lived at so-and-so address. Is this the family?" If the response to this inquiry was "No," the conversation was terminated forthwith, and all danger of violation of confidentiality was obviated. The next name on the list was then phoned and the same query made. This procedure continued either until the list of directory names was exhausted without having located the sample family in question or until one call elicited the response that the family had indeed lived at the previous address mentioned by the investigator. When this occurred the latter, after identifying himself as someone working with the placing agency, stated that the agency was conducting a research study in which it wished to enlist the family's participation and that the family would soon receive a letter supplying more information about the project.

It is apparent that this phase of the location procedure was immensely time-consuming since dozens of sample families had to be traced in this manner. Moreover, the calls required very careful handling lest a family acknowledging itself to be the sample family refuse at that juncture to have anything further to do with the study. This happened on a few occasions, but for the most part families showed a willingness to await and read the introductory letter before deciding whether or not to cooperate in the investigation.

5. This letter was sent within two days to each sample family identified in the above manner and also to every family located directly in the initial search of the telephone directories. Written on the letterhead of the agency which had originally placed the adoptee and over the signature of the current executive, it briefly outlined the purpose of the study, stressed its potential value to future prospective adoptive parents, requested the family's participation, and informed the adoptive parents that one of the study directors would phone within the week to describe what participation would entail for them and to answer whatever questions they might have. The study was

presented as being under the auspices of the four participating agencies together with the cooperation of the Child Welfare League of America.

6. The follow-up phone call was perhaps the most crucial step taken in actually launching the study because it was at this stage that a sample family could either be lost to the project or its interest captured and its participation assured. The family's option of refusing to cooperate was made particularly easy by the impersonal nature and lack of face-to-face contact in the telephone conversation. Accordingly, the approach to be followed in these calls was worked out carefully in advance. Strong emphasis was placed upon allaying the fears and anxieties of the adoptive parents and candidly answering all questions necessary to assure them of the legitimate professional nature of the study. All calls were made by the two authors.

If at the time of the phone call the adoptive family consented to participate in the research, an interview appointment was made for both parents at their convenience. If, however, the parent answering the phone hesitated to commit himself and/or his spouse at that point —a fairly frequent occurrence—telephone call-backs were arranged and made. In the main, most parents were quite amenable to cooperating in the research. Several families, however, exhibited considerable resistance and reluctance to participate but were unable to make firm refusals in several successive contacts. Others remained clearly ambivalent for periods up to a month, which necessitated numerous repeat calls. However, careful effort was made to follow through on each such family until the indecision was resolved either way.

The interview

INTERVIEW PRETEST

Both the format and content of the interview, as well as the attitude questionnaire, were subjected to an exhaustive pretest before being finalized for the study. Pretest interviewees were recruited through an article which appeared on the Women's Page of a Sunday issue of the *New York Times*. It described the study's nature and purpose, asked for volunteers to help test its instruments, and made clear that all pretest subjects had to be adoptive parents whose adopted children were currently twenty-one years of age or older.

The response to this brief announcement surprised us by its volume. Phone calls and letters began coming in the day after the appearance of the article and continued almost unabated for three weeks, with occasional volunteers continuing to contact us for as long as two months. The result was that we obtained a pool of some seventy-five adoptive families willing to be interviewed, forty of whom actually participated in the pretest.

It should be made clear that these families were in no way representative of the adoptive families who were to be the focus of our study. In the first place, the fact that they had volunteered for the pretest immediately introduced a possible bias stemming from self-selection. Furthermore, many of them had obtained their children by means of independent adoptions, and our inquiry was focused upon the adjustment of children adopted through agencies. Finally, even among the volunteer families who met this latter criterion, very few had adopted through one of the four agencies whose rosters constituted our study population.[3] However, all the forty pretest families *were* comparable with our final sample families in the crucial respect of having reared to adulthood one or more adopted children, and it was precisely the multifaceted nature of this experience and its outcome which we wished to study. We consequently concluded that we could justifiably draw from the volunteers' reactions and responses to the interview and the questionnaire valid deductions about how effectively these instruments were tapping the study's crucial variables.

The pretest confirmed the soundness of the interview content and format; no major modifications had to be made in either. However, the test did bring to light certain deficiencies in the wording of some of the items in the original version of the questionnaire. These were then rectified in the manner described in Chapter III.

FORMAT AND CONDUCT OF THE INTERVIEW

The two-parent interviews took the following form. Both parents were seen together briefly to answer any questions regarding the pur-

pose and sponsorship of the study which had not been sufficiently resolved in the earlier telephone conversation arranging for the interview. They were then asked to decide between themselves the order
in which they would be interviewed separately. As they had been prepared in the phone contact for this eventuality, it occasioned no difficulty in most instances.[4] Moreover, acceptance of this format was
made even easier by our use of the parent questionnaire in tandem
with the face-to-face aspect of the interview.[5]

The content of these separate interviews was not required to be,
and usually was not, identical. The wide scope and great detail of the
interview outline militated against covering all of it with each partner.
To have striven to do so would have been to place an exhorbitant
time demand upon the couple and possibly to have jeopardized both
their willingness to cooperate and the quality of their responses.

There was no specification of what material was to be discussed
with what parent, but as a matter of course the interviewers tended to
select topics traditionally linked in our culture to the parent's sex role.
For example, adoptive mothers were more apt to be queried about
child-rearing practices; adoptive fathers, about the family's socioeconomic status over the years. At the same time there was also substantial overlap, with many topics—particularly those tapping the study's
major conceptual dimensions—being taken up in both interviews.

The order in which the two parents were seen also tended to influence which areas would be explored with each. In the first of a pair
of interviews, the interviewer was apt to range somewhat freely
among various topics, tending to follow the parent's lead. In the second interview, he was likely to be more focused, seeking to touch
upon subjects which had not come up earlier. Finally, of course, the
relative articulateness and verbal facility of the two spouses was also
a partial determinant of how much material would be covered in the
respective interviews. Thus, although the average two-parent interview session lasted approximately three hours,[6] this time was often
not allocated completely equally to the two interviews.

THE INTERVIEW CODEBOOK

1. *Special coding procedures* Although each spouse in a two-parent family was interviewed separately, we decided, as discussed in Chapter III, to use in our data analysis a single composite family response for each item contained in the codebook by which the discursive interview material was translated into objective, categorized form. This decision required that we develop a special coding procedure to cope with the contingency of disparate responses by the two members of a given couple to the same codebook item. To obtain the single composite datum we needed, such disparities had to be resolved. But how? Was one partner's reply to be given full or partial preference over the conflicting reply of the other partner? If so, on what basis was the preferred parent to be designated? Or, was it imperative that the discordant responses be given equal weight? In that case, how could the conflicting reports be resolved into a single final coding?

Fortunately, this problem was susceptible of a variety of solutions. In the simplest case, when the interviewer had assigned one parent's reply to a substantive response category in the codebook item but had classified the mate's response as nondefinitive (i.e., "unable to determine" or "not covered"), the substantive response was utilized in the data analysis. When the discrepant responses had been equally definitive, one of the authors examined the codebook and resolved the conflict in one of several ways. Responses to other related items were scrutinized for evidence of inconsistency or self-contradiction on the part of one of the two spouses. If such evidence were found, the dissensus was resolved in favor of the partner showing the greater degree of consistency in his answers. If no such evidence appeared, discordant replies were handled as follows: when the conflicting codebook entries were two or more response categories apart, a category representing the average of the two numerical codes was used. Where, on occasion, entries were in adjacent response categories, the discrepancy was resolved by the toss of a coin.

2. *Test of codebook reliability* To conduct this test, we first had to resolve a practical problem with important methodological overtones. Ideally, a reliability check would have involved a complete and

exhaustive item-by-item comparison of two codebooks for each adoptive family interview; the original one filled out by the interviewer and a second one completed by another professional staff person listening independently to the interview tape. However, time and budgetary limitations militated against using such a procedure to test the reliability of each of the several hundred entries in even a small sample of codebooks.

We therefore restricted our reliability check to the thirty-seven different codebook items which comprised our eleven indices of adoption outcome.[7] Included in these indices were items representing all of the study's major dependent variables. A test of the reliability of the entries in these items would thus cover a goodly portion of the study's most crucial data from which our most important findings would be drawn. We were satisfied that if an assessment of these codebook items yielded high reliability scores, both we and our readers would be able to place confidence in our answers to the basic questions which gave rise to our investigation.

The reliability test was conducted in the following manner. We drew a 20 percent random sample of the one hundred interview tapes, sampling proportionately from each interviewer's tapes according to the total number of interviews he had conducted. Each of the authors then listened to ten of the sample tapes, among which, of course, none of his own interviews was represented. Next, without reference to the original codebooks, he completed for each interview enough of a second codebook to permit the development of scores for the eleven outcome indices as well as a summated score representing the adoptee's overall adjustment. The twenty cases were then rank-ordered twice: once on the basis of the twelve sets of new outcome scores and then again on the basis of the twelve sets of comparable scores generated from the interviewers' original codebooks. This provided two independent sets of ordered rankings, the association between which was tested by means of Kendall's Tau, a measure of rank-order correlation. The results, presented in Table A–1, reveal that each test produced a correlation coefficient significant at at least the .001 level. This statisfied us that the original codebook entries, upon which our subsequent data analysis and findings would rest, were quite reliable.

Table A–1 / *Kendall's tau coefficients showing*
results of rank-order correlations between
two independent sets of rankings of
a random sample of 20 cases for
11 outcome index scores and
for overall adjustment scores

OUTCOME INDEX	KENDALL'S TAU
Overall Adjustment Score	.726 *
Educational adjustment	.559 *
Personality adjustment	.586 *
Past parent-adoptee relationship	.598 *
Current parent-adoptee relationship	.698 *
Economic adjustment	.718 *
Personal and social adjustment	.653 *
Social relations adjustment	.531 *
Heterosexual relationship adjustment	.714 *
Outstanding talents	.808 *
Health status	.713 *
Parental dissatisfactions with adoption experience	.500 **

* Significant at <.01 level. ** Significant at .001 level.

The interviewers' rating instrument

TEST OF RELIABILITY OF RATINGS

Utilizing the same twenty cases involved in the foregoing description of the codebook reliability check, we also conducted a reliability check of the scaler judgments made by our caseworker-interviewers on the *Interviewer's Rating Form*. Pearsonian product-moment correlations were calculated for those rating scales which had been included in the *Interviewer Global Factor Rating Scores*.[8] The resulting correlation coefficients—between the original interviewer's ratings and those of the "listener"—are as follows:

SCALE	CORRELATION
1. Overall parental satisfaction with adoptive experience	.66
2. Stress encountered in the parental role	.55
6. Parental comfort in discussing biological parents	.70
7. Parental projection of difficulties upon adoption	.77
8. Closeness of parent's relationship with adoptee	.54
11. Global assessment of parent's ego-strength	.45
12. Parental satisfaction with current parent-adoptee relationship	.82
13. Current parental negative feelings towards adoptee	.55
14. Parental defensiveness in discussing relationship with adoptee	.43

A number of the above correlations are sufficiently low to raise some question about the utility of the ratings as a measure of the adoptive family's experience. Fortunately, as we have shown in the immediately preceding section of this appendix the scores derived from the codebook achieved a much higher level of reliability, and it is these scores which are emphasized in the present report.

appendix B / *Interviewing the adoptees*

IN CHAPTER III, which deals with the method of our study, we discussed the reasons why we shifted from our original intention of securing the direct reports of adult adopted children about their life experiences to the alternative of studying the phenonenon from the perspective of their adoptive parents. To recapitulate briefly, two factors were responsible for this major shift in focus: one was our growing awareness as we developed the adoptive parent interview that these parents had played a role in the adoption drama equal in importance to that of the adoptee himself, and that therefore their perceptions of the experience had to be included as an essential source of data. The second factor accounting for the ultimate focus of the study was related to a realistic constraint. Only one-third of the adoptees whose parents were interviewed—thirty-three in all—were themselves accessible for study interviews. In other words, in sixty-seven instances, although we were able to speak with one or both adoptive parents, it was not possible to obtain an interview with the adoptee who was the focus of study.

The purpose of this appendix is twofold: to acquaint the reader

with the reasons why two-thirds of the adoptees could not be interviewed, and to examine briefly the extent to which the thirty-three
adoptees who did participate in the study may be considered representative of the total sample of a hundred whose experiences and adjustment were described by the adoptive parents. An analysis of the
data obtained directly from the adoptees will be completed shortly.
The degree to which those reports agreed with the parental parents is
of course a matter of considerable interest.

Nonparticipation of two-thirds of adoptees

ACCESS TO ADOPTEES THROUGH PARENTS

The reader will recall that there were two compelling reasons
why access to the adoptees had to be gained through the adoptive
parents. First, we did not know how many of the adopted children
had been told of their adoptive status, which thereby made a direct
approach to them undesirable on a number of ethical and legal
grounds. In this regard, the initial phone contact with the adoptive
parents was handled with considerable planfulness to avoid the possibility of inadvertently divulging such information to an unsuspecting
adoptee who happened to answer the telephone.

Our second reason for seeking contact with the adoptees through
their adoptive parents was that there seemed no feasible way to locate
the former without parental assistance. Mobility of the American population being such a widespread phenomenon, it was difficult enough
to find the adoptive parents after the passage of two to three decades.
It would have been an even more formidable task—certainly outside
the scope of the time and financial resources available to us—to locate
the adoptees whose ties to the New York area were likely to be
weaker than those of their adoptive parents. We would, moreover,
have encountered still further difficulty in tracing the female adoptees
who had married and whose married names were unknown to us or
the agencies.

Our interviewers broached the topic of involving the adoptees in
the study only at the end of the parent interview. We believed that this

timing would optimize the chances for obtaining permission to contact the adoptees, since the interviewer would hopefully have established some rapport with the parents by the conclusion of the interview. We feared that any reference at the outset of the parent interviews to our wish to see the adoptees would not only fail to yield a greater number of consents; it might also result in the loss of a substantial number of parent interviews. Our thinking and our decision in this matter proved to be well founded in several instances where the adoptive parents revealed that they had anticipated a possible request for access to their child. They stated at the beginning of their interviews that they would not permit this and clearly implied that if the granting of such permission were a condition for their own participation, they would not consent to being interviewed.

In discussing with the parents our desire to interview the adoptee, we emphasized the usefulness of obtaining an "adoptee's eye view" of the adoption experience. We also gave assurance that care would be taken not to arouse undue anxiety in the adoptee and that we would protect the confidentiality of the parent interview as far as the adoptee was concerned. Parents who were unsure of their attitudes about having the adoptee interviewed were given several days to consider the matter. Every effort was made to reduce the potential threat the adoptee interview might be to the adoptive parents and to enlist their participation and cooperation as partners in the research undertaking.

REASONS FOR NONPARTICIPATION
OF SIXTY-SEVEN ADOPTEES

Notwithstanding our efforts to elicit a positive response from the parents, only thirty-three of the hundred adoptees were eventually interviewed. Table B–1 presents the reasons why the remaining sixty-seven adoptees did not participate in the study. The reader will note that in more than half (55 percent) of the cases where the adoptees proved unavailable to us, failure to interview was due directly to parental refusal to consent to the adoptee being involved in the research. In an additional one-fifth of the instances, the adoptee himself was reported by the parents to have refused to participate despite ostensible parental approval of his doing so. One in ten adoptees was not interviewed because his mental or emotional condition at the time was considered so fragile or precarious [1] that an interview seemed professionally contra-indicated. In another tenth of the cases, we encountered the problem that while the parents were most amenable to their children being contacted and interviewed, the adoptees lived in distant and widely scattered sections of the country. They were consequently considered geographically unavailable to us because time and budget limitations militated against the long and costly field trips which would have been necessary to interview these subjects. Finally, in 4 percent of the sixty-seven cases, either the parents did not know the whereabouts of the adoptees or—in one instance—the adoptee suffered an accidental death during the course of the study, prior to his parents' decision whether they would permit him to be interviewed.

Why did the majority of the parents of the uninterviewed adoptees deny access to their children? Table B-1 we note that in 6 percent of the cases—four instances—parents reported never having told their children that they were adopted. We were not surprised that, after two to three decades of carefully attempting to shield their children from this truth about their backgrounds, these adoptive parents steadfastly refused to consider altering such a fundamental decision for the sake of a study.

The refusals of the remaining parents can be divided into three general categories. In a few families, the adoptee had been told only once or twice in his entire life that he was adopted, usually when he was quite young. It appeared evident to us that the adoptive parents in these families had taken great pains to keep adoption as invisible as possible without actually concealing the information entirely. In one family, for example, the child had been informed of his status only once, at the age of four or five. According to the parents, the topic was never again broached, nor did the adoptee ever ask about his being adopted. In another family, reference to the adoptee's status had been very infrequent over the years. He was currently married and the father of several children, but he still had not informed his wife that he had been adopted. It seems understandable and consistent with past behavior that these parents, like their counterparts who had never talked about adoption at all, would not wish—after so long a history of "playing down" adoption—to suddenly make thi status visible to their children in a way required by a study interview.

In a second category of families, the adoptees had experienced or were currently undergoing adjustment problems of varying degrees of severity. One young man, for instance, had just returned home from a tour of duty in the armed forces and was encountering substantial difficulty in readjusting to civilian life. His adoptive parents, highly cooperative as far as their own participation was concerned, ruled out an interview with him. They, like some of the other adoptive parents who were burdened with similar concerns, contended that they did not like to "stir things up" any further while their children were contending with their current problems.

The rationale behind the third category of refusals is initially less easy to understand. In these families, according to parental reports, adoption has been made visible to the adoptees over the years. The latter had apparently accepted and integrated this information without undue difficulty or anxiety, and they were now seemingly comfortable and self-accepting with regard to their adoptive status. This very fact, however, constituted the main reason offered by the adoptive parents for withholding approval for interviewing the adoptees. Their efforts over the years had been concentrated upon allowing adoption "to assume its natural place" in the children's concept of themselves, to be accepted as part of their identity in much the same way as their sex or hair coloring. These parents had tended to "play it cool" in dealing with the topic of adoption, and once the adoptees had appeared able to absorb the knowledge, the parents had apparently attempted to simulate as closely as possible the biological parent-child relationship. They therefore saw no reason after twenty to thirty years to focus a spotlight upon the adoption phenomenon as would be required in an interview with the adoptees.

This posture is reminiscent of the "denial of difference" orientation of adoptive parents described by Kirk,[2] and it is difficult to appraise its latent meaning and the thinking and feeling underlying it. On the one hand, many of these adoptive parents were quite open and candid in all aspects of their account of the adoptees' life experiences and told stories of healthy adjustment which rang true and were thoroughly consistent throughout, even upon careful interviewer probing. On the face of it, in other words, there seems no basis for suspecting that the refusal of such parents to grant us access to their children was *invariably* a defensive maneuver. We would not preclude the possibility that the above rationale which they offered for their opposition to the adoptees' involvement in our research was in fact the true one as they perceived it. Given their general orientation to the role which adoption should play in theirs and their children's lives, it seems not inconsistent that they should wish to avoid a situation which by its nature would inevitably throw the adoptive status into bold relief, and thus possibly out of proportion, for their children.

On the other hand, if the adoptees had actually been as successful as they were reported to be in integrating the information of their adoptive status and in achieving the highly satisfactory life adjustment claimed for some of them, the expectation would be that they would not have encountered any undue difficulty in discussing their perceptions of their adoptive status. Nor would it be reasonable to anticipate that such an interview was likely to have any really adverse consequences for their emotional well-being. Their parents, in other words, should realistically not have been as threatened at the prospect of an adoptee interview as they appeared to be. From a clinical standpoint, therefore, the parents' stance might be interpreted as a defensive one, perhaps symptomatic of their unresolved feelings about adoption. Their refusal to let their children be contacted might be seen as reflecting their uncertainty about the strength and quality of their relationship with the adoptees, actual adjustment problems encountered by the latter and concealed by the parents, or qualms about just how thoroughly the children had in fact accepted their adoptive status as normal and natural.

When we examine the sixty-seven adoptees according to their outcome classification, we note in Table B-1 distinct differences in the reasons they were not interviewed. Approximately two-thirds of the noninterviewed adoptees in both the low-problem and middle-range adjustment groups did not participate in the study due to their adoptive parents' refusal to consent to such participation. This reason, however, is applicable to less than one-third the noninterviewed adoptees classified as having had high-problem adjustments. Part of the difference is accounted for by the substantial proportion of Group III adop

*Table B–1 / Reasons for not interviewing
uninterviewed adoptees—percentage
distribution by outcome*

REASON FOR NOT INTERVIEWING	GROUP I	GROUP II	GROUP III	TOTAL
Parent refusal of consent: adoptee did not know he was adopted	9%	4%	4%	6%
Parent refusal of consent: adoptee did know he was adopted	59	61	27	49
Parent report of adoptee refusal to participate despite parental approval	23	22	14	19
Study staff decision or agreement that adoptee should not be interviewed due to mental or emotional condition	—	4	27	11
Adoptee geographically unavailable	9	9	14	11
Adoptee dead or whereabouts unknown	—	—	14	4
	(22)	(23)	(22)	(67)

tees—more than one-fourth—where failure to interview resulted from staff assessment that the adoptees' mental or emotional condition militated against such an interview. This is not a surprising finding in view of the fact that Group III by definition comprises the adoptees who showed more problematic adjustments. In addition, however, that group also included all the adoptees whose whereabouts were unknown, plus the one adoptee who died during the course of the study. Finally, it also encompassed a larger proportion than did the other two groups of adoptees who were geographically unavailable to us for interviews.

Representativeness of the interviewed adoptees

The meaningfulness of any future analysis of the data obtained in the interviews with the thirty-three adoptees who did participate in the study will rest upon how possible it is to regard these interviewees as representative of the total original sample of one hundred. On the face of it, there would seem to have been some biases operating in the fact that the parents of the thirty-three permitted them to be con-tacted for the study and that they consented to be interviewed while this was not true for the remaining sixty-seven adoptees. The nature of these biases can be very roughly ascertained from the reasons given by the refusing parents and the refusing adoptees. At the same time, the implication of these biases for the quality of the life adjustment achieved by the adoptees cannot be accurately assessed.

Hence, the only way to shed some light on the question of repre-sentativeness is to explore the only relevant data which are available, viz., those obtained in the adoptive parent interviews. The purpose would be to determine whether or not, on the basis of such data, the thirty-three interviewed adoptees emerged as differing in significant ways from the uninterviewed sixty-seven. The parent interview data offered two avenues of inquiry, both of which have thus far been ex-plored to a limited degree: an examination of the outcome variables, and an examination of the major background variables.

EVIDENCE FROM THE OUTCOME VARIABLES

The adoptees' overall adjustment in the eleven life-space areas ex-plored in our study was reflected in each adoptee's Overall Adjust-ment Score, such score being derived from the adoptive parent re-ports in the manner described in Chapter XI. Consequently, the rank ordering of the hundred Overall Adjustment Scores was inspected to determine how the scores of the thirty-three interviewed adoptees were distributed.

We might justifiably have expected that these young adults would constitute a highly skewed subsample of well-adjusted individuals. It would not be unreasonable, after all, to anticipate that the adoptive parents of the reportedly better adjusted adoptees would have most readily consented to their children's participation in the study and that the more secure and better adjusted adoptees might also have been most willing to submit to interviews. We would therefore not have been greatly surprised had we found the thirty-three interviewees clustered at the high end of the rank ordering. This would have meant that as a group they could not be regarded as being representative of the total sample of one hundred adoptees.

Such, however, turned out not to be the case. Instead, the opposite was true. We discovered that the adoptees whom we interviewed were distributed very evenly throughout the entire rank ordering. At least one such interviewee—and more commonly three or four—appeared within *every* tenth of the range, from the best to the poorest adjustment poles. The actual distribution, presented in Table B–2, clearly indicates that the interviewed adoptees comprised a representative subgroup of the total sample with respect to their adjustment as perceived by their adoptive parents. This finding, in turn, suggests that had the other sixty-seven adoptees also been interviewed, their perceptions of and reactions to their adoptive experience, as a group, would not have differed appreciably from the data actually provided by the thirty-three interviewees.

There is of course one possible caveat to be borne in mind in this regard. While the interviewees were well distributed among the total group of adoptees with respect to scores based on the content of parental reports, the interviewed and noninterviewed subjects might be

Table B–2 / Distribution of interviewed adoptees within rank ordering of total sample of adoptees based on overall adjustment scores derived from adoptive parent interviews

RANK ORDERING BY TENTHS	NO. OF INTERVIEWED ADOPTEES WITHIN TENTH
1st tenth	3
2nd "	1
3rd "	5
4th "	3
5th "	4
6th "	4
7th "	4
8th "	3
9th "	5
10th "	1
Total	33

*Table B–3 / Comparison of 33 interviewed and
67 noninterviewed adoptees with respect to
8 background variables*

	MEAN, PERCENTAGE OR FREQUENCY		
	INTERVIEWED ADOPTEES	NON-INTERVIEWED ADOPTEES	
VARIABLE	$(N = 33)$	$(N = 67)$	DIFFERENCE
ADOPTEE CHARACTERISTICS			
Sex distribution (percent male)	42.4	52.2	9.8 *
Mean age at placement (in months)	11.6	14.4	2.8 *
Mean number of preadoption placements	3.2	3.3	.1 *
ADOPTIVE FAMILY CHARACTERISTICS			
Adoptee an only child (percent of families)	39.4	44.8	5.4 *
Mean age of adoptive father at application	33.8	34.3	.5 *
Mean age of adoptive mother at application	31.0	31.9	.9 *
Mean SES score [a]	13.4	13.6	.2 *
Religious affiliation (no. of families)			
Protestant	18	24	$\chi^2 = 4.12$ **
Catholic	6	24	(3 d.f.)
Jewish	8	17	
Mixed marriage	1	2	

* $p < .10$. ** $p < .20$.

[a] See Chapter IV for discussion of components and computation of SES score.

differentiated on the basis of the candor and reliability of those reports. It is possible, in other words, that candid parents as a group tended to allow us to see their children, regardless of the quality of the latter's adjustment, while the less-than-candid parents tended to deny us access to their children. Within the context of the research design utilized in our study, this issue cannot be resolved.

EVIDENCE FROM THE BACKGROUND VARIABLES

The interviewed and noninterviewed adoptees were also examined and compared with respect to eight major and theoretically important background variables utilized in the study. The result of this analysis, presented in Table B–3, discloses that the differences between the two groups are not striking and could be accounted for by chance.

This finding would seem to justify the following conclusion: to the degree that the independent variables employed in this subanalysis do in fact exert a meaningful influence upon the subsequent life adjustment of individuals and condition their responsiveness to various kinds of life experiences, the sixty-seven noninterviewed adoptees were given a start in their adoptive lives substantially similar to that experienced by the thirty-three interviewed adoptees. They were also exposed over the years to comparable influences resulting from these variables. On the basis of this criterion, there is support for generalizing to the total sample of a hundred adoptees from the data obtained in the interviews with the thirty-three who did participate in the study.

Notes

one / Introduction

1. *Supplement to CHILD WELFARE STATISTICS—1965: Adoptions in 1965,* Children's Bureau, U.S. Department of Health, Education, and Welfare (Statistical Series No. 84), 1966.

2. *Ibid.,* plus *Child Welfare Statistics*—1961–1964, Children's Bureau, U.S. Department of Health, Education, and Welfare (Statistical Series 66, 1961; 72, 1962; 75, 1963; 82, 1964; and 84, 1965).

3. Release by Children's Bureau, U.S. Department of Health, Education, and Welfare, dated November 13, 1966 (HEW-N81).

4. *Adoptions in 1965,* Children's Bureau.

5. *Ibid.*

6. See Michael Shapiro, *A Study of Adoption Practice,* 3 volumes (New York: Child Welfare League of America [CWLA], 1956). Also, *Child Welfare League of America Standards for Adoption Service* (New York: CWLA, 1959).

7. The selection of agencies was restricted to those located in New York under a specific condition of the grant financing the study.

8. See Leon Yarrow, "Research in Dimensions of Early Maternal Care," *Merrill-Palmer Quarterly of Behavior and Development,* Vol. IX, No. 2, 1963, pp. 101–14.

two/ Conceptualizing the study

1. Some of the material discussed here has been previously presented in D. Fanshel, "Approaches to Measuring Adjustment in Adoptive Parents," in *Quantitative Approaches to Parent Selection*, Child Welfare League of America, 1962, pp. 18–35.

2. Otto Pollak, "Design of a Model of Healthy Family as a Basis for Evaluative Research," *Social Service Review*, Vol. 31, No. 4, 1957, pp. 369–76.

3. See, for example, Florence Brown, "What Do We Seek in Adoptive Parents?" *Social Casework*, Vol. 32, No. 4, 1951, pp. 155–61.

4. Viola Bernard reports that the majority of physicians in a survey believed that adoption could trigger pregnancy. See: Viola Bernard, "Adoption," *The Encyclopedia of Mental Health*, Vol. I, Franklin Watts, Inc., 1963, pp. 70–108.

5. Lili Peller, "Comments on Adoption and Child Development," *The Bulletin of the Philadelphia Association for Psychonanalysis*, Vol. 11, No. 4, Dec. 1961, and Vol. 13, No. 1, March 1963.

6. Marjorie Brooke, et al., *How Adopted Children Turn Out: A Research Report*. Group Masters' Project. The New York School of Social Work, Columbia University, 1962.

three / The study method

1. A fairly accurate picture of the ways in which the adoptees' accounts would differ, if at all, from those of their adoptive parents might be obtained from a comparison of the data provided by the 33 interviewed adoptees with the information obtained from their adoptive parents. Such an analysis is being planned for the future. Appendix B of this report contains a discussion of the basis upon which one could conclude that the data from the reports of one-third of the adoptees in the study might be generalizable to the total sample of 100.

2. Elizabeth Gertrude Meier, *Former Foster Children as Adult Citizens*. Unpublished doctoral dissertation, Columbia University School of Social Work, 1962; Helen L. Witmer, et al., *Independent Adoptions: A Follow-Up Study* (New York: Russell Sage Foundation, 1963). H. M. Skeels and Marie Skodak, "Techniques for a High-Yield Follow-Up Study in the Field," *Public Health Report*, 1965, 80, pp. 249–57.

3. The actual number of located families for each agency is as follows: Catholic Home Bureau = 34; Chapin Nursery/Spence Alumnae = 30; Free Syngagogue Committee = 28; and State Charities Aid = 29.

4. Of the remaining two families, one each came from the reserve rosters of Catholic Home Bureau and State Charities Aid.

5. This refusal group was broken down by placing agency as follows: Catholic Home Bureau = 9 families; Chapin Nursery/Spence Alumnae = 10 families; Free Syngagogue Committee and State Charities Aid = 3 families each.

6. Of the 130 families located—121 from the primary sample and 9 from the reserve sample—103 consented to participate in the study, another family remained undecided about participating until our deadline for interviewing had passed, and one family expressed sympathy with the study's objectives but did not participate because of illness and eventual death in the family. Of the 103 who agreed to participate, 2 were actually not interviewed; in one instance, because the family was geographically unavailable to our interviewer staff and in the second instance, because severe illness in the family precluded our being able to arrange an interview. A third family was interviewed but was subsequently eliminated from the study when it was learned that the adoptee had been related to the adoptive parents.

7. Donald T. Campbell and Donald W. Fiske, "Convergent and Discriminant Validation by the Multitrait-Multimethod Matrix," *Psychological Bulletin*, 65, No. 2, March 1959, pp. 81–105.

8. Space and other publishing considerations unfortunately preclude the presentation in this volume of the results of our factor analysis of the questionnaire material and of the correlation of factor scores with the outcome measures derived from the interview data.

9. Copies of this schedule are available from the Child Welfare League of America (CWLA).

10. Copies of the complete outline are available from CWLA.

11. A full discussion of the rationale and method by which measures of the outcome of the adoptive experience were developed will be found in Chapter XI.

12. In these 38 cases, the following five factors accounted for our being able to interview only one adoptive parent: (a) one partner was deceased —26 cases; (b) an adoptive couple was separated or divorced—6 cases; (c) one spouse resisted or refused outright to be interviewed—3 cases; (d) one partner was too ill to be interviewed—2 cases; and (e) a foreign language barrier made an interview with one member of the couple impractical—1 case.

13. We were, of course, also aware of the potential drawback inherent in this timing. After recounting and reliving some of the possibly painful aspects of their adoptive experiences, some parents might be prone to refuse access to the adoptee out of a desire to shelter him from similar discomfort or due to their own misgivings over having divulged too much emotion-laden material. Nevertheless, we believed that the only feasible alternative,

viz., broaching the subject at the outset of the interview, was fraught with the even greater danger of losing the parent interview altogether. Several couples raised this issue at the beginning of the interview by stating unequivocally that they would not permit us to contact their children. Moreover, they made it clear that if their participation in the study were made contingent upon their granting such permission they would not cooperate. Faced with this prospect, we concluded that postponing raising the subject until the end of the interview, while certainly not foolproof or totally satisfactory, was the least risky solution.

14. As might be expected, this arrangement necessitated more diligent follow-up efforts to maximize the return of completed and usable questionnaires than was the case for the average two-parent interview.

15. Copies of this instrument are available from CWLA.

four / Describing the adoptive families

1. The rationale underlying this classification and the manner in which the three groupings were developed are discussed in detail in Chapter XI. However, in order to facilitate the reader's understanding and assessment of the data and findings contained in this and the following chapter, we shall summarize briefly here the procedures by which outcome scores were generated and the 100 families assigned to outcome categories on the basis of these scores.

Thirty-seven items of information stemming from the parent interviews and pertaining to the adoptees' adjustment were grouped on the basis of conceptual relevance into 12 clusters or adjustment indices. Each of these referred to the adoptees' functioning in a different life-space area.

Each index item was scored to reflect the reported adoptee functioning in that segment of the life-space area, and the scores of all component items in each index were then summed to arrive at a total index score. The total scores of 11 indices were in turn summed to obtain an all-inclusive measure of the adoptees' overall adjustment termed the Summated Index Score. (For reasons detailed in Chapter XI, this overall score did not include the score on the vocational adjustment index.) The Summated Index Scores were then rank ordered (with the lowest score indicating the last problematic adjustment), and this rank ordering was trichotomized to generate the three outcome categories now to be described.

2. Of four families in which the adoptee had biological children as siblings, there was one each in the low-problem and the high-problem groups and two in the middle-range adjustment group.

3. Otto Pollak, "Design of a Model of Health Family Relationships as the Basis for Evaluative Research," *Social Service Review*, 1957, 31, pp. 369–76.

4. W. L. Warner, Marcia Meeker, and Kenneth Eells, "Occupational Composition of Social Classes," in Sigmund Nosow and William A. Form (eds.), *Man, Work and Society* (New York: Basic Books, 1962).

5. In order that the scales for each of the three SES components have the same direction, viz., the higher the scale the more desirable or positive the value of the component, it was necessary to reverse the ratings assigned to the various occupational levels by Warner, Meeker, and Eells. Thus, their rating "1" designating those occupations with the highest prestige were redesignated as rating "7"; their rating "2" was renumbered "6" for our purposes, etc.

6. Where the adoptive father had died or where the adoptive parents had been separated before the adoptee was 12 years old, ranking was based upon a combination of both adoptive father's and adoptive mother's occupations. There were 2 such instances among the 100 cases.

7. Where the adoptive father had died or where the adoptive parents had been separated before the adoptee was 12 years old, the education of the adoptive mother was substituted for that of the adoptive father. There were 2 such instances among the 100 cases.

8. In Group I there was one Protestant–Roman Catholic couple and one Protestant–Greek Orthodox marriage. The one mixed marriage in Group II comprised a Protestant and a Roman Catholic.

9. H. M. Skeels and Marie Skodak, "Techniques for a High Yield Follow-Up Study in the Field," *Public Health Report,* 1965, 80, pp. 249–57.

10. In this group there was one instance each where a widowed adoptive mother, a widowed adoptive father, and a divorced adoptive mother had been remarried prior to the inception of our study.

11. *Abridged Generation Life Tables for White Males and White Females, Cohort Born in the United States,* 1930 (cited by Skeels and Skodak in *Public Health Reports,* 1965, 80, p. 249, footnote).

12. See, for example, E. A. Haggard, et al., "On the Reliability of the Anamestic Interview," *Journal of Abnormal and Social Psychology,* 1960, 61, pp. 311–18; Sarnoff A. Mednick and John B. P. Shaffer, "Mother's Retrospective Reports in Child-Rearing Research," *American Journal of Orthopsychiatry,* 1963, 33, pp. 457–61; Lillian Cukier Robbins, "The Accuracy of the Parental Recall of Aspects of Child Development and of Child-Rearing Practices," *Journal of Abnormal and Social Psychology,* 1963, 66, pp. 261–70; Alexander Thomas, et al., *Behavioral Individuality in Early Childhood* (New York: New York University Press, 1963), p. 5; Marion Radke Yarrow, "Problems of Methods in Parent-Child Research," *Child Development,* 1963, 34, 215; and Marion Radke Yarrow, et al., "Reliability of Maternal Retrospection: A Preliminary Report," *Family Process,* 1964, 3, pp. 207–18.

13. David Fanshel, *A Study in Negro Adoption* (New York: CWLA. 1957), p. 53.

14. H. David Kirk, *Shared Fate* (Glencoe, Illinois: Free Press, 1964), pp. 123–45.

15. The reader is reminded that the study sample had been restricted to families whose adopted children had been three years of age or younger at adoption. This helps account for the absence of any reported willingness to have accepted a child older than age three.

five / Describing the adoptees

1. Helen Witmer, Elizabeth Herzog, Eugene A. Weinstein, and Mary E. Sullivan, *Independent Adoptions: A Follow-Up Study*, Russell Sage Foundation, 1963, pp. 280–81.

2. H. D. Kirk, *Shared Fate*, pp. 123–45.

3. Leon J. Yarrow, "Research in Dimensions of Early Maternal Care," *Merrill-Palmer Quarterly of Behavior and Development*, Vol. 9, No. 2, 1963, pp. 101–14.

4. It should be brought to the reader's attention that with respect to each type of school problem, the interviewers failed to cover the material sufficiently in about 20% of the cases to allow for subsequent coding.

5. This was in regard to physical disabilities affecting school performance. No adoptees in the high-problem category were reported to have experienced such disabilities, whereas one adoptee in the middle-range outcome group and two adoptees with low-problem overall adjustments had reportedly encountered this type of problem.

6. Subcommittee on Juvenile Delinquency, Committee on the Judiciary, United States Senate (85th Congress, 1st session), *Juvenile Delinquency*, March 4, 1957 (Report No. 130), p. 101.

7. Conflict over heterosexual matters may not have been as pronounced for the families in this category as it might seem; in 12% of the cases the information was not obtained by the interviewers.

six / Background for adoption

1. See Leo Srole, Thomas S. Langner, Stanley T. Michael, Marvin K. Opler, and Thomas A. C. Rennie, *Mental Health in the Metropolis* (New York: McGraw-Hill, 1962); and Arnold Gurin, Joseph Veroff, and Sheila Feld, *Americans View Their Mental Health* (New York: Basic Books, 1960).

2. "Correlation" is a statistical measure of association between two variables. When a change in one variable is associated with a change in the other variable, the two are said to be correlated. The more pervasive this concomitant change among all cases in a given sample, i.e., the more the

two variables covary, the stronger is the correlation between them. When a change—either an increase or a decrease—in one variable tends to be associated with a change in the same direction in the second variable, the correlation between them is said to be positive. When the change in one variable tends to be accompanied by a change in the opposite direction, the correlation with the other variable is referred to as negative.

The "correlation coefficient," designated by the symbol "r," is a numerical concept which indicates the extent or degree of the association prevailing between the two variables. When this association is positive, r takes a positive, or plus, value although common usage tends to omit the $+$ sign in referring to positive correlation coefficients. In the case of a negative correlation, r takes a negative or minus ($-$) value. The correlation coefficient may vary in magnitude between $+1.00$ and -1.00, these two polar values representing perfect correlation or association while an r of 0.00 represents no association at all.

A "partial correlation" is a subclass of correlations involving the relationships among three or more variables. Such correlations express the degree of association existing between two variables under statistical conditions which control for, or remove the influence of, one or more additional variables which might hypothetically affect the two-variable relationship under study. The partial correlation coefficient possesses the various other attributes of the two-variable correlation outlined briefly above. In our analysis, the partial correlation coefficient will be represented by the symbol "$r_{12.3}$" with the subscripts signifying the relationship between variables 1 and 2, controlling for variable 3.

When a correlation coefficient for a given sample of cases is termed "statistically significant," reference is being made to the probability that a correlation of such magnitude could have occurred simply by chance in the sample if in fact there had been no correlation at all between the variables in the population from which the sample had been drawn. A correlation referred to as "significant at the .05 level" is a correlation of such magnitude in a sample that there is probability of one in twenty (or of five in 100) that it could have occurred by chance under the condition of no correlation in the universe. Comparably, a correlation significant at the .01 level denotes a one-in-one hundred probability that the correlation referred to was purely a chance occurrence.

In the social sciences, the .05 level is generally regarded by convention to be the highest probability level acceptable if correlations or other statistics are to be considered substantively meaningful and not simply chance occurrences. In some settings and disciplines, however, the .01 level of significance is preferred and even demanded. In discussing the correlations in this and the subsequent chapters in which our correlation analysis is set forth, we shall in general abide by the above convention in assessing and highlighting our most noteworthy findings. At the same time, we believe it to be dysfunctional for researchers in social work—where so many of our measuring instruments are still crude and so much of our resulting data still "soft"—to be overly rigid and purist in the application of the .05 and .01 norms. We also question the utility of endowing these norms, which have been arbitrarily selected, with a sacrosanctness they do not warrant. The state of tested knowledge being as limited as it is in social work, should we and can we afford to disregard findings with a probability of, say, six out of 100 (the .06 level) or even one out of ten (the .10 level) of having occurred by chance? To exclude *ipso facto* findings which fall just short of the conventional criterion from further scrutiny, analysis, and disciplined research rumination might well be to deprive the field of potentially fruitful insights and leads for further research. In our analysis, therefore, we will call attention to, and examine the implication of, those correlations which approach the .05 level of significance as well as those which attain or surpass it.

3. Alfred Kadushin, "A Study of Adoptive Parents of Hard-to-Place Children," *Social Casework*, May 1962.

4. The intercorrelation matrix available from the Child Welfare League of America gives the actual correlations between each of the latter two agencies and reported strength of motivation to adopt.

5. This does not mean that they tended to request boys, however. In fact there was only a weak and nonsignificant relationship between Catholic Home Bureau families and male sex preference. Our finding is phrased in the negative because in dichotomizing the range of responses on this item for correlational analysis, the two resulting categories were: "desire for a girl" and "all other categories of response." Hence, while we found that Catholic Home Bureau families tended not to fall in the former category, this finding does not indicate the specific nature of the requests of these families concerning the sex of the child they desired.

6. The negative nature of this correlation as contrasted with the positive sign of the comparable coefficient relating to the request for a girl is the result of having dichotomized the nominal variable, adoptee's sex, for purposes of correlational analysis. "Female" was assigned a 0 code and male, a 1 code. When both sexes are related in the same direction to another variable, the resulting correlation coefficients therefore take opposite signs.

7. The explanation for the negative phrasing of this finding is similar to that presented in footnote 5, *supra*. In the present instance, the dichotomized categories developed for the correlation analysis were: "infant and baby (preferred)" and "all other categories of response."

8. *Child Welfare League of America Standards for Adoption Service* (New York: CWLA, 1959), p. 24.

9. The actual correlation coefficients are $r = -.01$ and $r = -.03$ for the relationship between age of the adoptee at placement and the ages of the adoptive father and adoptive mother, respectively.

10. See Chapter IV for a discussion of the components of the SES measure and the method used in developing it.

seven / Revelation of adoptive status

1. Michael Shapiro, A *Study of Adoption Practice*, Vol. 1. Child Welfare League of America, 1956, p. 87.

2. Viola W. Bernard, "Adoption," appearing in *The Encyclopedia of Mental Health*, Vol. 1, Albert Deutsch and Helen Fishman (Editors), Franklin Watts, Inc., N.Y., 1963, p. 102.

3. Bernard, *Ibid.*, p. 103.

4. Lili Peller, "Comments on Adoption and Child Development," *The Bulletin of the Philadelphia Association for Psychoanalysis*, Vol. 11, No. 4, Dec. 1961, Vol. 13, No. 1, March 1963, p. 22.

5. Marshall D. Schechter, "Observations on Adopted Children," *A.M.A. Archives of General Psychiatry*, Vol. 3, July 1960, pp. 21–32.

6. Povl W. Toussieng, "Thoughts Regarding the Etiology of Psychological Difficulties in Adopted Children," *Child Welfare*, Vol. XLI, No. 2, February 1962, p. 62.

7. H. D. Kirk, *Shared Fate*, Free Press, New York, 1964, pp. 45–46.

8. See Chapter VIII, pp. 161, 163, and 164.

9. This figure includes the 40 families distributed among the 7 specific age categories in Table 7-2 plus 5 families in Group III where the two spouses concurred that the adoptee had been told of his adoption at a specific age but disagreed as to what that age was and were consequently included in the "disparate response" category.

10. Of the remaining three couples, the content of the revealed information was not covered by the interviewer in two instances. In the third instance, the two spouses gave disparate accounts of this content, and this couple is not included in the analysis discussed in this section.

11. In one family, the adoptee was apprised of his adoptive status for the first time when he was 28 years of age.

12. The remaining 17% of the 100 families gave disparate or "other" responses or else the interviewers had not covered this topic or had been unable to determine the exact nature of the adoptee's behavior in this area.

13. Kirk, *Shared Fate*, pp. 24–35.

14. An exploration of field interviews with 33 adoptees will subsequently be reported by Benson Jaffee.

eight / Child-rearing practices

1. The reader should note, however, that for more than one-fourth of the adoptive couples either this topic was not covered in the interview or the parents' responses to it could not be definitely coded by the interviewer.

2. We attempted to obtain data on a closely related point by asking the parents to recall which kinds of behavior on the part of the adoptees had tended to produce altercations that had required disciplining of the children. Our interviewers referred to 6 potential conflict-producing behaviors and asked the parents to mention others, but their efforts in this area proved quite unfruitful. A substantial majority of parents denied that there had been any specific behavior by the adoptees over the years which had provoked the parents into disciplining them.

3. Claire Selltiz, Marie Jahoda, Morton Deutsch, and Stuart W. Cook, *Research Methods in Social Relations* (revised), Holt, Rinehart and Winston, 1963, pp. 351, 352.

nine / Context of adoptive family life

1. The matrices depicting all the relevant relationships existing among the variables being discussed are available from the Child Welfare League of America.

2. Relationships alluded to in this section and in the following sections of the present chapter for which correlations are not specifically cited in tabular form or within the text will be found in Table 2 among the matrices available from CWLA.

3. $r = .17$ and $.19$ for the association between the ages of the adoptive father and adoptive mother, respectively, and the source of the initial revelation.

4. "Use of parental substitutes" was taken to refer most commonly to the use of baby-sitters, but we defined this practice broadly enough to include the employment of housekeepers and other live-in domestic help in whose charge the adoptees were left for relatively brief periods of time. This broader interpretation is of importance in assessing the meaning of some of our findings, as will be evident presently.

5. For the two periods studied, $r = .52$ and $.53$.

6. $r = .20$ while $r_{12.3} = .01$.

7. To be reported upon in greater detail in a subsequent paper.

8. The relevant correlations controlling for SES were as follows:
adoptee below age 5: $r = .52$ and $r_{12.3} = .31$;
adoptee age 5–10: $r = .51$ and $r_{12.3} = .30$.

9. The pertinent correlations controlling for degree of religious investment were these:

    adoptee below age 5: $r = .52$ while $r_{12.3} = .44$
    adoptee age 5–10: $r = .51$ while $r_{12.3} = .45$.

The failure of religious investment to account for an appreciable amount of the Catholic Home Bureau families' tendency to avoid using parent substitutes leads us to conclude that their involvement in religious activity may be less strongly linked to their more traditional child-rearing orientation than we had initially postulated it might be.

10. Partial correlations between placement by Catholic Home Bureau and degree of parental control, eliminating the influence of SES, yielded an $r_{12.3} = -.16$ for both age periods covered, whereas $r = -.22$ for each of these periods.

11. Cf. the preceding section of this chapter and footnote 8, *supra*.

12. A partial exception is socioeconomic status, which we have already examined separately and which shows some of the strongest associations with two child-rearing variables, viz., use of parental substitutes and affording the adoptee separation experiences.

13. Controlling for SES, $r_{12.3} = .16$.

14. Catherine V. Richards and Norman A. Polansky, "Reaching Working-Class Youth Leaders," *Social Work*, Vol. 4, No. 4, October 1959, pp. 31–39.

15. This statement must be partly qualified by the recognition that the intake period covered by our study, viz., 1930–1940, was also the era of the Great Depression when quite conceivably some of the higher-SES adoptive mothers might have needed to work to enable their families to weather the economic crisis confronting them.

16. For the two age periods covered, $r = -.26$ and $-.27$.

17. For the two age periods covered, $r = .18$ and $.19$.

18. $r = -.20$.

ten / Adoptee's life situation at follow-up

1. Otto Pollak, "Design of a Model of Healthy Family as a Basis for Evaluative Research," *Social Service Review*, Vol. 31, No. 4, 1957, pp. 369–76.

2. The reader should be aware that the items used to rank order the 100 adoptees, and thus determine their location within the three outcome groups, included some parental perceptions reported in this chapter. Hence, the frequent association between an adoptee's location in one of the three outcome groups and his adjustment in a given life-space area is partially accounted for by the nonindependence of the data which is being cross-tabulated.

3. The remaining seven cases involved disparate responses on the part of the parents or the failure of the interviewer to make inquiry in this area.

4. The reader is reminded of the statement set forth in footnote 2 above.

5. The analysis of the interviews with the adoptees and the degree of confirmation of parental reports about their adjustment will be reported in a subsequent publication.

eleven / Measuring the outcome of the adoptive experience

1. Seymour M. Lipset, Martin Trow, and James Coleman, *Union Democracy* (Glencoe, Illinois: Free Press, 1956), pp. 425–27.

2. The only area excluded from this multifaceted outcome score was that dealing with the vocational adjustment of the adoptee. This life-space area did not appear applicable for a fairly large group of female subjects who had eschewed the development of vocational careers in favor of marriage and homemaking responsibility.

3. The index scores reported for Table 11–8 are based upon the summation of items in each profile area. These profile area scores were then correlated with each other.

4. For a discussion of the interviewers' rating instrument see Chapter III, pp. 30–32. A factor analysis of the ratings revealed that a single evaluative factor accounted for most of the variation in ratings. Therefore a single score was developed to account for the interviewer's ratings for each family.

5. The index for this life-space area was not previously discussed because it consisted of a single item portraying the parental perception of the degree to which the adoptee possessed outstanding talents in any area functioning.

6. Leo Srole, Thomas S. Langner, Stanley T. Michael, Marvin K. Opler, and Thomas A. C. Rennie, *Mental Health in the Metropolis* (New York: McGraw-Hill, 1961).

twelve / Background and variables

1. The reader is referred to footnote 2, Chapter VI, for a brief exposition of the meaning and major characteristics of correlation as a statistical measure of association between variables.

2. Needless to say, the following findings in no way reflect invidious comparisons of either the clientele or of the service offered by the four agencies. We wish to reiterate the cautionary note which has been stated in

earlier sections of this report: it cannot be stressed too strongly. The findings of this investigation concern adoptions consummated 20 to 30 years ago, at a point when each of the agencies participating in this study was largely or wholly staffed by nonprofessional personnel whose practice was qualitatively quite different from current-day practice. Furthermore, there is some reason to believe that the characteristics of the clientele served by each agency in those days were different from the characteristics of clientele it now serves in ways potentially relevant to the areas explored in this study. Finally, and perhaps of greatest importance, a scrutiny or an evaluation of the quality of agency practice, either three decades ago or currently, was never considered to fall within the purview of this investigation.

3. These correlations were as follows:

ADOPTION THROUGH:	PERSONALITY ADJUSTMENT		GLOBAL INTERVIEWER RATING FACTOR	
	NO CONTROL ($r =$)	CONTROL FOR SES ($r_{12.3} =$)	NO CONTROL ($r =$)	CONTROL FOR SES ($r_{12.3} =$)
Catholic Home Bureau	15	04	−14 *	−01
Chapin Nursery/Spence Alumnae	−11	−08	−04	−08
Free Synagogue Committee	−21 *	−15	35 **	29 **
State Charities Aid Association	17	16	−17	−19

* Significant: $p < .05$. ** Significant: $p < .01$.

4. Correlation between sex of adoptee and educational adjustment was $r = .28$, with female coded "0," male coded "1" and low score signify low-problem outcome. All correlations not present in tables within the body of this chapter will be found in Table 5 among the correlation matrices available from the Child Welfare League of America.

5. For example, the *Child Welfare League of America Standards for Adoption Service* states explicitly that: "Infants should be placed in the adoptive home at as early an age as possible, preferably in the first weeks or at least by three months of age. . . ." (CWLA p. 20.)

6. *Ibid.*

7. Leon J. Yarrow, "Separation from Parents During Early Childhood," pp. 122, 123, in Martin L. Hoffman and Lois Wladis Hoffman (eds.), *Review of Child Development Research* (New York: Russell Sage Foundation, 1964).

8. The actual partial correlations between age of adoptee at placement and social relations adjustment, controlling for adoption through each of the four agencies, were as follows:

CONTROLLING FOR ADOPTION THROUGH $r_{12.3}$

Catholic Home Bureau	−09
Free Synagogue Committee	−12
State Charities Aid	−20 *
Chapin Nursery/Spence Alumnae	−19

9. Correlation of the number of preadoptive placements and health adjustment was $r = .22$. Number of such placements correlated with manifestations of outstanding talents at .17.

10. Three of the outstanding contributions to this literature are: World Health Organization, *Deprivation of Maternal Care: A Reassessment of its Effects*, Public Health Papers, No. 14, Geneva, 1962, 165 pp.; Leon J. Yarrow, "Maternal Deprivation: Toward an Empirical and Conceptual Reevaluation," pp. 3–41, in CWLA, *Maternal Deprivation*, New York, 1962; and Leon J. Yarrow in *Review of Child Development Research*, pp. 89–136.

11. *Ibid.*, p. 89.

12. *Ibid.*, pp. 91–92.

13. Leon J. Yarrow, "Theoretical Implications of Adoption Research," *Child Welfare*, 44, 1965, p. 70.

14. The reader should also note in Table 1 of the matrices available from CWLA that there is a statistically significant though not exceptionally strong negative correlation $(r = -.24)$ between the presence or absence of other children in the adoptive home prior to, and following, the adoptee's appearance. In other words, these two variables were somewhat related even though their respective outcome correlates were quite different.

15. In fact, the partial correlation betwen age of adoptive father at application and adoptee's current economic adjustment controlling for adoptive family's SES was exactly the same as the original zero-order correlation.

16. The original correlation between adoptive parent's socioeconomic status, and adoptee personality adjustment was $r = .24$.

The partial correlations, controlling for adoption through each of the four agencies, was as follows:

CONTROLLING FOR ADOPTION THROUGH $r_{12.3}$

Catholic Home Bureau	.19
Chapin Nursery/Spence Alumnae	.23 *
Free Synagogue Committee	.19
State Charities Aid	.25 *

The original correlation between parental SES and adoptee social relations adjustment was $r = .17$. The partial correlations, controlling for adoption through each of the four agencies, was as follows:

CONTROLLING FOR ADOPTION THROUGH $r_{12.3}$

Catholic Home Bureau	.07
Chapin Nursery/Spence Alumnae	.16
Free Synagogue Committee	.11
State Charities Aid	.18

17. We are here, of course, reversing the procedure employed in footnote 3 where we used SES as a control variable in examining the relationship between agency and personality adjustment.

18. Thus, whereas SES and the global interviewer rating factor were correlated at $r = -.27$, when adoption through the Free Synagogue Committee was introduced as a control variable, the resultive partial correlation was $r_{12.3} = -.41$. When we utilized adoption through Catholic Home Bureau as a control, $r_{12.3} = -.23$, while $r_{12.3} = -.28$ when adoption through each of the other two agencies was used as a control variable.

thirteen / Revelation of adoptive status

1. The reader will recall from Chapter VII that the term "always" is used in the context of the adoptive parent having used the word "adopted" and having referred to the child's adoptive status "from the beginning," before the child was able to comprehend the meaning of the word or its underlying concept.

2. All correlations between revelation variables and outcome variables not presented in tabular form in this chapter can be found in Table 6 among the correlation matrices available from the Child Welfare League of America.

3. However, it is precisely around ages five and six, when the child is enmeshed in his Oedipal struggles, that at least two psychoanalytically-oriented therapists suggest that the adoptee is least able emotionally to cope with the profoundly disturbing knowledge that he has two sets of parents and that his adoptive status connotes his rejection by one of them. See Marshall D. Schechter, "Observations on Adopted Children," *A.M.A. Archives of General Psychiatry*, 1960, III, p. 31, and Lili Peller, "About 'Telling the Child' of His Adoption," *Bulletin of the Philadelphia Association for Psychoanalysis*, XI (1961), pp. 145–54.

4. Dorothy C. Krugman, "Reality in Adoption," *Child Welfare*, XLIII, July 1964, p. 349.

5. For a creative and insightful approach to the question of which of the two sets of parents in an adopted child's life are or can be considered his "real" parents, see Krugman, *ibid.*, pp. 351–58.

6. Some adoption agencies currently advocate such a policy, encouraging the adoptive parents to present as positive and sympathetic a picture as

possible of the adoptee's natural parents. On the other hand, the *Child Welfare League of America Standards for Adoption Service* states that ". . . caseworkers can give [the adoptive parents] no formula for telling the child about adoption and about his original family, but they can give adoptive parents some general guides and help them to be aware of their feelings. . . ." (Section 4–19, p. 29).

7. The incidence of purposefully inaccurate or false stories given to the adoptee does not play a significant role in this finding, at least insofar as the adoptive parents' interview reports are in fact valid. As the reader will recall from the data in Chapter VII, less than one parent in ten reported having falsified any of the information given the adoptive children regarding their biological forebears.

8. To a less marked degree, ($r = -.09$) the parents also tended to characterize past parent-adoptee relationships in the same way.

9. The reader will recall from the discussion in Chapter VII that more than three-quarters (76%) of these parents reported that their adopted children had at no time indicated a wish to learn more about their natural parents than the adoptive parents had voluntarily told them. From a methodological standpoint, this concentration of responses in one response category of an item is undesirable. Such a situation is not fully consonant with the assumption of continuous variables upon which the use of correlation analysis is predicated. The consequence can be that correlating such a variable with another one may result in a spuriously high coefficient. This point has the following implication: the findings presented below indicate that some relationship does exist between the adoptee's desire to learn more about his biological parents and the kind of adjustment he was likely to make in various life-space areas. However, this relationship may not in actuality be as strong as the magnitude of the correlation coefficients might seem to imply. The same holds true, of course, for findings in other sections of his report which are based upon items to which the responses showed the same kind of "clumping" in one response category.

10. One investigator, however, has directed some research attention to this general subject. H. David Kirk in his book, *Shared Fate,* deals with the issue of how adoptive parents cope with what he believes is a role handicap encountered by most childless couples entering into adoption. Some deny that their situation differs from that of natural parents ("rejection-of-difference") while others are able to admit that such a difference exists ("acknowledgement-of-difference"). His data indicate that in his subjects a high degree of "acknowledgement-of-difference" was associated with strong feelings of empathy with the child on the part of the adopting couple and also with a readiness to think about the adoptee's biological parents.

11. Edmund V. Mech, "Trends in Adoption Research," in *Perspectives on Adoption Research,* CWLA, New York, 1965, p. 31.

12. These data consisted of parental responses to the question of whether they had or had not tended to reveal the adoptee's status to six different

categories of persons. For purposes of correlational analysis, the responses in all six categories were treated as a single item, with coding scores based on the number of categories to whom parents did in fact tend to reveal the fact of adoption. However as the reader will recall from our discussion in Chapter VII, this item was not covered with a fairly sizable proportion of adoptive couples (between 22% and 39% for various of the six categories), thereby limiting its value in the correlational analysis.

fourteen / Child-rearing practices and environmental influences

1. The full range of these variables, and the strength and direction of their association with the outcome variables, will be found in Table 8 among the correlation matrices available from the Child Welfare League of America.

2. The partial correlation between the adoptive father's perception of his strictness and past parent-adoptee relationships, controlling for severity of the adoptive father's spanking, was $r_{12.3} = .23$. As can be seen in Table 14–2, the zero-order correlation was $r = .26$.

3. The pertinent correlations, controlling for the adoptive parents' SES, are as follows:

severity of parental spanking practices and adoptee education adjustment:
$r = .18; r_{12.3} = .18$

severity of parental spanking practices and adoptee social relations adjustment:
$r = .18; r_{12.3} = .17$

severity of parental spanking practices and global interviewer rating factor:
$r = -.19; r_{12.3} = -.18$

4. This and all other correlation coefficients not specifically cited in the text of the first part of this chapter will be found in Table 7 among the correlation matrices available from CWLA.

5. The zero-order correlation between intensity of control and social relations adjustment was $r = -.24$. Controlling for SES, the resulting partial correlation was $r_{12.3} = -.21$. Both coefficients are significant at the .05 level. Controlling for adoption through each of the four participating agencies results in the following partial correlations, all of which are also significant at the .05 level:

$r_{12.3} = -.20$, controlling for adoption through Catholic Home Bureau
$r_{12.3} = -.23$, controlling for adoption through Chapin Nursery/Spence Alumnae
$r_{12.3} = -.22$, controlling for adoption through Free Synagogue Committee
$r_{12.3} = -.24$, controlling for adoption through State Charities Aid

6. The agency through which the adoption took place also had some influence on the most pronounced outcome correlate of frequent baby-sitter use, viz., problematic personality adjustment. This influence, however, was not nearly as strong or as pervasive as was the effect of SES. Thus, we see from Table 14–5 that the original (zero-order) correlations between personality adjustment and frequency of use of baby-sitters when the adoptee was below age 5 and age 5–10 were $r = .25$ and $r = .26$, respectively. The partial correlations, controlling for each of the four agencies in turn, were as follows for the two age periods consecutively:

$r_{12.3} = .20$ [*] and .21,[*]   controlling for adoption through Catholic Home Bureau

$r_{12.3} = .24$ [*] and .25,[*]   controlling for adoption through Chapin Nursery/Spence Alumnae

$r_{12.3} = .19$ [*] and .20,[*]   controlling for adoption through Free Synagogue Committee

$r_{12.3} = .26$ [**] and .26,[**]   controlling for adoption through State Charities Aid

[*]   Significant: $p < .05$
[**]   Significant: $p < .01$

7. See Leon J. Yarrow, "Separation from Parents During Early Childhood."

fifteen / In summary

1. Helen L. Witmer et al., *Independent Adoptions*, pp. 70–71 and 136–38.

2. The only exceptions were the areas concerned with health and outstanding talents.

3. For descriptions of longitudinal studies of adopted children, see Edmund V. Mech, "Child Welfare Research: A Review and Critique," *The Annals*, Vol. 355, September 1964, p. 27 (describes the Delaware Family Study); Leon J. Yarrow, "Research in Dimensions of Early Maternal Care," *Merrill-Palmer Quarterly of Behavior and Development*, IX, No. 2, 1963, pp. 101–14 (describes study in the Washington, D.C., area); David Fanshel, "Indian Adoption Research Project," *Child Welfare*, XLIII, No. 9, 1964, pp. 486–88.

4. See Edgar F. Borgatta and David Fanshel, *Behavioral Characteristics of Children Known to Psychiatric Outpatient Clinics: With Special Attention to Adoption Status, Sex and Age Groupings*, CWLA, March 1965.

5. H. D. Kirk, *Shared Fate*.

6. Otto Pollak, "Cultural Factors in Child Welfare Work," *Child Welfare*, XXXVIII, No. 9, 1959, pp. 1–6.

appendix A

1. See pages 32–34 for a discussion of the nature and purpose of these summaries.

2. Families who despite uncommon names could not be found in any of the available directories during the first wave of searching were deemed unlocateable for purposes of the study, and no further efforts were made to track them down.

3. Two of the 75 volunteering couples later appeared in the random sample drawn from these rosters and were interviewed as part of the study rather than being included in the pretest.

4. In only four cases were the two partners adamant in their refusal to be separated. When interpretation of the rationale for separate interviews was seen to be of no avail, they were interviewed jointly rather than risk the loss of their cooperation entirely.

5. This procedure had the added advantage of enabling the interviewer in most instances to recover the completed questionnaires by the time the contact was terminated, thereby substantially reducing the questionnaire loss rate.

6. This figure is not a precisely computed mean since no effort was made to have the interviewers record the exact time they began and ended each interview. The three-hour average is an estimate derived from the extensive interviewing conducted by the two authors throughout the study and from informal reports of the other interviewers. The range in duration of two-parent interviews, derived in the same manner, was from approximately two to five hours.

7. The nature of these indices, their conceptual underpinnings, and the method by which they were generated are discussed at length in Chapter XI.

8. These scores were based on the factor analysis of the interviewer ratings referred to in footnote 4 of Chapter XI.

appendix B

1. This conclusion was reached on the basis of either parental reports or brief, initial telephone contacts with the adoptees concerned.

2. H. D. Kirk, *Shared Fate.*

Index